Database Nation
The Death of Privacy in the 21st Century

Also by Simson Garfinkel

Architects of the Information Society (edited by Hal Abelson)

Stopping Spam (coauthored with Alan Schwartz)

Web Security & Commerce (with Gene Spafford)

Practical UNIX & Internet Security (coauthored with Gene Spafford)

PGP: Pretty Good Privacy

The UNIX-HATERS Handbook (with Daniel Weise and Steven Strassmann)

NeXTSTEP Programming (coauthored with Michael Mahoney)

Practical UNIX Security (coauthored with Gene Spafford)

DATABASE NATION
THE DEATH OF PRIVACY IN THE 21ST CENTURY

Simson Garfinkel

O'REILLY®

Beijing · Cambridge · Farnham · Köln · Paris · Sebastopol · Taipei · Tokyo

Database Nation: The Death of Privacy in the 21st Century
by Simson Garfinkel

Copyright © 2000 O'Reilly & Associates, Inc. All rights reserved.
Printed in the United States of America.
Cover photograph of eye © John Feingersh/Stock Market.

Published by O'Reilly & Associates, Inc., 101 Morris Street, Sebastopol, CA 95472.

Editor: Deborah Russell

Production Editor: Madeleine Newell

Cover Designer: Hanna Dyer

Printing History:

> January 2000: First Edition.

Library of Congress Cataloging-in-Publication Data

Garfinkel, Simson.
    Database nation: the death of privacy in the 21st century / Simson Garfinkel.
      p. cm.
    Includes bibliographical references and index.
    ISBN 1-56592-653-6 (alk. paper)
      1. Privacy, Right of--United States. 2. Computer security--United States. I. Title.

JC596.2U5 G37 2000
323.44'8'0973--dc21   99-058637

[C]

For Sonia

who will be 55 in 2048

CONTENTS

CHAPTER ONE

PRIVACY UNDER ATTACK

You wake to the sound of a ringing telephone—but how could that happen?

Several months ago, you reprogrammed your home telephone system so the phone would never ring before the civilized hour of 8:00 a.m. But it's barely 6:45 a.m. Who could be calling at this time? More importantly, who was able to bypass your phone's programming?

You pick up the telephone receiver, then slam it down a moment later. It's one of those marketing machines playing a prerecorded message. Computerized telemarketing calls have been illegal within the United States for more than a decade now, but ever since international long-distance prices dropped below 10 cents a minute, calls have been pouring in to North America from all over the world. And they're nearly all marketing calls—hence the popularity of programmable phones today. What's troubling you now is how this call got past the filters you set up. Later on, you'll discover how: the company that sold you the phone created an undocumented "back door"; last week, the phone codes were sold in an online auction. Because you weren't paying attention, you lost the chance to buy back your privacy.

Oops.

Now that you're awake, you decide to go through yesterday's mail. There's a letter from the neighborhood hospital you visited last month. "We're pleased that our emergency room could serve you in your time of need," the letter begins. "As you know, our fees (based on our agreement with your HMO) do not cover the cost of treatment. To make up the difference, a number of hospitals have started selling patient records to medical researchers and consumer marketing firms. Rather than mimic this distasteful behavior, we have decided to ask you to help us make up the difference. We are recommending a tax-deductible contribution of $275 to help defray the cost of your visit."

The veiled threat isn't empty, but you decide you don't really care who finds out about your sprained wrist. You fold the letter in half and drop it into your shredder. Also into the shredder goes a trio of low-interest credit card offers.

Why a shredder? A few years ago you would have never thought of shredding your junk mail—until a friend in your apartment complex had his identity "stolen" by the building's superintendent. As best as anybody can figure out, the super picked one of those preapproved credit-card applications out of the trash, called the toll-free number, and picked up the card when it was delivered. He's in Mexico now, with a lot of expensive clothing and electronics, all at your friend's expense.

On that cheery note, you grab your bag and head out the door, which automatically locks behind you.

When you enter the apartment's elevator, a hidden video camera scans your face, approves your identity, and takes you to the garage in the basement. You hope nobody else gets in the elevator—you don't relish a repeat of what happened last week to that poor fellow in 4G. It turns out that a neighbor recently broke up with her violent boyfriend and got a restraining order against him. Naturally, the elevator was programmed to recognize the man and, if he was spotted, to notify the police and keep the doors locked until they arrived. Too bad somebody else was in the elevator when it happened. Nobody realized the boyfriend was an undiagnosed (and claustrophobic) psychotic. A hostage situation quickly developed. Too bad for Mr. 4G. Fortunately, everything was captured on videotape.

Your car computer suggests three recommended approaches to your office this morning. You choose wrong, and a freak accident leaves you tied up in traffic for more than half an hour. As you wait, the computer plays an advertisement for a nearby burger joint every five minutes. You can't turn it off, of course: your car computer was free, paid for by the advertising.

Arriving late at work, you receive a polite email message from the company's timecard system; it knows when you showed up, and it gives you several options for making up the missed time. You can forgo lunch today, work an extra 45 minutes this evening, or take the 45 minutes out of your ever-dwindling vacation time. The choice is yours.

You look up and force a smile. A little video camera on your computer screen records your smile and broadcasts it to your boss and your coworkers. They've told you that Workplace Video Wallpaper™ builds camaraderie—but the company that sells the software also claims that the pervasive monitoring cuts down on workplace violence, romances, and even drug use. Nowadays, everybody smiles at work—it's too dangerous to do otherwise.

The cameras are just one of the ways you're being continually monitored at work. It started with electronic tags in all the company's books and magazines, designed to stop the steady pilferage from the library. Then, in the aftermath of a bomb scare, employees were told they'd have to wear badges at all times, and that desks and drawers would be subject to random searches. (Rumor has it that the chief of security herself called in the bomb threat—a ploy to justify the new policies.)

Next month, the company is installing devices in the bathrooms to make sure people wash their hands. Although the devices were originally intended for the healthcare and food industries, a recent study found that routine washing can also cut down on disease transmission among white-collar workers. So the machines are coming, and with them you'll lose just a little bit more of your privacy and your dignity.

This is the future—not a far-off future, but one that's just around the corner. It's a future in which what little privacy we now have will be gone. Some people call this loss of privacy "Orwellian," harking back to *1984*, George Orwell's classic work on privacy and autonomy. In that book, Orwell imagined a future in which privacy was decimated by a totalitarian state that used spies, video surveillance, historical revisionism, and control over the media to maintain its power. But the age of monolithic state control is over. The future we're rushing towards isn't one where our every move is watched and recorded by some all-knowing "Big Brother." It is instead a future of a hundred kid brothers that constantly watch and interrupt our daily lives. George Orwell thought that the Communist system represented the ultimate threat to individual liberty. Over the next 50 years, we will see new kinds of threats to privacy that don't find their roots in totalitarianism, but in capitalism, the free market, advanced technology, and the unbridled exchange of electronic information.

WHAT DO WE MEAN BY PRIVACY?

The concept of privacy is central to this book, yet I wish I had a better word to express the aspect of individual liberty that is under attack by advanced technology as we enter the new millennium.

For decades, people have warned that pervasive databanks and surveillance technology are leading inevitably to the death of privacy and democracy. But these days, many people who hear the word "privacy" think about those kooks living off in the woods with their shotguns: these folks get their mail at post office boxes registered under assumed names, grow their own food, use cash to buy what they can't grow for themselves, and constantly worry about being attacked by the federal government—or by space aliens. If you are not one of these people, you may well ask, "Why should I worry about my privacy? I have nothing to hide."

3

The problem with this word "privacy" is that it falls short of conveying the really big picture. Privacy isn't just about hiding things. It's about self-possession, autonomy, and integrity. As we move into the computerized world of the twenty-first century, privacy will be one of our most important civil rights. But this right of privacy isn't the right of people to close their doors and pull down their window shades—perhaps because they want to engage in some sort of illicit or illegal activity. It's the right of people to control what details about their lives stay inside their own houses and what leaks to the outside.

To understand privacy in the next century, we need to rethink what privacy really means today:

- It's not about the man who wants to watch pornography in complete anonymity over the Internet. It's about the woman who's afraid to use the Internet to organize her community against a proposed toxic dump—afraid because the dump's investors are sure to dig through her past if she becomes too much of a nuisance.

- It's not about people speeding on the nation's highways who get automatically generated tickets mailed to them thanks to a computerized speed trap. It's about lovers who will take less joy in walking around city streets or visiting stores because they know they're being photographed by surveillance cameras everywhere they step.

- It's not about the special prosecutors who leave no stone unturned in their search for corruption or political misdeeds. It's about good, upstanding citizens who are now refusing to enter public service because they don't want a bloodthirsty press rummaging through their old school reports, computerized medical records, and email.

- It's not about the searches, metal detectors, and inquisitions that have become a routine part of our daily lives at airports, schools, and federal buildings. It's about a society that views law-abiding citizens as potential terrorists, yet does little to effectively protect its citizens from the real threats to their safety.

Today, more than ever before, we are witnessing the daily erosion of personal privacy and freedom. We're victims of a war on privacy that's being waged by government eavesdroppers, business marketers, and nosy neighbors.

Most of us recognize that our privacy is at risk. According to a 1996 nationwide poll conducted by Louis Harris & Associates, one in four Americans (24%) has "personally experienced a privacy invasion"[1] —up from 19% in 1978. In 1995, the same survey found that 80% of

Americans felt that "consumers have lost all control over how personal information about them is circulated and used by companies."[2] Ironically, both the 1995 and 1996 surveys were paid for by Equifax, a company that earns nearly two billion dollars each year from collecting and distributing personal information.

We know our privacy is under attack. The problem is that we don't know how to fight back.

THE ROLE OF TECHNOLOGY

Today's war on privacy is intimately related to the dramatic advances in technology we've seen in recent years. As we'll see time and again in this book, unrestrained technology ends privacy. Video cameras observe personal moments; computers store personal facts; and communications networks make personal information widely available throughout the world. Although some specialty technology may be used to protect personal information and autonomy, the overwhelming tendency of advanced technology is to do the reverse.

Privacy is fundamentally about the power of the individual. In many ways, the story of technology's attack on privacy is really the story of how institutions and the people who run them use technology to gain control over the human spirit, for good and ill. That's because technology by itself doesn't violate our privacy or anything else: it's the people using this technology and the policies they carry out that create violations.

Many people today say that in order to enjoy the benefits of modern society, we must necessarily relinquish some degree of privacy. If we want the convenience of paying for a meal by credit card, or paying for a toll with an electronic tag mounted on our rear view mirror, then we must accept the routine collection of our purchases and driving habits in a large database over which we have no control. It's a simple bargain, albeit a Faustian one.

I think this tradeoff is both unnecessary and wrong. It reminds me of another crisis our society faced back in the 1950s and 1960s—the environmental crisis. Then, advocates of big business said that poisoned rivers and lakes were the necessary costs of economic development, jobs, and an improved standard of living. Poison was progress: anybody who argued otherwise simply didn't understand the facts.

Today we know better. Today we know that sustainable economic development *depends* on preserving the environment. Indeed, preserving the environment is a prerequisite to the survivability of the human race. Without clean air to breathe and clean water to drink, we will all surely die. Similarly, in order to reap the benefits of technology, it is more important than ever for us to use technology to protect personal freedom.

Blaming technology for the death of privacy isn't new. In 1890, two Boston lawyers, Samuel Warren and Louis Brandeis, argued in the *Harvard Law Review* that privacy was under attack by "recent inventions and business methods." They contended that the pressures of modern society required the creation of a "right of privacy," which would help protect what they called "the right to be let alone."[3] Warren and Brandeis refused to believe that privacy had to die for technology to flourish. Today, the Warren/Brandeis article is regarded as one of the most influential law review articles ever published.[4] And the article's significance has increased with each passing year, as the technological invasions that worried Warren and Brandeis have become more commonplace.

Privacy-invasive technology does not exist in a vacuum, of course. That's because technology itself exists at a junction between science, the market, and society. People create technology to fill specific needs, real or otherwise. And technology is regulated, or not, as people and society see fit.

Few engineers set out to build systems designed to crush privacy and autonomy, and few businesses or consumers would willingly use or purchase these systems if they understood the consequences. What happens more often is that the privacy implications of a new technology go unnoticed. Or if the privacy implications are considered, they are misunderstood. Or if they are understood correctly, errors are made in implementation. In practice, just a few mistakes can turn a system designed to protect personal information into one that destroys our secrets.

How can we keep technology and the free market from killing our privacy? One way is by being careful and informed consumers. But I believe that government has an equally important role to play.

THE ROLE OF GOVERNMENT

With everything we've heard about Big Brother, how can we think of government as anything but the enemy of privacy? While it's true that federal laws and actions have often damaged the cause of privacy, I believe that the federal government may be our best hope for privacy protection as we move into the new millennium.

The biggest privacy failure of American government has been its failure to carry through with the impressive privacy groundwork that was laid in the Nixon, Ford, and Carter administrations. It's worth taking a look back at that groundwork and how it may serve us today.

The 1970s were a good decade for privacy protection and consumer rights. In 1970, Congress passed the Fair Credit Reporting Act. Elliot Richardson, who at the time was President Nixon's secretary of health, education, and welfare (HEW), created a commission in 1970 to study the impact of computers on privacy. After years of testimony in Congress, the commission found all the more reason for alarm and issued a landmark report in 1973.

The most important contribution of the Richardson report was a bill of rights for the computer age, which it called the Code of Fair Information Practices (see the shaded box). That Code remains the most significant American thinking on the topic of computers and privacy to this day.

CODE OF FAIR INFORMATION PRACTICES

The Code of Fair Information Practices is based on five principles:

- There must be no personal data record-keeping systems whose very existence is secret.

- There must be a way for a person to find out what information about the person is in a record and how it is used.

- There must be a way for a person to prevent information about the person that was obtained for one purpose from being used or made available for other purposes without the person's consent.

- There must be a way for a person to correct or amend a record of identifiable information about the person.

- Any organization creating, maintaining, using, or disseminating records of identifiable personal data must assure the reliability of the data for their intended use and must take precautions to prevent misuses of the data.

Source: Department of Health, Education, and Welfare, 1973.

The biggest impact of the HEW report wasn't in the United States, but in Europe. In the years after the report was published, practically every European country passed laws based on these principles. Many created data protection commissions and commissioners to enforce the laws.[5] Some believe that one reason for this interest in electronic privacy was Europe's experience with Nazi Germany in the 1940s. Hitler's secret police used the records of governments and private organizations in the countries he invaded to round up people who posed the greatest threat to the German occupation; postwar Europe realized the danger of allowing potentially threatening private information to be collected, even by democratic governments that might be responsive to public opinion.

But here in the United States, the idea of institutionalized data protection faltered. President Jimmy Carter showed interest in improving medical privacy, but he was quickly overtaken by economic and political events. Carter lost the election of 1980 to Ronald Reagan, whose aides saw privacy protection as yet another failed Carter initiative. Although several privacy protection laws were signed during the Reagan/Bush era, the leadership for these bills came from Congress, not the White House. The lack of leadership stifled any chance of passing a nationwide data protection act.

In fact, while most people in the federal government were ignoring the cause of privacy, some were actually pursuing an antiprivacy agenda. In the early 1980s, the federal government initiated numerous "computer matching" programs designed to catch fraud and abuse. (Unfortunately, because of erroneous data, these programs often penalized innocent individuals.[6]) In 1994, Congress passed the Communications Assistance to Law Enforcement Act, which gave the government dramatic new powers for wiretapping digital communications. In 1996, Congress passed a law requiring states to display Social Security numbers on driver's licenses, and another law requiring that all medical patients in the U.S. be issued unique numerical identifiers, even if they paid their own bills. Fortunately, the implementation of those 1996 laws has been delayed, largely thanks to a citizen backlash.

Continuing the assault, both the Bush and Clinton administrations waged an all-out war against the rights of computer users to engage in private and secure communications. Starting in 1991, both administrations floated proposals for use of "Clipper" encryption systems that would have given the government access to encrypted personal communications. President Clinton also backed the Communications Decency Act (CDA), which made it a crime to transmit sexually explicit information to minors—and, as a result, might have required Internet providers to deploy far-reaching monitoring and censorship systems. When a court in Philadelphia found the CDA unconstitutional, the Clinton administration appealed the decision all the way to the Supreme Court—and lost.

Finally, the U.S. government's restrictions on the export of encryption technology have effectively restrained the widespread use of this technology for personal privacy protection within the United States.

As we move forward into the twenty-first century, the United States needs to take personal privacy seriously again. The final chapter of this book explores ways our government might get back on track, and suggests a federal privacy agenda for the twenty-first century.

FIGHTING BACK

Privacy is certainly on the ropes in America today, but so was the environment in 1969. Thirty years ago, the Cuyahoga River in Ohio caught on fire and Lake Erie was proclaimed dead. Times have certainly changed. Today it's safe to eat fish that are caught in the Cuyahoga, Lake Erie is alive again, and the overall environment in America is the cleanest it's been in decades.

There are signs around us indicating that privacy is getting ready to make a comeback as well. The war against privacy is commanding more and more attention in print, on television, and on the Internet. People are increasingly aware of how their privacy is compromised on a daily basis. Some people have begun taking simple measures to protect their privacy, measures like making purchases with cash and refusing to provide their Social Security numbers—or providing fake ones. And a small but growing number of people are speaking out for technology *with* privacy, and putting their convictions into practice by developing systems or services that protect, rather than attack, our privacy.

Over the past few decades, we've learned that technology is flexible, and that when it invades our privacy, the invasion is usually the result of a conscious choice. We now know, for instance, that when a representative from our bank says:

> I'm sorry that you don't like having your Social Security number printed on your bank statement, but there is no way to change it.

that representative is actually saying:

> Our programmers made a mistake by telling the computer to put your Social Security number on your bank statement, but we don't think it's a priority to change the program. Take your business elsewhere.

Today we are relearning this lesson and discovering how vulnerable business and government can be to public pressure. Consider these three examples from the past decade:

Lotus Development Corporation. In 1990, Lotus and Equifax teamed up to create a CD-ROM product called "Lotus Marketplace: Households" that would have included names, addresses, and demographic information on every household in the United States, so small businesses could do the same kind of target marketing that big businesses have been doing since the 1960s. The project was canceled when more than 30,000 people wrote to Lotus demanding that their names be taken out of the database.

Lexis-Nexis. In 1996, Lexis-Nexis suffered an embarrassing public relations debacle when it was revealed that their P-TRAK database service was publishing the Social Security numbers of most U.S. residents. Thousands of angry consumers called the company's switchboard, effectively shutting it down for a week. Lexis-Nexis discontinued the display of Social Security numbers 11 days after the product was introduced.

Social Security Administration (SSA). In 1997, it was the U.S. Social Security Administration's turn to suffer the public's wrath. The press informed U.S. taxpayers that the SSA was making detailed tax history information about them available over the Internet. The SSA argued that its security provisions—requiring that taxpayers enter their name, date of birth, state of birth, and mother's maiden name—were sufficient to prevent fraud. But tens of thousands of Americans disagreed, several U.S. senators investigated the agency, and the service was promptly shut down. When the service was reactivated some months later, the detailed financial information could not be downloaded over the Internet.

Technology is not autonomous; it simply empowers choices made by government, business, and individuals. One of the big lessons of the environmental movement is that it's possible to shape these choices through the political process. This, I believe, justifies the involvement of government on the privacy question.

WHY THIS BOOK?

In this book we'll take a look at today's wide-ranging—and frightening—threats to our personal privacy:

The end of due process. Governments and businesses went on a computer buying spree in the second half of the twentieth century, replacing billions of paper files with electronic data processing systems. Today, humans often are completely absent from digital decision making. As a result, we've created a world in which the smallest clerical errors can have devastating effects on a person's life. It's a world where computers are assumed to be correct, and people wrong.

The fallibility of biometrics. Fingerprints, iris scans, and genetic sequences are widely regarded as infallible techniques for identifying human beings. They're so good, in fact, that 50 years from now, identification cards and passports probably won't exist. Instead, a global data network will allow anyone on the planet to be instantly identified from the unique markings of that person's own body. Who controls access to the databank, who has the power to change its contents, and what do we do if the infallible system is nevertheless wrong?

The systematic capture of everyday events. We are entering a new world in which every purchase we make, every place we travel, every word we say, and everything we read is routinely recorded and made available for later analysis. But while the technology exists to capture this data, we lack the wisdom to figure out how to treat it fairly and justly. The result is an unprecedented amount of data surveillance, the effects of which we're just beginning to grasp.

The bugging of the outside world. Orwell thought the ultimate threat to privacy would be the bugging of bedrooms and offices. Today, an equally large threat to freedom is the systematic monitoring of public places through microphones, video cameras, surveillance satellites, and other remote sensing devices, combined with information processing technology. Soon it may be impossible for most people to escape the watchful outdoor eye.

The misuse of medical records. Traditionally, medical records have been society's most tightly held personal records. The obligation to maintain patient confidentiality is widely regarded as a fundamental responsibility of medical professionals. But patient confidentiality is at odds with the business of health insurance—a business that would rather turn away the sick than cure them.

Runaway marketing. Junk mail, junk faxes, junk email, and telemarketing calls during dinner are only the beginning of the twenty-first century's runaway marketing campaigns. Marketers increasingly will use personal information to create solicitations that are continual and virtually indistinguishable from news articles, personal letters, and other kinds of noncommercial communications.

Personal information as a commodity. Personal identification information—your name, your profession, your hobbies, and the other bits that make up your self—is being turned into a valuable property right. But instead of being given to individuals to help them exert control over their lives, this right is being seized by big business to ensure continued profits and market share. If you don't even own your own name, how can you have a sense of self-worth?

Genetic autonomy. Breakthrough advances in genetics make it possible to predict disease, behavior, intelligence, and many other human traits. Whether or not these predictions are correct, they will change how people are perceived and treated. Will it be possible to treat people fairly and equally if there is irrefutable scientific evidence that people have different strengths, different weaknesses, and different susceptibilities to disease? If not, how is it possible to maintain a democratic society when this information is easily available?

The micromanagement of intellectual property. Businesses are becoming increasingly vigilant in detecting the misuse of their own intellectual property. But piracy is hard to prevent when technology can turn every consumer into an electronic publisher. To prevent info-theft, publishers are turning to increasingly intrusive techniques for spying on their customers. Once this technology is in place, it is unlikely that it will be restricted to antipiracy protection.

The individual as terrorist. Astonishingly lethal technologies are now widely available throughout society. How can society reasonably protect itself from random acts of terrorism without putting everyone under surveillance? How can society protect itself from systematic abuses by law enforcement officials, even when those abuses seem to be in the public interest?

Intelligent computing. The ultimate threat to privacy will be intelligent computers—machines that can use human-like reasoning powers, combined with blinding calculating speed, to assemble coherent data portraits, interpret and anticipate our mental states, and betray us with false relationships.

This is a broad collection of issues, but it's no less broad than the future itself. This book's purpose is to show the privacy implications of many ongoing technological developments, and to show good cause for abandoning today's laissez-faire approach to privacy protection. Once you have a good vision of the technological future we're shaping, you'll be better equipped to mold it.

Although this book is subtitled *The Death of Privacy in the Twenty-First Century*, it is designed to bring about a different end. Nearly 40 years ago, Rachel Carson's book *Silent Spring* helped seed the U.S. environmental movement. And to our credit, the silent spring that Carson foretold never came to be. *Silent Spring* was successful because it helped people to understand the insidious damage that pesticides were wreaking on the Earth's environment, and it helped our society and our planet plot a course to a better future.

This book, likewise, seeks to show the plethora of ways that technology is killing one of our most cherished freedoms. Whether you call this freedom the right to digital self-determination, the right to informational autonomy, or simply the right to privacy, the shape of our future will be determined in large part by how we understand, and ultimately how we control or regulate, the threats to this freedom that we face today.

CHAPTER TWO

DATABASE NATION

WASHINGTON, DC, 1965. The Bureau of the Budget's proposal was simple yet revolutionary. Instead of each federal agency's investing in computers, storage technology, and operations personnel, the United States government would build a single National Data Center. The project would start by storing records from four federal agencies: population and housing data from the Bureau of the Census; employment information from the Bureau of Labor Statistics; tax information from the Internal Revenue Service; and benefit information from the Social Security Administration. Eventually, it would store far more.

While the original motivation was simply to cut costs, it soon became clear that there would be additional benefits. Accurate statistics could be created quickly and precisely from the nation's data. By building a single national database, the government could track down and stamp out the misspelled names and other inconsistent information that haunts large-scale databank projects. A single database would also let government officials and even outsiders use the data in the most efficient manner possible.

The Princeton Institute for Advanced Study issued a report enthusiastically supporting the databank project, saying that centralized storage of the records could actually improve the security of the information, and therefore the privacy of the nation. Carl Kaysen, the Institute's director and the chairman of the study group, further urged that Congress pass legislation that would give the records additional protections, provide for privacy, and promote accountability of the databank workers. Others latched on to the idea, and the concept of the National Data Center slowly evolved into that of a massive databank containing cradle-to-grave electronic records for every U.S. citizen. The database would contain every person's electronic birth certificate, proof of citizenship, school records, draft registration and military service, tax records, Social Security benefits, and ultimately, their death records and estate information. The FBI might even use the system to store criminal records.

An article promoting the project appeared in the July 23, 1966 issue of the *Saturday Review*. Its title said everything: "Automated Government—How Computers Are Being Used in Washington to Streamline Personnel Administration to the Individual's Benefit."[1] But the article didn't have the intended result. Instead of applauding the technocratic vision, the U.S. Congress commenced a series of hearings on the threats of computerized databanks. Six months later, the *New York Times Magazine* ran an article titled "Don't Tell It to the Computer," which viciously attacked the idea of a centralized government data warehouse. Written by Vance Packard, author of *The Naked Society* (a best-selling book that describes the invasion of privacy by government, business, and schools), the *Times* piece articulated what was to become a key argument against the project:

> The most disquieting hazard in a central data bank would be the placing of so much power in the hands of the people in a position to push computer buttons. When the details of our lives are fed into a central computer or other vast file-keeping systems, we all fall under the control of the machine's managers to some extent.[2]

The tide was turning. By 1968, the Bureau of the Budget said that it was doubtful that a practical plan for the center would be presented to the Ninetieth Congress. Meanwhile, the House Special Subcommittee on Invasion of Privacy issued a report holding that privacy must be the primary consideration in establishing computerized databanks, that no work should be done on a National Data Center until privacy could be guaranteed, and that the Bureau was at fault for not developing procedures to ensure privacy.

A poll by the Harvard University Program on Technology and Society the following year found that 56% of Americans opposed development of the National Data Center, on the grounds that it would invade their privacy. That same year, in his book *The Death of Privacy*, Jerry M. Rosenberg opened with this grave warning:

> When Adolf Hitler was aspiring to the Chancellorship of Germany, he acquired the confidential European Census and used it to weed out some of his potential antagonists.

> With the advance of technology, centralized data accumulation becomes easier, the reward for intrusion is increased, and control shifts to still fewer people.[3]

The National Data Center was never built. Instead, each federal agency was told to continue building its own computer systems. In lieu of creating a single databank, which could be used by unscrupulous bureaucrats to exercise inappropriate control over some people's lives, the government created dozens of databanks.

American businesses followed the government's example, often purchasing the same computers that had first been developed to fill government needs. The political decision not to build a central data repository set the direction that computers would follow for the next 30 years. Whereas a central databank would have pushed the development of massive mainframes and high-speed communications networks, developers created smaller, regional mainframes with basically no interconnecting networks until the late 1980s. But the decision to kill the project also had a profound impact on personal privacy—and not necessarily the impact that was expected.

THIRTY-FOUR YEARS LATER

SEATTLE, 1999. I order a pair of white chocolate lattés, and hand my Mileage Plus First Card to the barista for payment. Although the drinks cost only $3 each, I'd rather charge the transaction than pay cash. By putting every single purchase on my credit card, I've managed to accumulate a balance of more than 50,000 frequent-flyer miles in less than a year—enough to buy my wife and myself a pair of round-trip tickets anywhere in the United States.

Thirty years ago, the idea of a centralized computer tracking one's every purchase seemed like part of an Orwellian nightmare. Fifteen years ago, the mathematical genius Dr. David Chaum invented "E-Cash," an anonymous payment system designed to let consumers buy things electronically without revealing their identities. Who could have imagined that the day would come when millions of people would not only wish to have their purchases tracked—but would complain when transactions were missed? Yet that is one of the most intriguing results of so-called loyalty programs such as United's credit card: they have created massive databanks that paint a detailed electronic mosaic of consumer behavior, and they have done so with the willing participation of the monitored.

I call my mother when I get home. In the back of my mind, I know that a record of my call is being kept in the phone company's computer system. My records will probably never be reviewed by a human being, but at least once a month I hear of some big crime in which the suspect's guilt was "proven," in part, with these kinds of telephone records. In trials after the bombing of the Murrah Federal Building in Oklahoma City in 1995, for instance, one critical piece of evidence presented by the prosecution was the telephone call records from pre-paid calling cards used by Timothy McVeigh and Terry Nichols. Right-wing extremists in the militia movement thought that calls made with these calling cards, purchased with cash, would be anonymous and untraceable. In fact, records of every call made with each card had been carefully kept. Prosecutors presented hundreds of pages of phone card records, with calls to auto racing tracks, chemical companies, motels, storage facilities, and rental truck outlets.[4] Those records allowed the prosecution to show that Timothy McVeigh and Terry Nichols had been in frequent contact by telephone during the months and weeks leading up to the most murderous act of terrorism in U.S. history.[5]

In the 1960s, the federal government operated most of the computers in the country. Commentators warned that the centralization of personal information might be planting the seeds of some future totalitarian regime. "My own hunch is that Big Brother, if he comes to the United States, will turn out to be not a greedy power-seeker but a relentless bureaucrat obsessed with efficiency," wrote Vance Packard in his *New York Times Magazine* article.

Articles written by journalists like Packard helped kill the National Data Center. But they did not stop data progress. Today, a mesh of computers operated by banks, utilities, and private businesses records an astonishing amount of information about us on a daily basis. In many cases, personal information is there for the taking. Instead of building a national databank, we have built a nation of databanks.

HOW WE GOT HERE

If you want to blame somebody for the computerization of America, blame George Washington, Thomas Jefferson, and the other framers of the Constitution. Way back in 1787, Jefferson and company decreed that the new republic would conduct a census every ten years. It sounded easy enough at the time, but as the United States expanded in both geographical size and population, the job of the census takers became increasingly difficult.

The problem wasn't just the growing numbers of "huddled masses" in search of freedom that were docking at U.S. ports. Like any government program, the census suffered mission creep. By 1880, the census was much more than a simple head count: it had become a tool for learning more about the people who made up the nation. Congress ordered the recording of people's gender, marital status, age, place of birth, education, occupation, and literacy status. All this information

Herman Hollerith

Herman Hollerith was an academic, a U.S. Census Office employee, and an inventor who built a machine that could automate the tedious process of counting the nation's census forms. Hollerith's quest to build an automatic tabulator nearly bankrupted his family, but ultimately led to the formation of his company, the Tabulating Machine Company, in 1896. In time, Hollerith's company was sold to a company that eventually became International Business Machines Corporation (IBM). [Photo courtesy The Computer Museum, Boston, MA, and The History Center, Mountain View, CA]

was sent to Washington, D.C. for tabulation. The whole process was strictly manual: census clerks made repeated passes over the forms, counting the number of responses that matched particular criteria. It took 18 weeks from start to finish, there were a lot of errors, and it was getting harder all the time.

Herman Hollerith was a young man who came to the census office after graduating from Columbia College in 1879. Hollerith saw the census problems and soon became obsessed with the idea of building a machine that would somehow automate the clerical work. He spent a year looking at the problem, then left and spent a year teaching mechanical engineering at MIT. He returned to Washington, this time spending a year in the Patent Office. Finally, he quit government service in 1884 to become a full-time inventor.[6]

Hollerith realized that information from each census form could be stored by punching holes on pieces of paper, and that by repeatedly counting the holes in different ways, he could perform the basic statistical operations the census office required. In 1889, he entered and won a competition organized by the census office, earning a contract to process the census forms with his tabulating machines the following year.

With these new machines, the census was tabulated in just six weeks, and Hollerith became the toast of census officials around the world.

In 1896, Hollerith incorporated his business, the Tabulating Machine Company. He sold the business in 1911, receiving $1 million for his stock and a promise of continued employment with the successor firm, the Computing-Tabulating-Recording Company (CTR). Three years later, CTR hired Thomas J. Watson, who in 1924 renamed the company the International Business Machines Corporation (IBM).

Throughout the 1920s, IBM continued to improve its tabulating machines and to find new markets for the equipment. The company built a Type 1 printing tabulator, which recorded counts on paper. It developed the Type 80 Sorter, which automatically sorted a stack of cards depending on the placement of the punched holes. In 1928, IBM developed a card that had 80 columns of ten rows each—a format which remained in use until the 1980s. (Those 80 columns live on to this day: the first Teletype terminals had platens that were 80 columns wide, as were the first video terminals. When IBM started selling its personal computer in 1981, it was only natural to make the PC's screen 80 columns wide as well.)

Ironically, IBM's biggest boost came from the Great Depression. A third of the nation's workers were unemployed, and people were starving. President Franklin D. Roosevelt's solution was to create the modern welfare state.

In 1935, Congress passed President Roosevelt's Social Security Act. Under the plan, a portion of each American's earnings would be deducted from his paycheck by his employer, who would add a matching "contribution," and send the money to the federal government, where it was put into the Social Security Trust Fund. Using this money, the Social Security Board, as it was known at the time, would send monthly checks to people who had retired or had become disabled, or to the families of workers who had died.

Greatly complicating things for the new Social Security Administration was the requirement that benefit payments received by each worker be dependent, in part, on the worker's lifetime contribution to the trust fund. This meant that the Social Security Board had to monitor how much money each employee in the United States earned, and it had to keep track of this information, from a worker's first day of employment until long after the worker died, when the worker's family finally stopped receiving death benefits.

When the Social Security Board opened for business in 1936, it was immediately "the largest bookkeeping operation in the history of the world."[7] The Board had expected that it would receive requests from 25 million workers; it received 45 million.[8] To keep the accounts straight, the Board assigned each worker a Social Security number (SSN). The number was sent back to each worker to keep for his or her records, and was additionally punched onto a "summary-of-earnings" punch card. Each year, the Social Security Board found each employee's card and punched it with that year's earnings. By 1943, Social Security had more than 100 million cards on file, filling six and a half acres of storage space.

Then, in 1951, Congress changed the rules under which Social Security benefits were calculated. Complying with the changes meant storing additional information on each card—information that would fill up the original cards within just five years. The newly renamed Social Security Administration couldn't give everybody a second card: that would have doubled the number of acres necessary to store all the information. With no other choice, Social Security turned to the young field of electronic data processing, and IBM's first generation tube-based computer, the IBM 705. The nation's work history would no longer be stored on punch cards, but on magnetic tape. The machines were installed in 1956, just as the first punch cards were reaching their eightieth column.

Punch Card

Invented by Herman Hollerith, punch cards were the primary way tabulating machines and computers stored information from the late 1880s until the 1960s, when the cards started to be replaced by magnetic tape. The punch card above uses a format (standardized in 1928) in which each card contains 80 columns of ten rows. A punched hole in a particular row and column is used to represent a single number. Combinations of holes in a single row represent letters. Punch cards were used through the 1980s, and there are doubtless some punch card systems still in use today. [Punch card courtesy Bradley Ross]

Social Security Numbers Grow in Popularity

The Social Security number was never designed to be a universal identifier for American citizens. Nevertheless, a decade after the number's creation it became just that:

- In 1943, President Roosevelt issued an executive order that required federal agencies to use the Social Security number for identifying people, rather than having each agency waste money developing its own numbering systems.

- The Department of Defense discarded military service "serial numbers" and adopted the Social Security number.

- The Veterans Administration used the number to keep track of returning soldiers' benefits.

- The FAA adopted SSNs as pilot license numbers.

- The Civil Service Commission adopted the number to keep track of federal employees.

Early into this process, some statisticians realized that the Social Security number was a bad choice for a national identifier. The first problem was the number itself: with just nine digits, the SSN simply wasn't long enough to handle every citizen, every visitor to the country, and every resident alien through the end of the twenty-first century. Because the Social Security number is so small, any randomly chosen nine-digit number has a good chance of being a valid SSN, raising the possibility of fraud and tax evasion. Another problem with the SSN is the way the number is assigned. Instead of assigning the number in a uniform manner at birth, the way many European nations do, SSNs are assigned when a letter is sent to the Social Security Administration. As a result, different people are issued SSNs at different times, and many citizens don't have an SSN at all! Lastly, the SSN lacks what's called a *check digit*—a digit that doesn't actually store information, but verifies that the other digits are correct. Without a check digit, there's no way to detect swapped digits or mistyped numbers. All of these problems only increase the amount of invalid information that will be stored in databanks using SSNs for identifiers. These factors made the United States Social Security number a singularly bad choice for any type of identification—even the original purpose of tabulating Social Security retirement and survivor benefits.

For all these reasons, in 1948 the U.S. National Office of Vital Statistics proposed that the U.S. adopt a national birth certificate number. Starting on January 1, 1949, each birth certificate would be stamped with its own unique number. In a few years, that number could replace the SSN.

But the country didn't want a uniform national number that was well-designed and properly administered. Wrote Columbia University professor Alan Westin in 1967:

> The idea was denounced in 1949 and 1950 in many newspapers as a potentially regimenting "police state" measure, and angry cartoons raised the "Big Brother" argument. The opposition was sufficiently strong to persuade twenty-four states to reject participation in the plan and to cause Congress to drop legislative proposals that had been put forward to provide for federal participation in the program.[9]

In 1961, the Internal Revenue Service tried to buck the trend and issue its own numbers. The plan was shot down as being too expensive. The IRS was told to use the Social Security number instead, which it did the following year.

For better or for worse, the U.S. government was saddled with using the SSN to identify the citizens in its computers. Certainly the government couldn't use names: more than one person can have the same name; spellings are easily changed by accident or on purpose; and names were too unwieldy for the computers of the time. But nobody was happy with the numeric alternative either. Speaking to a researcher from Harvard University in 1969, a respondent from Boston summed things up pretty well:

> Well, they have all this information . . . [and] if they're going to put it all together, there's nothing we can do about it. But I don't want to be known by my Social Security number. I have a name. No one else has this name. I'd like to have this name until I die, and I don't want to be known by a Social Security number.[10]

AMERICA ADOPTS THE SSN

The United States government wasn't the only organization to adopt the Social Security number. Many states adopted Social Security numbers for state income taxes and driver's license numbers; libraries used SSNs for library cards; colleges used SSNs for student ID numbers; hospitals used SSNs as patient identification numbers. And in the world of private business, some of the most aggressive users of the number were the consumer reporting bureaus, who were computerizing their files in the 1960s and found the SSN to be a valuable tool for the process.

Credit reporting didn't start in the 1960s, of course. Americans had been making major purchases on credit since the end of the Civil War. And since the turn of the century, specialized credit bureaus across the country had been keeping files on Americans that recorded people's ability and willingness to pay their debts. Credit bureaus had even created their own trade organization, the Associated Credit Bureaus, to facilitate the exchange of consumer credit information.

By 1969, credit bureaus were widely used by businesses, but most Americans were only dimly aware that consumer credit files even existed. Indeed, many credit bureaus had policies that forbade consumers from seeing their own files.

One reason for the secrecy was the content of the files themselves. The companies that held them said that the files contained factual information: loans that hadn't been repaid, overdue credit card payments, and multiple address changes by people constantly trying to escape creditors. But testifying before Congress in March 1970, Professor Alan Westin said that the files "may include 'facts, statistics, inaccuracies and rumors' . . . about virtually every phase of a person's life: his marital troubles, jobs, school history, childhood, sex life, and political activities." Apparently, business leaders of the time thought that if a person beat his spouse or engaged in certain sexual practices, he probably couldn't be trusted to pay back a loan. Not surprisingly, businesses were afraid of letting the public discover just what kind of information was being collected on Americans.

Between 1965 and 1970, three Congressional committees and five state legislatures held hearings on the practices of the growing credit reporting industry.[11] Lawmakers were attempting to understand this industry, which heretofore had largely been secret. At many of those hearings, the star witness was Alan Westin. The professor attacked the industry for its cavalier attitude toward the accuracy of its information on consumers, and criticized its practice of giving out that information to practically anyone who asked for it—except the consumers themselves.

But the biggest concern for both Westin and the lawmakers was that the coming wave of computerization would only make things worse. Unlike paper files, which must be periodically pruned, lest they become unmanageable, computers never need to forget. "Almost inevitably, transferring information from a manual file to a computer triggers a threat to civil liberties, to privacy, to a man's very humanity because access is so simple," argued Westin. Computers would make it possible to create an indelible history of a person's life mistakes, making it impossible for that person ever to get a second chance.

There was some evidence to support Westin's conjecture. In his book *The Naked Society*, Vance Packard recounted the story of an 18-year-old who couldn't get a job with any department store in Michigan, despite letters of praise from his teachers, clergy, and even his town's chief of police. The reason: when he was 13 years old, the man had been caught shoplifting. His name had been placed in a computerized file shared among all of the region's stores. Thanks to the power of the computer to store data away for years yet keep it instantly accessible, the man had been blacklisted forever by Michigan's merchants.

Westin and others uncovered numerous stories of people who were denied credit, insurance, or jobs because of a mistake—erroneous information that somebody had entered into a computer's databanks. Sometimes two people with similar-sounding names would have their records confused. Occasionally, a store would say that a customer owed money, but the customer denied it. In these cases, the customer was always wrong, because the businesses controlled what information was entered into the credit files.

Credit bureaus responded to the criticism by saying that their industry was a vital part of the nation's growing credit-based economy. Without these credit reports, the bureaus argued, how could you tell who was a good credit risk and who was not? Banks couldn't write mortgages. Department stores wouldn't be able to sell anything to anyone on credit. Not only would the growing credit economy collapse, millions of people would be denied the credit they deserved.

Congress saw the two sides at an impasse. Packard, Westin, and other commentators said that moving manual files to computers would create unprecedented opportunities for new kinds of abuse. For this reason, computerization should be stopped. But experts familiar with the technology said otherwise. The computer created "more opportunity for control than it does for hazard," said Dr. Harry C. Jordan, founder of the California-based firm Credit Data Corporation. (In 1968, Credit Data Corporation was bought by TRW, Inc., and the company's name was changed to TRW–Credit Data. The company was divested from TRW in 1996, and its name changed again, to Experian.) Testifying in 1968 before the Congressional Subcommittee on Invasion of Privacy, Jordan said that computers could even be programmed to enforce pro-privacy policies such as automatically discarding old data.[12]

As a result of the hearings, Congress ultimately passed the Fair Credit Reporting Act (FCRA) in April 1971.[13] Instead of putting the brakes on computerization, the act gave consumers new rights regarding information stored about them in credit-related databanks, including the right to view the contents of their own files, challenge erroneous information, and insert their own version of events if a creditor insisted that deleterious information in a consumer's file was correct.

The industry complained. Credit Data's executives said that the act would create a landslide of consumer requests to see their files. But the landslide failed to materialize. Westin's 1972 survey of the company found that the act had merely increased the number of inquiries from consumers requesting to see their own files from 0.5% to 0.7%.[14] Instead of creating a landslide, the act gave consumers a new right for fighting the most egregious practices of the industry. The states and federal government have used this right to sue the credit reporting companies on behalf of consumers.

Alan F. Westin

In March 1968, Professor Alan F. Westin of Columbia University testified before the Special Congressional Subcommittee on Invasion of Privacy about the threat posed by credit bureaus. Westin's dramatic testimony was influential in convincing Congress to adopt the Fair Credit Reporting Act. He also convinced Secretary Elliot Richardson to create the Advisory Committee on Automated Personal Data Systems. In 1972, the commission released a highly praised report outlining the Code of Fair Information Practices and concluding: "The federal government itself has been in the forefront of expanding the use of the SSN [Social Security number]." [Image Copyright © 1968 by The New York Times Co. Reprinted by permission.]

The 1970s and 1980s saw considerable consolidation in the credit reporting industry, to the point that today there are basically three U.S. companies in the business: Equifax (formerly Retail Credit); Experian (formerly Credit Data Corporation); and Trans Union. Each company's credit report contains more or less the same information: a list of credit cards, bank loans, student loans, and other credit that has been granted over the past seven years, for every man, woman, and child in the United States. (Negative credit assessments remain on the report for seven years, bankruptcy proceedings for ten years, and all "good" credit behavior can stay on your record for life, but in practice, it is cleared out after seven years as well.) For each loan, the companies record the person's payment history: how often a payment was made on time, and how many times payments were 30, 60, or 90 days late.

Equifax, Experian, and Trans Union do a lot more with this bulk data than merely report it. For an added fee, they will compute a credit "score." This score looks at a consumer's credit history and rates that person, for example, on a scale of one to ten. Other information that is collected includes demographics, population statistics, and purchasing habits. Although many consumers have demanded to see their scores, the reporting companies have never released them. You would think that this is a violation of the Fair Credit Reporting Act, but it isn't. The score is not technically part of the consumer's file.

Despite the 1971 reforms, many consumers have continued to complain that a significant amount of the information stored in the nation's credit banks is either misleading or just plain wrong—and that this inaccurate information turns people into innocent victims by denying them credit for no good reason.

The credit reporting firms have also fought for their right to release certain kinds of information in a consumer's file—the consumer's name, address, phone, and Social Security number—to anybody and for any purpose. The firms maintain that this information is not credit information and is thus not covered by the FCRA, which forbids the release of the information for noncredit or insurance purposes, such as direct marketing or "people-finding" services. Trans Union, in particular, has sued the Federal Trade Commission for the right to use this information for targeted marketing.

Of course, nobody is entitled to credit. But in a society where credit is required by all but the very richest families to buy a house, to buy or lease a car, or to get an education, denying somebody credit effectively denies that person the privileges of being a member of society. And the real tragedy of the credit bureaus is that a significant number of people who are denied credit are simply unlucky: they have a common name, they suffered some kind of clerical mistake, or they had their identity and credit history appropriated by some crook.

IT COULD HAPPEN TO YOU

Many people in American society do their best to follow the rules, but inadvertently get ground up by computer systems that have been poorly designed—systems that somehow can't quite cope with the messiness of day-to-day life. Just take the case of Steve and Nancy

Ross, who did a lot of traveling in the early 1980s and paid for it with a ruined credit report, courtesy of the Internal Revenue Service.[15]

In 1983, Nancy Ross won a fellowship to spend six months in Hawaii, paid for by the Japanese American Institute for Management Sciences. At the time, her husband Steve was a freelance writer and self-employed computer consultant, so the two of them packed up their kids and went off on their Pacific adventure. At the end of the trip, they returned to their home in Leonia, New Jersey.

A few months later, Nancy was invited to spend a year in the Far East and Japan. It was the chance of a lifetime for her kids, so they packed their bags again and left. By this time, Steve had accepted a job at the journalism department of Columbia University, so he stayed behind. To save money, the family rented out their house in New Jersey and Steve moved into a tiny apartment in New York City.

Shortly after Steve and Nancy moved back home, they received a nasty letter from the IRS: a lien had been placed on their house. "I immediately called the IRS in Holtsville [New Jersey] and said essentially, 'What are you talking about?'" recalls Steve Ross. "I reached a good clerk. We were on the phone for about half an hour. She figured it out. She said, 'I bet I know what happened.' She called out to California, and within six hours I had a call back from the IRS. She said 'Just to set your mind at ease, you are clean. We are sending you a letter.'" The lien was immediately removed.

What had happened was one of those weird confluences of errors that have a way of popping up whenever computers are involved. Because Steve and Nancy were both self-employed, they had to make quarterly income tax payments to the IRS. During the summer of 1983, they sent their $3,500 check from Hawaii to the regional IRS processing center on Long Island. But the post office mistakenly redirected the check to an IRS processing center in California.

Now, it turns out that during the summer of 1983, the IRS was deploying a new computer system, and that year the quarterly payments from the various regional processing centers weren't properly cross-posted to the other regions of the country. Instead, the California processing center simply opened a new account for the Ross family.

When the IRS processing center on Long Island got the Ross family's 1983 tax returns, its computers detected an inconsistency: the Rosses had reported paying $3,500 more in taxes than the IRS computers (in New York, at least) had received. So the computers sent Steve Ross a letter demanding the $3,500 payment.

By that time, Nancy was in Japan and Steve was living in a tiny New York apartment. Although they had arranged for their mail to be forwarded, the letter from the IRS had the words "do not forward" stamped on the outside. So Steve never saw it. The IRS also sent a "to whom it may concern" letter to the tenant at the family house, advising that a lien was about to be placed on the house, but the tenant refused delivery of the letter because the tenant was also in trouble with the IRS.

Next, the IRS tried to find the family's bank account in New Jersey, but the Ross family had closed that account and was using new accounts in Hawaii and New York. The IRS couldn't find the new accounts, so they put a lien on the New Jersey home.

I've gone into this level of detail because many of these stories of credit mishap are equally complicated. There's always a long story. But that story doesn't show up on the computers at Trans Union and Equifax. All these companies knew was that a lien had been placed on the Ross house for $10,000. So when the family's Mid Atlantic MasterCard came up for renewal in May 1985, instead of automatically renewing the card, the bank canceled it.

"I called up TRW first," says Steve Ross. "They said 'no problem, send a copy of the letter and an explanation, and we will put that with your credit report.' I said, 'Aren't you going to expunge the record?' They said 'No.' They don't do that. When you have an unfavorable note in your credit report, they don't take it out; they just put your explanation with it.

"We sent two copies off. And true to their word, they put in a notice—they summarized my explanation in a paragraph, and they confirmed that the IRS had sent a letter saying we were clean. The problem is that those two [TRW and Equifax] had already sold the credit data to something like 187 independent bureaus. And there was just no way that I could ever keep up with it," he says.

Like a computer virus, the information from the independent credit bureaus' computers kept reinfecting TRW's computer with the incorrect information—that the IRS had a lien on the family's house in Leonia. As far as the Ross family was concerned, the correction provisions of the Fair Credit Reporting Act just didn't work. "There was literally no way to get that information out of the system."

The Ross family eventually convinced Mid Atlantic to reissue the credit card. And it was a good thing, too: for the next seven years, the family couldn't obtain a new credit card from any other financial institution; they were also rejected for bank loans, and they were unable to refinance their house. And they were effectively grounded: with a credit report that said the IRS once put a lien on their home, they couldn't move and get a new mortgage on a new house.

The situation would have been much worse without that Mid Atlantic credit card: "I travel a lot on business. How can you rent a car without a credit card? How can you rent a hotel room without a credit card? It's just part of life. It would have destroyed my ability to make a living," says Steve Ross.

"By the end of the 1980s, our family income was well into six figures. But it was not until 1992, seven years later, that the obnoxious credit card salesmen began calling," and the offers for low-interest-rate credit cards started appearing in the mail. After seven years, the lien was removed from the credit reporting databanks, thanks to the Fair Credit Reporting Act.

As a side note, when the Rosses first received a copy of their credit report, they noticed something else on it that was wrong: a record of an item ordered from the Spiegel catalog in Chicago. "Spiegel claimed that we had ordered it and never paid for it. Now, the fascinating thing was we had never done business with them, and they had never dunned us. They had probably dunned someone in Texas [where the item was shipped]. TRW did investigate that one, [at least] they tried to. By the time we had noticed that, Spiegel no longer had those records in their computer, so they had no way of verifying it, except by hand. So it just stayed there," on the family's credit report.

The Ross family's experience is far from unique. In 1991, James Williams of Consolidated Information Service, a New York-area mortgage reporting firm, analyzed 1,500 reports from TRW, Equifax, and Trans Union, and found errors in 43% of the files. That same year, roughly 1,400 homeowners in the town of Norwich, Vermont (population: 3,000) were listed on TRW's computer system as tax delinquents "because [a] TRW contractor gathering home mortgage information mistakenly noted tax bills on town records as tax *liens*."[16] Despite considerable publicity on the case, some of the residents encountered difficulty convincing TRW to correct their files. The same thing happened in Cambridge, Massachusetts, in 1992, when an Equifax contractor mistakenly reported tax bills as tax liens.

Privacy activists say that more than 50% of all consumer files have a significant error in them. Some errors are relatively minor, such as an incorrect address. In other cases, the files mix credit information from two people with similar names. Or the files contain information that is simply wrong.

What's worse, reporting agencies frequently do not correct errors when the mistakes are brought to the agencies' attention. For example, in 1989 Bonnie Guiton, then the White House Advisor on Consumer Affairs, requested a copy of her credit report and discovered an account she knew nothing about: a stranger had apparently applied for, and received, a credit card under Guiton's name. So Guiton wrote to the bureau and asked that the erroneous information be deleted. "They wrote me back and indicated that they had corrected it, it had been taken off my record," Guiton testified before Congress in September 1989.[17] A few months later she requested her report again, and discovered the fraudulent account was still listed.

Errors are pervasive in credit files. When she testified, Guiton noted that her staff members had all requested their own credit reports; many found errors in their own files. In my personal experience, I do not know of a single person who has ever requested a copy of his or her own credit report and not found something in it that was wrong—not just a typo, but something that was detrimental to the overall credit rating.

Associated Credit Bureaus, the industry's trade organization, disputes the 50% figure. ACB claims that more than 550 million credit reports are sold each year with little mishap. According to a 1991 study funded by ACB and conducted by the consulting firm Arthur Andersen, errors critical to the decision of offering credit turn up in fewer than 1% of all consumer files. Still, that is more than two million people who are being denied credit unfairly.

Both studies are probably correct. Many people who see their credit reports spot errors on them, but usually they are not material. Indeed, there are so many errors on so many credit reports that credit card companies have come to expect them, and as a result, a single black mark no longer keeps a person from obtaining credit. But this approach is far from the most fair, because it invariably offers credit to some people who shouldn't get it, while it keeps credit from others who should.

IDENTITY THEFT: A STOLEN SELF

Stories like what happened to the Ross family made up the bulk of credit reporting problems in the 1980s and early 1990s. But in recent years, there has been a sudden and dramatic growth of a new kind of crime, made possible by the ready availability of both credit and once-private information on Americans. In these cases, one person finds another's name and Social Security number, applies for a dozen credit cards, and proceeds to run up huge bills. (Many banks make this kind of theft far easier than it should be by printing their customers' Social Security numbers on their bank statements.) Sometimes the thieves enjoy the merchandise for themselves, go on lavish trips, and eat in fine restaurants. Other times, the thieves fence the ill-gotten merchandise, turning it into cash. This crime has become so common that it has earned its own special name: *identity theft*.

Sometimes the crook gets the personal information from inside sources: in April 1996, federal prosecutors charged a group of Social Security Administration employees with stealing personal information on more than 11,000 people and selling the data to credit fraud rings, who used the information to activate stolen credit cards and ring up huge bills.[18] Other times, crooks pose as homeless people and rummage through urban trash cans, looking for bank and credit card statements.

A typical case is what happened to Stephen Shaw, a Washington-based journalist.[19] Sometime during the summer of 1991, a car salesman from Orlando, Florida with a similar name—Steven Shaw—obtained Stephen Shaw's credit report. This is actually easier than it sounds. For years, Equifax had aggressively marketed its credit reporting service to car dealers. The service lets salespeople weed out the Sunday window-shoppers from the serious prospects by asking a customer's name and then surreptitiously disappearing into the back room and running a quick credit check. In all likelihood, says the Washington-based Shaw, the Shaw in Florida had simply gone fishing for someone with a similar-sounding name and a good credit history.

Once Steven Shaw in Florida had Stephen Shaw's Social Security number and credit report, he had everything he needed to steal the journalist's identity. Besides stating that Stephen Shaw had excellent credit, the report listed his current and previous addresses, his mother's maiden name, and the account numbers of all of his major credit cards. Jackpot!

"He used my information to open 35 accounts and racked up $100,000 worth of charges," says Stephen Shaw. "He tagged me for everything under the sun—car loans, personal loans, bank accounts, stereos, furniture, appliances, clothes, airline tickets."

Because all the accounts were opened using Stephen Shaw's name and Social Security number, all of the businesses held the Washington-based Stephen Shaw liable for the money that the other Shaw spent. And when the bills weren't paid, the companies told Equifax and the other credit bureaus that Stephen Shaw, the man who once had stellar credit, was now a deadbeat.

Not all cases of identity theft start with a stolen credit report or a misappropriated bank statement. Some cases begin with a fraudulently filed change of address form, directing the victim's mail to an abandoned building. And no paper trail need be created at all. In May 1997, the *Seattle Times* reported that hundreds of people in the Seattle area had received suspicious crank phone calls. The caller claimed to be from a radio station that was giving away money; the check would be in the mail as soon as the people picking up the phone provided their Social Security numbers.

Some people found the calls suspicious and telephoned the station or the police. Others presumably handed over the information that the callers requested. Similar scams are epidemic on America Online, the world's largest online service, where they have been given the evocative name *phishing*.

Shaw says it took him more than four years to resolve his problems—a period that appears to be typical for most identity theft victims. That's four years of harassing calls from bill collectors, of getting more and more angry letters in the mail, of not knowing what else is being done in your name. Four years of having your creditors think of you as a deadbeat. During this period, it's virtually impossible for the victim to obtain a new credit card or a mortgage. One of the cruelest results of identity theft is that many victims find themselves unemployable; in addition to job references, many businesses routinely check the credit reports of their job applicants.

Identity theft is made possible because credit card companies, always on the lookout for new customers, don't have a good way to verify the identity of a person who mails in an application or orders a credit card over the telephone. So the credit card companies make a dangerous assumption: they take it for granted that if you know a person's name, address, telephone number, Social Security number, and mother's maiden name, *you must be that person*. And when the merchandise is bought and the bills aren't paid, that person is the one held responsible.

Of course, it's relatively easy to learn a person's name, address, telephone number, Social Security number, and mother's maiden name. Credit bureaus hand this data out to their customers. Lookup services make this information available, at minimal cost, over the Internet. And many consumers, unaware of the risk, will readily divulge this information to people who call on the phone and claim to be from a bank or credit card agency.

Identity theft isn't a fundamentally new kind of crime. There are many stories from fairy tales and from the American West of con men who scammed a place to stay, fancy meals, and even the affection of an unknowing lady, by claiming to be somebody else. What's different now is that corporate willingness to extend credit has made many more people vulnerable to having their identity and reputation exploited without their knowledge. And because the credit is offered by mail or by telephone—often by either a computer running a program or by a low-paid customer service representative reading a script—it has become nearly impossible for the hero to convince the lady that she has been duped by a rogue.

Nobody is really sure how prevalent identity theft is today—estimates vary between 100,000 and 400,000 cases a year—but it is definitely on the rise. Ideally, the perpetrators should be jailed, fined, and otherwise punished. But law enforcement agencies are overwhelmed, and the courts have not allowed the true victims—the people who have had their identities stolen—to press charges against the perpetrators. That's because the law sees the company that issued the credit as the aggrieved party, not the people who have had their identities stolen. And most banks won't prosecute; it is easier to simply write off the loss and move on.

There are lots of technical changes that could be made to lower the incidence of identity theft. One change, for example, would be to require a person applying for a credit card to show up in person and have a photograph taken, recorded, and put on the back of the credit card. This would act as a deterrent, since most identity thieves don't want to have records created that could be used to trace back to the their actual identity. But few credit card issuers would ever mandate the use of photographs, since it would effectively end the industry's marketing strategy of sending credit cards to new customers through the mail, without the need to have local branch offices.

Ultimately, identity theft is flourishing because credit-issuing companies are not being forced to cover the costs of their lax security procedures. The eagerness with which credit companies send out preapproved credit card applications creates the risk of fraud. When the fraud takes place, the credit issuer simply notes that information in the consumer's credit file and moves on; the consumer is left to pick up the pieces and otherwise deal with the cost of a stolen identity. It stands to reason, then, that the easiest way to reduce fraud would be to force the companies that are creating the risk to suffer the consequences. One way to do that would by penalizing companies that add provably false information to a consumer credit report in the same way we penalize individuals who file false police reports. Such penalties would force credit grantors to do a better job of identifying the individuals to whom they grant credit, and this, in turn, would do a good job of limiting the crime of identity theft.

LOOKING FORWARD BY LOOKING BACK

Looking back from thirty years later, there are a lot of lessons to learn from the failed federal National Data Center proposal and the nationwide system of databanks, access terminals, and computer networks that private industry built in the resulting vacuum.

Perhaps the most important lesson is that decisions made early on have far-reaching effects. Designed in 1932, the Social Security number has had its role in society constantly expanded over the last two-thirds of this century. No matter how you look at it, the SSN is a bad number. But our country has been unable to stop using it. Witness the huge number of uses that the number has today.[20]

Year	Authorized Uses of Social Security Numbers
1943	Federal agencies use SSN exclusively for employees.
1961	Civil Service Commission uses SSN as an employee identifier.
1962	Internal Revenue Service uses SSN as taxpayer identification.
1967	Department of Defense uses SSN as an Armed Forces identifier.
1972	U.S. begins issuing SSNs to legally admitted aliens at U.S. entry and to anyone receiving or applying for federal benefits.
1975	AFDC (Aid for Families with Dependent Children) uses SSN for eligibility.
1976	States use SSN for tax and general public assistance identification and for driver's licenses.
1977	Food stamp program uses SSN for household member eligibility.
1981	School lunch program uses SSN for adult household member eligibility.
1981	Selective Service System uses SSN for draft registrants.
1982	Federal loan program uses SSN for applicants.
1983	SSN required for all holders of interest-bearing accounts.
1984	States authorized to require SSN for AFDC, Medicaid, unemployment compensation, food stamp programs, and state programs established under a plan approved under Title I, X, XIV, or XVI of the Social Security Act.
1986	SSN may be used as proof of employment eligibility.
1986	SSN required for taxpayer identification for tax dependents age five and over (effective for 1988 returns).
1986	Secretary of Transportation authorizes use of SSN for commercial motor vehicle operator's licenses.
1988	SSN required for taxpayer identification for tax dependents age two and over (effective for 1990 returns).
1988	States use parents' SSNs to issue birth certificates.
1988	States and/or blood donation facilities use SSN for blood donor identification.
1988	All Title II beneficiaries required to have SSN for eligibility.
1989	National Student Loan Data System includes SSN of borrowers.
1990	SSN required for taxpayer identification for tax dependents age one and over (effective for 1991 returns).
1990	SSN required for eligibility for all Department of Veterans Affairs payments.
1990	SSN required for officers of food and retail stores that redeem food stamps.

Year	Authorized Uses of Social Security Numbers
1994	Use of SSN authorized for jury selection.
1994	Use of SSN authorized by Department of Labor for claim identification numbers for worker's compensation claims.
1994	SSN required for taxpayer identification for tax dependents regardless of age (effective for 1996 returns).
1996	SSN required for any applicant for a professional license, commercial driver's license, occupational license, or marriage license (must be recorded on the application). The SSN of any person subject to a divorce decree, support order, or paternity determination or acknowledgment would have to be placed in the pertinent records. SSNs are required on death certificates.
1996	The Attorney General authorized to require any noncitizen to provide his or her SSN for inclusion in Immigration and Naturalization Service (INS) records.
1996	Driver's licenses required to display an SSN.

Another important lesson is that large organizations that make technical mistakes rarely have to pay for their mistakes. Instead, it is users and the populace that pay. Today, banks and credit card companies offer easy, high-interest loans at the drop of an SSN; sometimes they screw up and offer these loans to a crook. When an error is made, it is often the defrauded customer who suffers the consequences of the unpaid loan. The banks don't really suffer at all: they simply raise their rates, spreading the cost throughout society as a whole.

Yet another lesson is that the details matter. Quick details and snippets that you might read in a newspaper or hear on TV don't convey the entire story. But all too often, that's the way complex issues involving technology and society are discussed in the media.

In the United States, it is almost an item of religious faith that the free market is all-powerful and always makes the correct decisions, while government regulation invariably creates problems. These beliefs are especially true among the digital elite, who see anything government does as bad and anything private enterprise does as good. Nevertheless, the reverse has been largely true in the area of computer privacy. Left to its own devices, private industry created a system in the 1960s that was tremendously unfair to private citizens. Yes, there was a free information market, but it was a market in which only businesses could participate. It was only after government interference—the Fair Credit Reporting Act—that people were given a right to look into their credit histories and to have inaccurate information removed. If anything, the acknowledged limitations in the FCRA suggest that the problem with government privacy regulation is not that we have too much, but rather that we don't have enough.

Hand-in-hand with the previous point, we've seen that business fights any attempt at privacy regulation, just as the chemical industry fought attempts at environmental regulation. Yet in both cases, the predicted dire consequences somehow failed to materialize. In fact, just as environmental regulations forced the chemical industry to be less wasteful—and thus more profitable—the few privacy regulations that have been adopted have generally improved the quality of the information stored in corporate and government databanks, thus making these systems more valuable, useful, and profitable. Indeed, protecting consumer privacy and freedom is in the best long-term interests of both business and society. But because most business leaders are focused on the next 12-month cycle, they don't tend to appreciate this simple fact.

OUR DATABANKED FUTURE

And what if we look in the other direction? Looking forward, we can see a future in which technology will increasingly be used to limit ambiguity. Anything that can be known will be known, and it will be known to a greater degree of precision than was ever thought possible. Left to its own devices, it's quite likely that business will repeat the mistakes of the past, designing systems that are fundamentally unfair, undemocratic, and unaccountable.

Back in 1965, the United States government stood at a computational crossroads. On the table was a proposal to create a massive government database. But when details of the project reached the public, the project was terminated. Instead, the U.S. Congress held hearings on the threat of computers to privacy, a U.S. government commission formulated the idea of data protection, and a (relatively) small part of the U.S. government's executive branch was given the mission to enforce a new set of laws.

We blew it. A national database could have headed off the excesses of the credit reporting industry. If the system had allowed strong user controls, or had avenues for redress, it further could have prevented the sea of errors that exist in the plethora of private databanks today. Moreover, with a public system, uses of the data for purposes other than those originally intended would have been debated in public, rather than proposed and approved behind closed doors.

Today, we stand at another computational crossroads. We are moving past the 1960s vision of computers that hold important financial, educational, and credit information. We are moving into an integrated future in which computers will track the most mundane and the most intimate aspects of our lives. They will measure and record the happenings on our planet. They will let us distinguish one person from another with the most fine-grained precision. Once again, there may be a need for the government to step in and set the rules for what can and cannot be done with this advanced information technology. Otherwise, we risk recreating the information abyss that we handled so deftly before. Sadly, this level of analysis is missing from most public discourse on credit card fraud, unauthorized uses of database information, and identity theft.

Databank technology has a fundamental problem: there is no way to guarantee that the information in the databank is correct. We should focus on this problem, and try to build computer and societal systems that are resilient in the face of error. Instead, we are doing the reverse. Bankers, law enforcement and immigration officials, and policymakers are looking for a quick technological fix to the problem of identifying individuals. In the next chapter, we'll see why this approach ultimately can't work.

CHAPTER THREE

ABSOLUTE IDENTIFICATION

Confronted with database discrepancies, identity theft, illegal immigration, and unsolved crimes, many policymakers have put their faith in the technological promise of biometric identification. These technologies, their boosters say, will ultimately usher in a regime of absolute identification in which each individual can be precisely known by the unique characteristics of that person's body.

Absolute identification is a policy goal that is within our grasp. Indeed, a growing number of scientists, engineers, and politicians now see identification of human bodies not as a technical problem, but rather as a political one. If society has the will, they argue, we could uniquely register every person in the United States, Europe, Asia, and possibly the entire planet. We could then routinely identify individuals at banks, at school, at work, and on the road. Absolute identification could eliminate mismatched computer records, stolen identities, and the ambiguity that comes with the messiness of day-to-day life. By replacing anonymity with absolute identity, we would create a society in which each person could be absolutely granted the privileges that come with his or her station in life, and each person could be held uniquely and absolutely accountable for his or her own actions.

Absolute identification is a seductive idea. It's a pity that it is also fundamentally flawed. To understand why, you need to understand the technology and its shortcomings.

ON THE IDENTIFICATION OF INFANTS

Three thousand years ago, two women in Jerusalem came before King Solomon. Both women had recently given birth to a child. Now one child was dead, and both women claimed the remaining child as their own. Solomon needed to identify the child and assign it to its rightful mother.

Today, Solomon's dilemma would be easy to solve. Unless the women were identical twins, they would have different genetic make-ups. By testing blood from both adults and the child, the baby's true mother could be easily determined. Indeed, such genetic tests are routinely performed in the modern world to determine the paternity of children in child support cases.

But Solomon didn't have modern biology at his disposal. So Solomon called for his sword. Since the women could not decide between themselves, he said, the child would be divided in half. Solomon knew that the baby's true mother would rather yield custody than see her child killed. And moments later, when one of the women hastily gave up the baby, Solomon knew that the other woman was the liar.

Twenty-five hundred years later, the explorer João de Barros wrote about a different way to identify young children. In his book *Décadas da Ásia*, published in 1563, de Barros described how Chinese merchants identified young children by stamping their palm prints and footprints on paper with ink. These weren't just any pieces of paper, of course: they were deeds of sale.[1] Once recorded in this way, there could be no chance of mistaking one child for another, which is quite important when human beings are being bought or sold.

Had Solomon wanted to, he could have instituted a similar system for registering the prints of every Israelite child at birth. Ancient Israel certainly had the necessary technology—parchment and ink—to carry out such a project. Ancient Israelites also knew that fingerprints were unique: in recent years, archeologists digging in Israel have discovered caches of clay pottery in which a thumbprint is clearly visible on each piece. Presumably, the potter had used his thumbprint as his own personal mark. But the idea of a national identification system never would have occurred to Solomon or any of his courtiers, because identification of adults was generally not a problem until the modern age.

Literature is filled with stories of mistaken identification: consider Mark Twain's *The Prince and the Pauper*, the stories of the Doppelgänger, and many Shakespearean plays. These stories appealed to our ancestors precisely because swapped or mistaken identities were not the stuff of everyday life. Before the Industrial Revolution, the world had no real need for a formal system of strong identification. In Europe, there wasn't even a need for last names until the Middle Ages! Most people were born in a place and lived there all their lives. People knew who you were. Outsiders were clearly identifiable.

ANTHROPOMETRICAL SIGNALMENT

A constellation of events in the late nineteenth century forced governments to find better ways to identify the people within their borders. The first was the rise of the modern city, in which people routinely carried out their day-to-day business with strangers. In the city, citizens needed a way of identifying each other so they could avoid being cheated: identity promotes accountability. The second event was the improved ease of travel, which created waves of immigrants seeking new homes. In short order, xenophobic lawmakers throughout Europe and the United States passed strict immigration laws to keep out the newly mobile foreigners. This, in turn, created a need for strong identification systems to let officials distinguish citizens from noncitizens. The third reason for strong identification was the nouveau concept of criminal rehabilitation—the idea that people who committed a crime could be rehabilitated and set on a new path, rather than simply put to death or exiled. Some sort of identification system was required to distinguish a first-time pickpocket from a habitual offender.

It was the problem of identifying convicted criminals that caught the attention of Alphonse Bertillion (1853–1914), a Parisian anthropologist. How do you identify a pickpocket who has been caught for the fourth time, if each time the crook is arrested he gives a different name? How is it possible to establish the continuity of identity without the cooperation of the individual?

Bertillion realized that even if names changed, even if a person cut his hair or put on weight, certain elements of the body remained fixed. He created a system called *anthropometrical signalment* for measuring these bodily invariants. The system was remarkably straightforward:

- When a person was arrested for a crime, Bertillion would have one of his assistants make careful measurements of the suspect's head, arms, feet, and ears. Also recorded were distinguishing scars, marks, and other unique bodily information. These measurements and the person's name were then recorded on an index card and stored at the central police station.

- Instead of arranging the cards by the arrested person's name, as others might have done, Bertillion placed them in files that were indexed by the measurements themselves. All of the men with heads that were longer than average were placed in one set of files, average in a second, and less than average in a third. Each of these files was then divided in threes according to the length of the arrested person's middle finger. The process was repeated for each of the six measurements that Bertillion recorded. The result was $3 \times 3 \times 3 \times 3 \times 3 \times 3 = 729$ different groups of cards.

- When an officer went to file a criminal's card, he would systematically check through the other cards for which the six signalment quantities were similar. If he found a card that was an exact match, the officer would know that the person had been previously arrested. By looking at the name on the older card, the officer could tell if the criminal had given the same name both times, or different ones.

Bertillion's system was a criminological breakthrough. A person could be arrested in 1881 and have his signalment recorded by one police officer. Three years later, after that police officer had left the force, the criminal could be rearrested, have his signalment rerecorded by a second officer, and have the match discovered as a matter of routine when the second card was filed. Bertillion had created a system for identifying people from records, whereas in the past such identifications could be performed only by using the eyesight of trained human beings.

Bertillion spent six years refining his system, then published a 95-page pamphlet for the 1879 International Prison Congress in Rome. Over the next decade, he oversaw the signalment of more than 120,000 criminals in Paris.

Today, much of Bertillion's work seems primitive and tinged by racism. (Bertillion was most impressed that his system could be used to distinguish one Gypsy from another, since few Frenchmen, apparently, had this ability.) But it worked. In the decade following December 1882, when the system was formally adopted, Parisian police used anthropometrical signalment to identify 4,564 individuals who had given the police false names. Bertillion made it possible for French judges to impose stiffer sentences on repeat offenders. Within a few years, various crime rates in Paris started to drop. Bertillion asserted that this was because the pickpockets were moving to places where they would have less chance of being identified.

By 1896, the Bertillion system had been adopted by 20 prisons and seven police departments in the United States alone. But boosters realized that the real potential of anthropometrical signalment wasn't merely identifying criminals. In the American edition of Bertillion's book, Major R. W. McClaughry, Warden of the Illinois State Penitentiary, clearly articulated the ultimate goal of any strong identification system: the identification of the entire populace. McClaughry imagined it as a strong tool for social control:

> According to the theory of the system, and in order for society to reap its full benefit, every human being should be partially signalized (especially by that part of the descriptive signalment relating to the ear) at the age of ten years, and completely so at the age of maturity; and every country

should have a national signaletic office where all the signalments of its inhabitants should be filed. The process of signalment would take the place of passports at every national frontier, and signalments would appear on all life insurance policies, permits and other papers whose value depends upon the establishment of personal identity. It would then be possible to find any person at once whenever desired, whether for his own good or that of society at large, in whatever place he might be and however he might alter his appearance or his name. Crime could thus be rooted out, elections purified, immigration laws effectively enforced, innumerable misunderstandings and much injustice prevented and all business relations greatly facilitated.[2]

A century later, American lawmakers are still looking for a strong identification system to enforce immigration laws, eliminate consumer fraud, and identify the dead. Of course, we're not measuring each other's ears and middle fingers.[3] But Bertillion's basic ideas carry forth in today's biometric and DNA-based identification systems, both of which extend the promise of allowing the authorities to find any person at once, whenever desired, for any purpose, and wherever they may happen to be.

THE SCIENCE OF FINGERPRINTS

Two black brothers, identical twins, are accused of a grisly murder in Missouri. The weapon is a bloody knife found at the scene of the crime. At the trial, the defense lawyer shows the jury that the murderer's fingers have each left their own characteristic prints on the weapon, and those prints match not the twins, but another person in the courtroom. The court is stunned: clearly, the wrong people are on trial!

The story is Mark Twain's *Pudd'nhead Wilson*, first published in 1893 by *Century Magazine*. Wilson's address to the jury gave many Americans their first introduction to the science of fingerprints:

> Every human being carries with him from his cradle to his grave certain physical marks which do not change their character, and by which he can always be identified—and that without shade or doubt or question. These marks are his signature, his physiological autograph, so to speak, and this autograph cannot be counterfeited, nor can he disguise it or hide it away, nor can it become illegible by the wear and mutations of time.[4]

Our understanding of fingerprints has changed little to this day. Determined by a combination of genetics and random processes inside the womb, fingerprints are fixed by birth and remain fixed for life. The marks truly are a unique signature: there is so much room for variation that no two people ever have shared, or ever will share, the same pattern.

Perhaps most importantly, fingerprints are permanent. I learned this firsthand when I took a chemistry course at Bryn Mawr College. I was performing a series of experiments with anhydrous acetic acid. After a few weeks, I noticed that the tips of my fingers had become smooth; the acid had actually etched away my fingerprints. But within a month after finishing the experiments, my fingerprints were back, exactly as they had been before and no worse for their absence.

The reason for this permanence is that the fingerprint pattern is determined by the very bottom layers of the epidermis. The only way to change an individual's fingerprints is to remove the skin entirely and replace it with new skin from elsewhere on the body. This painful and disfiguring operation was employed by a few gangsters in the 1930s, but hasn't found much use since.

Despite the fact that humans have long known that each person's fingerprints are unique, it wasn't until the late nineteenth century that scientists turned their attention to the possibility of using fingerprints for identification. Henry Faulds (1843–1930) published a letter in an 1880 edition of the scientific journal *Nature*. In his letter, Faulds noted that he occasionally left fingerprints on objects and conjectured that a criminal might leave similar monographs in oil at the scene of a crime. Should a suspect be apprehended, Faulds reasoned, it should be possible to compare that suspect's fingerprints with the prints left behind and see if they matched.

The value of fingerprints for crime-fighting, then, wasn't just that they were unique, but that they were left behind. And unlike Bertillion's system, it wasn't necessary to measure the fingerprints of an entire populace in order to make use of the system: you could simply compare latent prints with the prints of a suspect.

W. J. Herschel, an English official stationed in India, saw Faulds's letter and wrote to *Nature* that he had been using a similar crime-fighting technique for nearly 20 years. But whereas Faulds had thought that fingerprints would be useful only for establishing the identity of criminals, Herschel envisioned a much grander scheme of using fingerprints as a general-purpose system to establish identity and prevent impersonations. (Clearly, racism was operating here as well: Herschel, charged with maintaining order in a colony, couldn't tell the people apart without fingerprinting them.) Five years later, a photographer in San Francisco named Tabor noticed his own fingerprint made by an inky hand on a piece of paper. After carrying out some experiments, he suggested that fingerprints could be used as a means of registering Chinese immigrants, who presumably all looked the same to the people who were running San Francisco at the time. A similar proposal was made in 1885 in Cincinnati for putting fingerprints on railroad tickets.[5]

THE RISE OF THE IDENTIFICATION STATE

Both Bertillion and Herschel realized that identification technology had two uses in a modern society. On the one hand, identification technology is clearly useful for law enforcement. Using a universal fingerprint registry, you could simply take a latent print from a crime scene, search for a match in the registry, and know who had left the print behind. This same registry might have many positive social uses, such as protecting individuals from fraud and identifying the deceased.

Law enforcement agencies have long advocated the creation of such a registry. And until the 1980s, they were always met with sizable opposition. The only question is, why? Proponents of the infallibility of fingerprinting are continually baffled by public opposition to their plans for mass registration. For example, in the book *Finger Prints, Palms and Soles*, published in 1943 at the height of World War II, the authors, Harold Cummins and Charles Midlo, wrote:

> It is apparent that the day is soon coming when there will be no longer a significant objection to finger-printing. The feeling against it is on the wane, though there are still some who regard finger-printing as a stigma because they associate it with police records of criminals. It is not too much to hope that universal registration of prints will be eventually realized. Objections can be based only on misconceptions, namely that the method is tainted by its criminal application and that compulsory registration would violate principles of liberty.[6]

Why does the public fear mass registration? Perhaps because we know that fingerprints are not foolproof and that a registry, once created, could be misused. Here are some examples to ponder:

- Fingerprint identification is done by humans, and humans make mistakes.

- There is a risk that a person's fingerprint might have a legitimate reason for being at a crime scene. The presence of an identifiable fingerprint creates a presumption of guilt.

- A fingerprint might have been swapped, accidentally or intentionally, in a police laboratory.

- The fingerprint files maintained by the police might be surreptitiously modified, in order to frame an innocent person.

- A report from a fingerprint expert might be swapped or intentionally changed.

The more trust we place in an identification technology, the more rewarding fraud becomes. And the possibility of intentional fraud can never be eliminated. That's because fingerprints do not really identify a person: they merely link a particular finger to a record in a file. Change the file, and you change the identification.

The other side of the fingerprint coin is that strong identification systems are frequently used as a tool by oppressive or totalitarian societies. The people running these societies remain in power, in part, because the people who oppose the society are identified and subjected to increasing degrees of threats and punishment until they either accept the social order or are killed. The pass system in apartheid South Africa and the identification cards issued to Palestinians under Israeli occupation are both examples of such identification systems. Nondemocratic regimes require good identification systems: punishing the wrong people can create more enemies and, perhaps more importantly, can allow the real troublemakers to go free.

The United States never embarked on a mandatory fingerprint registration program. Instead, states and the federal government built their fingerprint files by fingerprinting people who were arrested and those who applied for particular jobs. These prints were recorded on a so-called "ten-print card"—one print for each finger. The cards were then classified by an expert and stored in a file cabinet. Sometimes police departments would create two cards: one for local use, and one that was sent to the FBI.

As the twentieth century progressed, the push for mandatory fingerprint registration began to ebb. The reason had to do with a fundamental contradiction inherent in the whole identification project: the larger the fingerprint files became, the harder it was to identify somebody from their fingerprints alone.

By 1987, the FBI had 23 million criminal fingerprint cards on file; the state of California alone had 7.5 million.[7] Realistically, this size made the files unusable for anything other than identity confirmation: given a name, an investigator could look up a fingerprint card and see if the prints matched. But for practical purposes, it was all but impossible to take a set of prints, cold, and determine a person's name. Fingerprint files had grown so large that they were no longer usable for their intended purpose! In the mid-1980s, for example, a crime scene investigator in San Francisco estimated that if he worked eight hours a day, seven days a week, it would take him 33 years to conduct a manual search of the city's 300,000 fingerprint cards.[8]

AFIS

Clearly, though, fingerprinting systems are still in use. This is due in large part to the Automated Fingerprint Identification System, also known as AFIS. AFIS completely changed the role of fingerprints in the 1980s. The systems combined relatively simple computer graphics, special-purpose algorithms for analyzing and matching fingerprint images, and parallel processing computers to create spectacularly effective forensic results.

Computers don't match fingerprints the way human beings do. Instead of looking at the patterns of arches, loops, and whorls, AFIS systems reduce the fingerprint image to a table of two-dimensional vectors. Called *minutiae,* these vectors correspond to the places on a fingerprint where a ridge begins, ends, or splits from one ridge into two. Each minutia has an exact (x,y) position within the fingerprint, as well as a direction in which it points.

A typical fingerprint has 90 or more minutiae; taken together, these points create a series of relationships that is absolutely unique. The typical AFIS search compares the set of minutiae points for a person's ten fingers, or roughly 900 points, against all of the other records stored in the database. The search is performed by a special-purpose computer called a *matcher.* In 1987, a typical matcher could search a candidate print against the database at a rate of 500 to 600 prints per second. (Today's matchers are roughly ten times faster.) Thus, a single database of a million prints could be searched in a little over 30 minutes. To speed the search, a police department could simply add a second matcher. The two units would operate in parallel, each scanning through half of the database and completing the task in 15 minutes. Actual systems might have five or ten matchers, reducing a typical search to minutes.

AFIS systems made it possible for police to search latent prints against the entire database. The systems could even conduct partial print searches, where only a part of a print is found at a crime scene. The following excerpt from a 1987 U.S. Department of Justice report extols the wonders of the then-new technology:

> The first latent print run against the San Francisco Police Department's AFIS database had been the subject of thousands of hours of manual search methods over an eight-year period. The print belonged to the killer of Miriam Slamovich, a World War II concentration camp survivor, who was shot point blank in the face by an intruder in her home in 1978. Her assailant left a full, perfect print at the scene, but with no suspect and no other clues, there was little chance of making a match on existing file prints by conventional manual searching methods. Police detectives doggedly pursued the case, however, and when the AFIS system was implemented in 1985, it matched the print in six minutes. Slamovich's alleged killer was in custody the same day.[9]

In 1988, I attended a conference on AFIS in Boston. There, I met Detective Ken Moses of the San Francisco Police Department. Moses told me that in 1984, the first year after the SFPD installed its automatic fingerprint identification system, the city's burglary rate dropped 26%.[10] Here's why: fingerprints are found at 40% of all burglaries;

28% of these fingerprints result in positive identifications. A positive fingerprint identification results in a conviction 93% of the time. By the end of 1985, San Francisco had identified, convicted, and sentenced more than 900 burglars using AFIS.

AFIS also allowed San Francisco do something that had never before been possible: turn back the clock and reinvestigate old, unsolved crimes. Starting with the case of Miriam Slamovich, police were able to clear 816 outstanding cases, including 52 homicides. (The previous year, only 58 cases in total had been cleared through the use of latent prints.)

San Francisco's experience was repeated in other jurisdictions. California's infamous "Night Stalker" case was similarly solved with an AFIS search using a latent print that was lifted from a stolen car. Within a few months after installing an AFIS system in Baltimore, the state of Maryland correctly identified 525 people who had been arrested and given false names to the police. The early AFIS successes were so stunning, in fact, that the Department of Justice report gushed: "AFIS may well have the greatest impact of any technological development on law enforcement effectiveness since the introduction of computers to widespread use in the criminal justice system in the 1960's."[11]

The rush by police forces to implement AFIS systems ignored one crucial factor: questions about the accuracy of the underlying technology. In part, this is because the uniqueness of fingerprints had long been established in American law. But another reason was that even a lay person could visually confirm an AFIS match by comparing the two fingerprints. And because the initial AFIS databases were built by scanning in cards that were already in the possession of police departments, the systems were largely adopted without public discussion. For law enforcement, the only serious policy questions were pragmatic ones: settling jurisdictional disputes between AFIS systems operated by cities, states, and the federal government; assuring that AFIS systems from different manufacturers used compatible file formats; and figuring out how to get more fingerprints digitized and stored in the computers.

Far more controversy surrounded the adoption of DNA identification systems, the technology popularly misnamed *DNA fingerprinting*.

DNA IDENTIFICATION

Deoxyribonucleic acid, better known as DNA, is the molecule that separates us and connects us. DNA is an intergenerational messenger, the basis of family and clan identity, and the imaginary binder of many nations. And yet, DNA is also the basis of most people's individuality.

Automatic Fingerprint Identification System

This terminal is used by a technician to view the results of a computerized search through a databank of digitized fingerprints. To look up a fingerprint, the AFIS system first analyzes the print and makes a list of the print's minutiae points—the points where a fingerprint ridge starts, stops, or forks. The matrix of these points is then used as a key into the computer's databank. Searches are very fast and very accurate: it can take less than a minute to search a database of a million prints and find an exact match.

The system shown here was developed by NEC Technologies' AFIS Division, which introduced one of the first biometric applications nearly 30 years ago and continues to lead the market today. Today, NEC's biometric identification technology is being used at more than 300 installations in 14 countries. Specially tailored systems are available for healthcare, licensing, welfare, and security. Many cities and states are aggressively deploying this technology, seeking to build a master database containing the fingerprints of every citizen, whether or not that person has committed a crime. Such a database, advocates say, would have a tremendous impact on both crime-fighting and identification of the dead or missing. [Photos courtesy NEC Technologies]

Just as our DNA connects us to both of our parents, our own unique pattern separates us from them.

DNA identity testing uses the genetic code as the basis of a near-perfect identification system. Today, this testing has three primary uses:

- Paternity testing

- Identification of blood and semen left at crime scenes

- Identification of human remains

Since half of a person's DNA fingerprint comes from each parent, it's relatively easy to use the molecule to determine paternity: all that's required are a few cells from the child, the mother, and the suspected father. Over the past decade, DNA testing has also worked its way into thousands of court cases. The test is ideal for crimes where no fingerprints are found, and needs only tiny amounts of genetic information for success—a drop of blood, saliva, or semen, a single hair root, or a piece of skin. As Dr. Michael Baird from Lifecodes Labs told me: "If you have a piece of blood on your shirt that matches the blood of the victim, chances are that you are the murderer."[12]

And increasingly, DNA testing is being used to identify human remains. Because DNA is an incredibly stable molecule, DNA necessary for identification can be retrieved from a body years, or even thousands of years, after a person's death. For this reason, the U.S. military has built a DNA identification database for every soldier in the armed services. Never again will the United States bury the remains of an unknown solider.

Meanwhile, the nature of the controversy surrounding DNA identification systems has subtly changed. When the technology was first introduced, scientists, lawyers, and civil libertarians argued over whether the underlying science was sound, and if the technology actually worked. Today, DNA identification is widely accepted as absolutely accurate—and we are struggling with the social implications of this newfound precision.

SETTLING THE SCIENCE: DNA TESTING 1986–1996

At the heart of DNA identity tests is the human genome itself. Each person carries a unique genetic code, a sequence of roughly 3 billion nucleic acid *base pairs*—adenine (A), guanine (G), cytosine (C), and thymidine (T). Every cell of a human body contains its own copy of that person's genetic code, determined at conception—a code that is different for every person on the planet. Unlike fingerprints, there's no way to change a person's DNA by surgery or by cutting off the person's hands.

Yet, while DNA identification techniques are quite powerful, the system suffers from fundamental problems. The first problem is that, unlike fingerprints, not everybody's DNA is unique: identical twins, by definition, share the same genetic pattern. And identical twins are fairly common: in North America, one in every 83.4 births is a twin, and 28.2% of twins share identical DNA from an original cell. Thus, roughly 0.338% of the population are identical twins—three people out of a thousand. Adopting DNA as the country's sole identification system would instantly create a million genetic doppelgängers.

A second problem inherent in DNA identification systems is that they do not use the entire human genome—at 3 billion base pairs, the genome is too big. The complete genome is also largely irrelevant for identification, since more than 99% of the DNA between two individuals is identical. Instead, the DNA tests look at particular regions of the DNA that don't seem to serve any function—what's commonly called *junk DNA*. Because these parts of the genome aren't involved in keeping the cell or the organism alive, random changes or mutations get passed down from generation to generation. DNA identification tests look at these regions in two different samples and report if they are the same or different.

If the two samples have patterns that don't match, then the test is conclusive: they didn't come from the same person. But what if there is a match? If two samples have the same pattern, they might be from the same person—or it might just be a random, coincidental match between two individuals. There is no way to know for sure. Indeed, the typical DNA test can only resolve a hundred or so different genetic patterns— meaning that the chance of a random match is one in a hundred. To deal with this uncertainty, identification labs typically combine the results from four or five tests. Provided that the tests are actually looking at different regions of the genome, and provided that the genetic patterns aren't "structured" within a community by inbreeding, using multiple tests can reduce the chance of a false match from one in a hundred to one in a million or even one in 500 million. But they can't entirely eliminate the chance of a false match. "DNA testing is not a fingerprint," says Dr. David Bing, former director of the Human Identification Trade Association. "You can never be sure. There is no DNA test that says that this person is unique."[13]

A third problem is that DNA identification tests need to be performed in a laboratory by a skilled technician. The jury in *Pudd'nhead Wilson* could look at the fingerprint on the murder weapon and compare it with the suspect's actual fingerprint. But because the DNA identification process relies on outside experts, there's always room for professional disagreement. And there's always a chance that a sample of blood or semen taken from a crime scene might be contaminated en route—either by accident or on purpose. (Indeed, the DNA evidence at the 1996 trial of O. J. Simpson was attacked by Simpson's defense team not on scientific grounds, but using the argument that the evidence had been contaminated by a racist cop intent on framing the former football player.)

When DNA testing first moved into American courtrooms in 1987, few defense lawyers knew enough about the science to raise these objections. Prosecutors presented DNA identification to judges and juries as a well-established scientific theory—despite the fact that the idea itself

DNA Identification

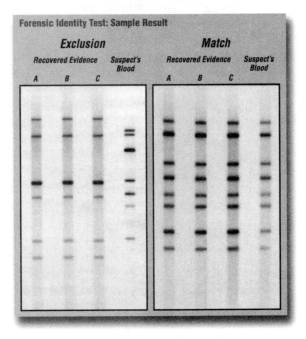

These two identity tests show the use of DNA evidence to exclude a suspect from a crime scene and to confirm a match. To perform this test, DNA is collected from a crime scene and from a suspect's blood. The DNA is then treated with an enzyme that cuts it into fragments of different sizes. The fragments are put on a piece of gel and placed in an electric field, which sorts the fragments by size. The fragments are then treated with a probe that adheres to unique patterns of DNA on the chromosome. A black line, or band, appears where the probe sticks. If a DNA sample has the same-sized fragments as DNA collected from a suspect, the DNA samples are said to match. This example is from Cellmark Diagnostics, one of the leading laboratories performing forensic DNA identifications. [Photo courtesy Cellmark Diagnostics, Inc., Germantown, Maryland]

had been first proposed only a year before. By 1991, DNA evidence had been used in hundreds of felony prosecutions. But there were problems. In the 1989 case *People v. Castro*,[14] the trial court accepted the state's DNA evidence, ruling that DNA testing was generally accepted by scientists—then the appellate court threw out the evidence because of apparent irregularities on the part of the testing laboratory. In November 1989, the Supreme Court of Minnesota threw out DNA evidence in *State v. Schwartz*:[15] the court criticized the testing laboratory for poor quality control and for failing to share the population-frequency data on which the lab's statistical conclusion was based. But that same year, the Maryland Court of Special Appeals ruled in the case *Cobey v. State*[16] that DNA evidence could be admitted—but that DNA evidence should not necessarily be "admissible willy-nilly in all criminal trials."

Suddenly, whenever the prosecution wanted to use DNA testing as evidence, the trial quickly became a trial about the scientific merit of DNA testing itself. Many scientific studies and papers argued the validity of the technique; however, all of them were written by people who were either on the payroll of testing labs or had been paid by the FBI or a state district attorney to testify at trials. Nobody in the scientific community could give an unbiased opinion about the technique; everyone who understood the science seemed to have a vested interest in it!

To help put the controversy to rest, in 1989 the National Research Council formed the Committee on DNA Technology in Forensic Science to study DNA-based identification techniques. Part of the National Academy of Sciences, the NRC is the United States' most prestigious research organization, widely regarded as the benchmark of fair and objective scientific wisdom. The Committee found that the underlying science was basically correct. But the industry needed to standardize on the particular probes being used, and it needed a bigger database of population genetics. And then the Committee made a serious mistake. Trying to settle a statistical dispute between practitioners of the DNA tests and a group of population geneticists, the Committee recommended that DNA tests be performed using a new statistical technique that it called the *interim ceiling principle*. The principle was a new mathematical formula for computing the chances of a mismatch—a formula that was much more conservative than those that were being used at the time.

"It created a legal snafu," Mark Stolorow, manager of forensic sciences at Cellmark Diagnostics, explained to me.[17] The problem was that the legal standard for the admission of scientific evidence in a court—called the Frye standard—requires that the scientific technique be peer reviewed and generally accepted by the scientific community. But the NRC's interim ceiling principle wasn't generally accepted; the members of the NRC committee invented it themselves.

In April 1993, FBI director William Sessions asked the NRC to do a follow-up study, in order to eliminate the confusion. Although this sort of reevaluation of a report was unprecedented, it was clearly necessary. Nevertheless, the whole process stumbled. NRC convened a new committee on August 30, 1993, but the committee didn't have its first meeting until September 1994 because of funding uncertainties. The report wasn't issued until 1996.

By the time that the NRC issued its second and final report on genetic identification testing, the issue was already settled. In November 1995, *Nature* published an article titled "DNA Fingerprinting Dispute Laid to Rest."[18] True to its title, the article was coauthored by the most vocal proponent of DNA testing, Eric S. Lander, and one of its most vocal opponents, Bruce Budowle. In the article, Lander, a geneticist at the Whitehead Institute Center for Genome Research, and Budowle, head of the FBI's Forensic Science Research and Training Center, agreed that the science behind DNA was sound. Provided that laboratories take care to avoid contamination, DNA can be as accurate as any other technology for assuring identification.

DNA FINGERPRINTING TODAY

It is hard to overstate the power of DNA identification testing. Today the tests have completely changed paternity testing for child support. "Do you know how they used to do paternity testing in the old days?" Dr. David Bing asked me. "They brought the child into the court and said 'does it look like him?'"

DNA testing is also being used by people who want to *know* if they are siblings, or half-siblings, but aren't interested in following up in court. CBR Laboratories has performed several of these tests for "sibship," says Bing, who was previously associate director of the lab. To perform the test, DNA samples are needed from both suspected siblings as well as from as many other relatives as possible. At $200 per person, the tests are not very expensive for the peace of mind that they produce. And people can be tested without their knowledge or permission—it's easy to get a DNA sample from a used tissue.

"Generally speaking, we wouldn't write up a report, but we will do the test," says Bing. The test wouldn't hold up in court because there is no chain of custody associated with the samples. But the tests do answer questions of the heart. Bing's laboratory will answer those questions for anybody—provided that the person is represented by a lawyer, physician, counselor, social worker, or private investigator.

Today, the ironclad certainty of DNA evidence is being used to overturn convictions from the days before the technology was available. The Innocence Project at Yeshiva University's Cardozo School of Law specializes in using DNA evidence to force the retrial and acquittal of those who have been falsely convicted of crimes. A 1996 report by the National Institute of Justice detailed 28 cases in which wrongly convicted men had been freed after DNA testing proved they were innocent. The men had served, on average, seven years in prison.[19] DNA testing is also being used to reunite children kidnapped during

Argentina's "Dirty War" with their grandparents and remaining family members.

Even the dead can be exonerated. In Cleveland, the son of Dr. Sam Sheppard hoped DNA evidence would prove once and for all that his father was innocent of the 1954 murder of his wife, Marilyn Sheppard. Sam Sheppard, who was imprisoned for ten years, was acquitted in a 1966 retrial of the case, but doubts remained in many people's minds. The doctor's son, Sam Reese Sheppard, successfully obtained an order in July 1997 to have his father's body exhumed so that his father's DNA could be compared with blood and bodily fluids found at the murder scene.[20] The testing proved that blood found at the scene of the crime belonged not to Sheppard, nor to his wife, but to another man.

THE DNA DATABANK

On the morning of November 25, 1991, a masked man broke into the home of a newlywed couple near Springfield, Illinois, shot and killed the husband, raped the wife, shot her, and left her for dead. Miraculously, the woman survived. Investigators took the murderer's semen from the woman and performed a routine DNA identification test. The pattern was searched against other DNA patterns stored inside a computerized DNA index system, but there was no match. And with the woman unable to identify her attacker, the police quickly ran out of clues. The case went cold.

The following April, in an unrelated case, Springfield police took a DNA sample from a man who had been convicted of raping a 17-year-old girl and entered the information into the same computer. This time, the computer reported a match—with the DNA taken from the November rape. A jury eventually convicted the man, Arthur Dale Hickey, of first-degree murder, attempted murder, aggravated criminal sexual assault, and home invasion. Hickey was sentenced to death.

According to the FBI, 67% of rapists commit more than one offense—with the average number of offenses being 2.8 detected, and 5.2 undetected. DNA identification technology promises to help solve many of these cases. As a result, the U.S. government passed legislation forcing every state to establish DNA registries for convicted sex offenders. And many of the state laws don't stop at sex offenders. Some states require that all convicted violent criminals provide samples. Others require that people convicted of nonviolent crimes be genetically fingerprinted as well. Some states even collect and databank the genetic patterns from people accused of crimes.

These DNA patterns are stored in the FBI's Combined DNA Index System, or CODIS. Authorized by the 1994 DNA Identification Act, the system is actually a network of computer systems designed to be used by local, state, and federal authorities as they acquire DNA profiles and search for matches. The pilot program has been operational since 1991.

DNA profiles are created from evidence left at crime scenes, as well as from convicted offenders. When a new profile is entered into CODIS, it is automatically searched against the profiles from all of the other unsolved crimes that the database contains. If a match is found, an email message is sent to the lab that entered the original information.

Keeping up with the number of samples coming into the system has been a problem. In the summer of 1997, the CODIS system had roughly 125,000 samples from convicted offenders and 20,000 samples from unsolved cases on file. Another 400,000 DNA samples from convicted offenders were in storage, waiting to be analyzed and fed into the computers. By November 1998, the number of untested samples had grown to 450,000 DNA samples throughout the United States.[21] At that time, the FBI asked for an additional infusion of $22.5 million, specifically designed to profile the backlog.

An even larger DNA databank is being constructed by the U.S. Department of Defense (DoD). The purpose of the Department of Defense DNA Registry is to identify the remains of lost soldiers. As of December 31, 1995, the Registry's Specimen Repository had 1.15 million DNA specimens.

According to a written statement about the repository that appeared on the DoD's web site:

> The blood is placed on special cards with the service member's Social Security number, date of birth, and branch of service designated on the front side of the card. On the reverse side of the bloodstain card are a fingerprint, a bar code, and signature attesting to the validity of the sample. Ultimately, the bloodstain card is stored in a vacuum-sealed barrier bag and frozen at −20 degrees Celsius, in the Specimen Repository. The oral swab (buccal scraping) is fixed in isopropanol and stored at room temperature. Great care is taken to prevent the possibility of error from sample switching or mislabeling.

But it is likely that this DNA databank may one day be used for more than just identification, since the DoD is storing whole blood cells, rather than simply the results of a particular DNA screening. DoD, after all, is creating the world's largest archive of well-preserved genetic material, and for each sample, the department has detailed medical and performance information. As the years pass and the databank grows, its guardians will be increasingly pressured to release samples for scientific research—and perhaps for criminal investigations as well. Some sort of mission creep seems likely, given the history of other federal databank projects.

COMPUTERIZED BIOMETRICS

Despite their apparent accuracy, neither fingerprints nor DNA samples are suitable for identifying individuals on a day-to-day basis. Fingerprints may be a lost cause: after more than 100 years, proponents have still been unable to shake the stain of criminality from their use. DNA identification is unworkable because the biological reactions on which DNA testing is based require minutes or hours, rather than seconds, to take place. Fortunately, for the past 100 years, the world has relied on another kind of biometric that can be nearly as good as a fingerprint or a DNA sample. That biometric is the photograph.

The most common form of identification today is a photograph fixed to an official document. Worldwide, the "universal currency" for personal identification is the passport. Most European countries supplement passports with identity cards. In the United States, the photo driver's license is the most common form of identification for both private industry and government.

The reliability of a driver's license depends on two factors. First, the state must be sure that the driver's license is being issued to the correct person. Second, the driver's license itself needs to be reasonably *tamper-proof*, so it can't be changed once it is issued. (A driver's license that can be easily modified is an invitation to crime, since the license can be stolen, altered, and then used for fraudulent purposes.) States have increasingly, and somewhat successfully, turned to exotic materials to make driver's licenses more difficult to forge. But they generally do only a fair job of verifying the identity of the prospective driver. An even bigger problem with the U.S. driver's license system is that each state's license looks radically different from every other's. It can be very difficult for a check casher in Massachusetts to know if an offered driver's license really came from the state of Montana or if it is a forgery.

Now the move is on to computerize identification systems. Like AFIS, modern biometric systems have two parts. The first is a device that is able to measure an aspect of the human body, and reduce that measurement to a series of numbers. The second is a large database, recording the biometric measurement for hundreds or thousands or millions of people. In many cases, an online database can do away with the problem of forgeries: while a fake piece of plastic can be produced, it is considerably harder to put fake entries into a government database.

A variety of computerized biometric systems have been proposed and developed over the past decade. The simplest involve merely creating an online database of every driver's license photograph. But more sophisticated biometrics are constantly being proposed and tested. Here are some of the more popular ones.

Retina prints. Eye prints are similar to fingerprints, but instead of capturing the minutiae on the tips of the fingers, these systems record and analyze the patterns inside a person's eye. In the 1980s, retina prints, based on the veins and arteries in a person's retina, were popular. But unlike fingerprints, retina prints are not fixed: when a woman is pregnant, the fetal hormones can cause new arteries and veins to branch in the mother's eye. If widely adopted, retina prints could prove to be a remarkably intrusive identification system, with women being forced to explain if they were pregnant, why they were pregnant, and perhaps what happened to the fetus, every time a retina print didn't quite match.

Iris prints. In the 1990s, iris prints have surged in popularity. The patterns on the human iris are fixed while the eyes are formed *in utero*; they remain constant for an individual's life; and they can be captured with a standard video camera, rather than an expensive and somewhat intrusive retinal scanner. One of the leaders in this field is IriScan, whose technology has been used inside prisons, at automatic teller machines, and, soon, in subway stations. British Telecom, a partner in the venture, has developed a high-speed iris scanner that can capture the iris print of a person in a car driving at 50 miles per hour. Today, the automotive scanner is quite expensive, as it requires special optics, a high-resolution camera, and a servo-mounted, computer-controlled lens. But as technology advances and prices drop, this technology is likely to become democratized.

Signature and handwriting analysis. Signature and handwriting analysis was one of the world's first biometrics. Today, signatures can be digitized and electronically compared with stored templates. If the signature is written on an electronic pad, the computer can also record the speed at which the pen moves and the pressure exerted. Combined, these three sets of values (position, speed, and pressure) create a biometric that is nearly impossible to forge.

Palm prints and hand geometry. Palm prints and hand geometry are two systems that rely on the wrinkles in a person's hand or the relative lengths of the fingers to establish identity. Both lack the consistency over a lifetime that fingerprints provide. On the other hand, these systems don't have the stigma of fingerprints. A hand geometry system was used to identify athletes at the 1996 Summer Olympics in Atlanta.

Voice prints. Voice print systems attempt to determine a speaker's identity by comparing a spoken phrase with one that has been previously recorded. Today's computer voice systems can perform either speaker identification, in which they determine who is speaking, or voice recognition, in which the computer determines what is being said. Today's computers can't perform identification and recognition at

Iris Scan

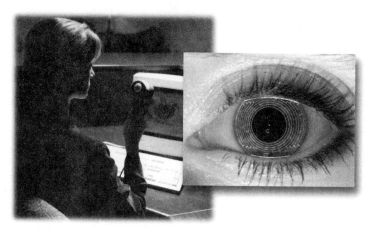

Of all the biometric identification systems made possible by the human body, iris scanning appears to be the most robust and most accurate. The subtle patterns in the iris of each person's eyes are fixed before birth and remain unchanged throughout life (barring an accident or surgery, of course). The patterns can be read using a standard high-resolution video camera, and there is so much variation between individuals that the probability that two irises would have the same biometric value is approximately 1 in 10^{78}. (The population of the earth is approximately 10^{10}.) Even identical twins have dramatically different irises.

Nevertheless, remember that an iris scan does not uniquely identify a person: an iris scan identifies an iris. Turning that identification into a name requires looking up the scan in a computerized database. If the database has been tampered with or altered, the iris scan will not yield the person's true identity. [Photos courtesy IriScan, Inc.]

the same time, but humans can, so it's reasonable to assume that as computers get faster they will be able to do the same. It's unlikely that computers will ever be able to identify speakers with 100% accuracy. After all, people can't do it either. Sometimes there just isn't enough information available for the task.

Face recognition. Face recognition systems attempt to identify people based on what they look like. Today's systems require that a person's face fill the computer's video camera and that the background be reasonably controlled. Future systems should be able to recognize a person in a crowd, the same way that people do (and probably with similar rates of success). Because there is no stigma attached to face recognition, and no fear of something scanning the eye, face recognition systems are poised to become quite popular in the coming century, which

Face Recognition

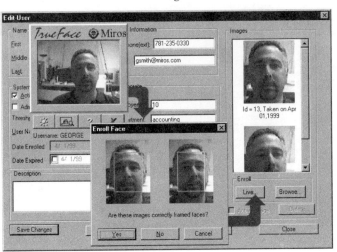

Unlike other biometric identification technologies, face recognition is largely passive: it can be performed without a person's knowledge, allowing the person to be identified in an elevator or as they walk through a doorway. Today, biometric systems are increasingly being used for identification at ATM machines, in banks, and by security-conscious businesses. Several states are evaluating whether face recognition should be applied to their databank of driver's license photos, allowing them to determine if the same person has been issued a driver's license in more than one name. [Image courtesy Miros, Inc.]

might have many unforeseen results. "Undercover people are scared about facial recognition," says Stephen Shaw, editor of *Identity World* magazine. "It doesn't just suck up terrorists—it gets diplomats and spooks and undercover cops."[22]

Facial thermograms. Facial thermograms identify people based on the patterns of veins and arteries underneath their skin. Although it's possible for a person to change their facial appearance with makeup or to grow or cut their facial hair, it's much harder to rearrange one's circulatory system. As a result, it's believed that facial thermograms might be more reliable than simple face recognition systems.

Silhouette identification and gait prints. Silhouette identification and gait prints are my own names for the next category of biometrics, but others in the identification field are considering them as well. When you see a friend at a distance, you can usually tell who they are without actually seeing their face. You make the identification based on a variety of parameters, including the person's size and proportions, the way they walk, and the kind of clothes they are wearing. Once again, if people can do this kind of identification, it's reasonable to think that computers will eventually be able to do it as well.

Performance. It is also possible to identify people based on their performance at a certain task. As an undergraduate at MIT, I developed a computer program that could identify people based on their typing speed and the pressure with which they hit the keyboard. While he was on staff at AT&T, researcher Thomas Speeter developed floor tiles that can identify who is walking on them.[23] Several computer intrusion programs can detect if somebody has broken into a computer system; the systems operate on the principle that intruders use computers differently from their legitimate users.

Writing style. A growing body of techniques can be used to identify the author of a creative work—be it a play, a novel, or a musical score—based on patterns in the work. In 1996, Donald Foster, a computer scientist at Vassar College, analyzed the best-selling novel *Primary Colors* and concluded that the "anonymous" author was in fact Joe Klein, a columnist for *Newsweek* magazine.[24] (Interestingly enough, Klein didn't admit to being the book's author until the *Washington Post* surreptitiously obtained a handwriting sample from Klein and from the book's original manuscript, and had the two compared by Maureen Casey Owens, a former chief document examiner for the Chicago Police Crime Laboratory.[25]) Likewise, Ted Kaczynski was identified as the Unabomber only after his manifesto was published and his brother recognized the writing style and ideas.

It's important to realize that *none* of the techniques mentioned here have gone through the kind of thorough peer review that was required of DNA fingerprinting in the 1980s and early 1990s. Instead, individuals and companies are testing them the way an undergraduate might test spaghetti boiling in a pot of water to see if it is done: throw it against the wall and see if it sticks. If we are to use biometrics for serious future applications, then they must be subjected to significantly higher standards of accuracy than they are today. Otherwise, it's likely that there will be numerous misidentifications and false identifications that will cast doubt and suspicion, and that could even imprison people who have done nothing wrong.

BIOMETRICS TOMORROW

Between 1989 and 1995, I lived in a house that had a voice print lock on its front door. The lock gave me freedom and power. It gave me the freedom to walk around without fear of losing my keys: as long as I had my voice, I knew that I would always be able to get back into my house. And it gave me the power to control access to my home with tremendous precision. For example, I could voice print a contractor who was doing work on my house, knowing for sure that he would not give the key to one of his employees or make a copy for himself. And I never had to ask somebody for his keys back: all I had to do was erase his voice from the lock's memory.

But the voice print lock was not without its faults. After a few months, I discovered that I could not enter my house if a jet was flying overhead, or during a particularly loud rainstorm. I also discovered that biometrics are not democratic. Certain individuals could not be reliably identified by the system, while others were always identified on their first try. (Similar problems have been reported with fingerprint identification systems.) As a result, I eventually created "voiceless codes" that would let people in without requiring that they first speak a pass-phrase.

As we move into the next century, experiences such as mine will become widespread, as biometrics increasingly replace keys and identity cards. Biometrics will be used to open the doors of office buildings and to unlock computer files. Your computer will recognize you when you sit down in front of it, either by voice or by using its built-in video camera. It's easy to see why people are likely to prefer biometrics-based systems: there will be no passwords to forget and no access cards to lose. Yet at the same time, some people will be discriminated against because their biometrics are not easily read or reproduced.

Imagine a university in the year 2020. At the cafeteria, students take a tray, pick up the food that they want, and then simply walk to the dining room. A computerized system scans each student's tray, calculating the cost of the food they've taken, then looks at the student's face to figure out whose account should be debited. At the library, another face recognition system has long since replaced the student's library card. When the student walks into a laboratory, the computer scans his face to make sure that he has authorized entry—this is especially important for labs that contain material that could be subverted and used by terrorists. And when the student sits down at a computer, the system automatically logs the person in and opens his files.

This university of the future won't need to issue its students identification cards: a smart video camera and a connection to the university's computer network will work just as well. But the university will probably continue to issue student IDs so students can prove their university affiliation to area businesses and other organizations. After all, no university is going to let outsiders tap into its biometric database!

The university biometric identification system works because a university is a total environment and students are voluntary members. Because students are paying a lot of money to earn academic credit, and because a university's library privileges, athletic facilities, and dorms are not available to the general public, the students have a vested interest in being properly identified by the institution.

Many stores now have video cameras that record the image of everyone who walks inside. (Frequently, these cameras are positioned in such a way that they also record the person's height.) Soon these cameras will likely be connected to computers and networks that use the person's face and other information to determine his or her identity. The store's computers might consult public records to find out if the person who just entered is wanted by the authorities. The computer might check other databases to find out if the person has a history of violent behavior, or if they owe too much money on their credit cards, or if they are suspected shoplifters. Place the camera outside the store and you can have the computer automatically lock the store's doors when a disreputable person tries to enter. Because these identification systems won't be perfect, places that use them will have to weigh the risk of not using the technology versus the risk of lawsuits, civil penalties, or simply poor customer relations that might result from misidentifications. In fact, the computer would probably be programmed to weigh the risk for each shopper.

Building a database of all the nation's faces would not be very difficult, since much of the data is already in public hands. In the 1990s, most states began digitizing photographs that were recorded on driver's licenses. These photographs, which are now part of the public record, will increasingly be sold to private businesses unless the sales are prohibited by legislation. The process has already started. In February 1999, the South Carolina Public Safety Department sold photographs of the state's 3.5 million drivers to Image Data LLC of Nashua, New Hampshire. The price was a bargain basement $5,000, or roughly a penny for seven photos, according to an article in the *Washington Post*.

The *Washington Post* also revealed that Image Data LLC had received a $1.46 million grant and technical assistance from the U.S. Secret Service in 1998. The company was charged with building a national photo ID database to fight check and credit card fraud, as well as to fight terrorism and verify immigration status.[26]

Image Data's plans cause alarm because photographs provide tremendous potential for abuse. For example, a racist programmer operating inside a bank might gimmick a bank's loan calculation program to automatically factor in a person's skin tone as part of the loan approval process. Alternatively, a bug in a computer program, especially one based on "neural net" technology, might inadvertently factor in this information without anyone's conscious planning. Such calculations could be exceedingly difficult to locate during a routine audit.

Ironically, there is a far cheaper and easier approach for using photography to prevent check and credit fraud. Instead of building a computerized database with all of the nation's faces, simply put each person's photograph on the front of his or her credit cards and checks. The Polaroid Corporation developed a photo credit card in the 1960s, but most banks resisted using the cards. One reason was that photographs, while they decrease fraud, marginally increase costs. The second reason is that if a person's photograph needs to be snapped before that person can be issued a credit card, then banks cannot acquire new customers by target marketing: in order to get a photograph onto the card, the customer needs to come into the bank in person.

The national database of photographs is well on its way to being created. But we as a society need to discuss what this database will be used for, who will have access to it, and how erroneous information will be corrected. It would be a mistake to give private industry unrestricted use of this data without any checks and balances.

BIOMETRIC PIRACY

When the *Washington Post* published word of South Carolina's impending sale of driver's license photographs, it caused an uproar. Immediately, the state tried to get out of the contract, arguing that the sale would violate the privacy of its citizens. But a state judge rejected the argument, saying that no law prevented the sale.

As a result of this and other cases, it's likely that some states will soon pass legislation to prevent states from selling driver's license photographs to private businesses. But it will be harder to prevent businesses from using their own resources to construct national image databanks. Video cameras behind checkout counters already record the image of each person using a credit card. It would be simple for a business to match up this information with names taken from the subject's credit card or courtesy card. In fact, such data collection is so easy that it is likely to happen unless lawmakers outlaw the practice.

Steve Mann, now a professor at the University of Toronto, Department of Electrical Engineering, calls the capture of a person's image without his or her permission *likeness piracy*.[27] Mann is quick to point out that likeness piracy is different from copyright infringement: copyright only protects specific creative works that are in a fixed form. Copyright infringement is the appropriation and use of a specific image; likeness piracy is the appropriation and use of a person's image in general.

Some laws in the United States and other countries regulate likeness piracy. In the state of New York, for instance, it is a crime to use somebody's image in conjunction with an advertisement without his or her permission. This law dates to the early twentieth century, when

Smart Card–Based Identification

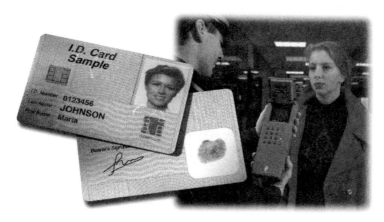

A "smart card," like this one from Gemplus, is a plastic card that contains a tiny microchip. The chip can hold both a microprocessor and several kilobytes of memory. One popular application of smart cards is as "stored value cards," in which the cards are used to store a kind of digital money. Another way to use a smart card is as a mobile databank that cannot be easily accessed or modified by the cardholder. In this example, the smart card is used as an identity card that contains a digitized photograph and possibly a fingerprint. Here, the border guard can compare the face of the woman standing in front of him with the image of the woman stored in the card. Because it is presumably more difficult for a person to tamper with the digitized image stored inside the smart card than to tamper with the image printed on the card's surface, smart card identity cards are considered by their promoters to be more secure. Although this may be true today, the presumption that smart cards are more secure means that there will be a higher reward for creating counterfeit or falsified cards. Ultimately, the smart cards of the future may be no more secure than credit cards are today. [Photos courtesy Gemplus]

marketers put people's faces on boxes as a form of product endorsement—without first going through the formality of obtaining the person's permission. It's anyone's guess if these laws will prevent likeness and biometric piracy in the twenty-first century. They won't if biometrics policy becomes an established business practice.

Already, the United Parcel Service, the nation's largest package delivery service, is also the nation's leader in biometric piracy. For most packages, UPS requires that a signature be written to serve as proof of delivery. In 1987, UPS started scanning the pen-and-ink signatures recorded for each package delivery. These images were stored in a database and faxed to any person who called UPS's 800 number and asked for a "proof of delivery" receipt. In 1990, UPS improved its piracy technology by equipping its drivers with portable electronic computers called DIADs (Delivery Information Acquisition Devices). Each computer has a built-in bar code reader and a signature pad. When a delivery is made, the UPS driver scans the bar code on each package and then has the person receiving the delivery sign for the package. The bar code number and the handwritten signature are recorded inside the DIAD, and ultimately uploaded to the company's databanks.

The push to make signatures available in electronic form came from UPS customers, Pat Steffen, a spokesperson for UPS, told me when I called the company to complain about the practices. Signatures are considered proof of delivery. Digitizing that proof allows UPS to manipulate it like any other digital data. The faxed proof-of-delivery certificates are sent automatically from UPS computers, she explained. It's also possible for UPS customers to download tracking software and view the signatures directly on their personal computers.[28]

Ironically, by making a person's written signature widely available, UPS is helping to dilute the written signature's very value. Once the signature is digitized, it's easy to manipulate it further with a computer—for example, you can paste it at the bottom of a contract. UPS's system is particularly vulnerable: any package can be tracked as long as you know the package's airbill, and UPS issues its preprinted airbills in sequential order—for example, "0930 8164 904," "0930 8164 913," and "0930 8164 922." An attacker can easily learn a company's UPS airbill, use that airbill to obtain a comprehensive list of every delivery recipient—and then make a copy of every recipient's signature.

UPS understands the vulnerability, but it can't address the problem very well. A note on the company's web site says:

> UPS authorizes you to use UPS tracking systems solely to track shipments tendered by or for you to UPS for delivery and for no other purpose. Any other use of UPS tracking systems and information is strictly prohibited.

But, realistically speaking, UPS can do little to prevent this kind of attack. "If someone wants to go out of their way to get package numbers, it can be done. If someone wants to go out of their way to do anything, I suppose that's possible. It is not an easy thing to do," said Steffen. Guessing would be harder, of course, if UPS used longer airbill numbers and didn't issue them in a predictable sequence.

The financial community has found a better way to incorporate biometrics into its business practices. Historically, crooks have been able to either steal blank checks or print their own, fill them out, and then take them to a bank and cash them. So in 1997, SeaFirst and a number of other West Coast banks started recording thumbprints on the back of checks whenever they were cashed by a person who didn't already have an account at the bank. The fingerprint itself was recorded with a new kind of ink: the person simply puts his thumb on the ink-pad, presses his thumb against the check's back, then wipes off the rest of the ink. This way, if it turns out that the check was forged, SeaFirst has the thumbprint of the actual crook—and it's the crook's actual thumbprint, rather than a copy of the thumbprint that was stored inside a computer (where it could be electronically manipulated to implicate somebody else). Since SeaFirst knows the exact time that the check was cashed—that's also recorded on the check, as well as in the bank's computer—it's a simple matter to go to the videotape and get a photograph of the crook's face. Thumbprints can also be searched through a variety of AFIS systems. Alas, while this technique may be laudable from a technical point of view, it has the unfortunate side-effect of making people who cash checks feel as if they are being treated like criminals.

Biometrics *are* a powerful means to ascertain somebody's identity, but only for the person or the machine that actually does the measuring. Once a biometric is stored inside a computer, all of the security provided by biometric identification is lost. A stored biometric could easily have been copied from another computer, rather than being directly measured. This is a critical distinction to understand when using biometrics. It is a distinction that is so subtle that it frequently is overlooked by the people implementing and using biometrics-based systems.

IDENTIFYING BODIES, NOT PEOPLE

Absolute identification is a seductive idea. Unfortunately, it's an idea that is fundamentally flawed. All of the identification techniques discussed in this chapter share a common flaw: the techniques do not identify *people*, they identify *bodies*. In modern society, people are legal entities. People have names, Social Security numbers, and histories. People buy and sell property. People have obligations. Bodies, on the other hand, are the warm-blooded, two-legged animals that are walking around on our planet's surface. Bodies are born, and bodies die.

When a murder is committed in our society, one body has taken the life of another body. It is then the job of the police to determine the people involved—that is, identifying the victim and finding the perpetrator. Bodies are imprisoned, but people go to jail. Any identification databank, whether it's the passports issued by the U.S. State Department or the FBI's CODIS system, attempts to draw lines connecting legal people with the bodies that they inhabit. This is an imperfect exercise.

Today, it is remarkably easy for a criminal to adopt an assumed name and construct an alias, complete with a state-issued driver's license. Many underground and semi-underground tracts give precise directions on how to create a fraudulent identity: first, search public records and find somebody who was born at roughly the same time and died in early childhood. Next, request a duplicate birth certificate and Social Security card. Subscribe to magazines in the stolen name. Just start using it. At some point, take a driver's license test.

The United States does not operate a central computerized registry of every birth and death in the country. Instead, cities, counties, and states all operate their own record systems. Sometimes records get lost—hospitals burn down, computer files get destroyed. Sometimes there are duplicate records, sometimes there aren't. Many record-keeping systems are antiquated. This lack of centralization can be exploited by people who know how. Once the identity of a dead child is appropriated in this manner, it can be remarkably difficult to disprove. Just about the only way one of these constructed identities can unravel is if the individual was previously arrested or fingerprinted—and if that information has been stored in some biometrically indexed, computerized database, such as a police department's fingerprint files. The databanks don't prove that the new identity is false. All they prove is that the biometrically identified body once used some other person's name.

Crooks aren't the only ones who create new people for old bodies: the government does it as well. New identities are routinely created for undercover officers, spies, defectors, and participants in the Federal Witness Protection Program. These needs of the state assure that no ironclad biometric identification system will ever be adopted in the United States or anywhere else: there will always need to be a means to introduce erroneous information into any government-sponsored identification database, or to change correct information that is no longer politically appropriate.

Some biometric identification systems have another problem as well: they can be subverted by a person who is suitably motivated. In the 1930s, gangsters had their fingerprints surgically removed and replaced with skin grafts from other parts of their bodies. Today, a person's hand prints or retina prints could be similarly removed—with the person's permission, or without. The risk or danger of mutilation will only increase as society increases its reliance on biometrics.

Instead of relying on technology to solve the social problem of bodily identification, we might want to consider social solutions. One possibility would be to use relatively weak identification systems and have very strong penalties for people who engage in identity fraud. Next, we should create statutory damages not just for the bank or business that was defrauded, but also for the person who had their identity appropriated.

Biometrics are sure to be an omnipresent part of tomorrow. But because of their recognized limitations, and because of the legitimate civil liberties concerns that these systems create, our civilization will probably not experience the full realization of a totally biometrically tracked future. Instead of tracking people, our civilization will increasingly turn to the much simpler project of tracking things, as the next chapter explores.

CHAPTER FOUR

WHAT DID YOU DO TODAY?

When I was teenager, I tried keeping a diary. I took out my fountain pen every night before I went to sleep and wrote down the details of the previous day. I had just started dating and soon the book's pages were filled with stories of my teenage romances: I'd write down who I liked and who I didn't; who I had seen at school and who I had talked to on the phone. And, of course, I wrote down the details of my dates themselves: who they were with, where we had gone, what we had eaten, and what we had done.

After a month or so I had created quite an impressive historical record of my teenage exploits. But as time passed, my entries started getting shorter and shorter. It was just too much work to write down all of the details. Ultimately, my project collapsed under the weight of its own data.

Keeping that diary in today's world would be much easier. Every time I buy something with a credit card, I get back a little yellow slip telling me the exact time and location of my purchase. I get a much more detailed receipt at my neighborhood supermarket that lists the name and size of everything in my shopping cart. My airline's frequent flyer statement lists every city that I've flown to over the past year. Should I accidentally throw out the statement, all of this information is stored safely in numerous computer databanks.

Even my telephone calls are carefully recorded, tabulated, and presented to me at the end of each month. I remember in college when my girlfriend broke up with me during a long-distance phone call. We talked for 20 minutes, then she hung up. I called her back again and again; I got her answering machine each time. A few weeks later, the phone bill came in the mail, and there were the calls: one for 20 minutes, and then five calls in rapid succession, each one lasting just 15 seconds.

But by far the most detailed records of my life reside on my computer's hard drive: my stored email messages, going back to my freshman year in college. All told, there are more than 600 megabytes of information—roughly 315,000 pages of double-spaced text, or 40 pages of text for every day since September 3, 1983, when I got my first email account at MIT.

"Keep all your old email messages," my friend Harold told me just before I graduated. "When historians look back at the 1980s, we are the ones they're going to be writing about." And he was right: with keyword searching and advanced text-processing algorithms, it will be a simple matter for some future historian to assemble a very accurate record of my life as a college student—and my life ever since—by examining the written electronic record I've left behind.

But this archive of facts and feelings is a rapier that can slice two different ways. More than my own digital diary, I have also been casting a vast "data shadow" that reveals the secrets of my daily life to anyone who can read it.

Alan Westin coined the term *data shadow* in the 1960s. Westin, a professor at Columbia University in New York, warned that credit records, bank records, insurance records, and other information that made up America's emerging digital infrastructure could be combined to create a detailed digital dossier. The metaphor, with its slightly sinister feeling, was uncannily accurate: just as few people are aware of where their shadows fall, few data subjects in the future, Westin conjectured, would be able to keep track of their digital dossiers.

In the three decades that have passed since then, the data shadow has grown from an academic conjecture to a concrete reality that affects us all.

We stand at the brink of an information crisis. Never before has so much information about so many people been collected in so many different places. Never before has so much information been made so easily available to so many institutions in so many different ways and for so many different purposes.

Unlike the email that's stored on my laptop, my data shadow is largely beyond my control. Scattered across the computers of a hundred different companies, my shadow stands at attention, shoulder-to-shoulder with an army of other data shadows inside the databanks of corporations and governments all over the world. These shadows are making routine the discovery of human secrets. They are forcing us to live up to a new standard of accountability. And because the information that makes up these shadows is occasionally incorrect, they leave us all vulnerable to punishment or retaliation for actions that we did not even commit.

The good news is that we can fight back against this wholesale invasion of personal privacy. We can fight to stop the capturing of everyday events. And where capture is inevitable, we can establish strong business practices and laws that guarantee the sanctity of our privacy—protection for our shadows to live by. We have done so before. All that's is needed is for people to understand how this information is being recorded, and how to make that recording stop.

THE INFORMATION CRISIS

As an experiment, make a list of the data trails that you leave behind on a daily basis. Did you buy lunch with a credit card? Write that down. Did you buy lunch with cash, but visit the automatic teller machine (ATM) beforehand? If so, then that withdrawal makes up your data shadow as well. Every long distance phone call, any time you leave a message inside a voice mailbox, and every web page you access on the Internet—all of these are part of your comprehensive data profile.

You are more likely to leave records if you live in a city, if you pay for things with credit cards, and if your work requires that you use a telephone or a computer. You will leave fewer records if you live in the country or if you are not affluent. This is really no surprise: detailed records are what makes the modern economy possible.

What is surprising, though, is the amount of collateral information that these records reveal. Withdraw cash from an ATM, and a computer records not just how much money you took out, but the fact that you were physically located at a particular place and time. Make a telephone call to somebody who has Caller ID, and a little box records not just your phone number (and possibly your name), but also the exact time that you placed your call. Browse the Internet, and the web server on the other side of your computer's screen doesn't just record every page that you download—it also records the speed of your computer's modem, the kind of web browser you are using, and even your geographical location.

There's nothing terribly new here, either. In 1986, John Diebold wrote about a bank that seven years earlier

> had recently installed an automatic teller machine network and noticed "that an unusual number of withdrawals were being made every night between midnight and 2:00 a.m." . . . Suspecting foul play, the bank hired detectives to look into the matter. It turns out that many of the late-night customers were withdrawing cash on their way to a local red light district![1]

An article about the incident that appeared in the Knight News Service observed: "there's a bank someplace in America that knows which of its customers paid a hooker last night."[2] (Diebold, one of America's computer pioneers in the 1960s and 1970s, had been an advocate of the proposed National Data Center. But by 1986, he had come to believe that building the Data Center would have been a tremendous mistake, because it would have concentrated too much information in one place.)

I call records such as banks' ATM archives *hot files*. They are juicy, they reveal unexpected information, and they exist largely outside the scope of most people's understanding.

Over the past 15 years, we've seen a growing use of hot files. One of the earliest cases that I remember occurred in the 1980s, when investigators for the U.S. Drug Enforcement Agency started scanning through the records of lawn-and-garden stores and correlating the information with data dumps from electric companies. The DEA project was called Operation Green Merchant; by 1993, the DEA, together with state and local authorities, had seized nearly 4,000 growing operations, arrested more than 1,500 violators, and frozen millions of dollars in illicitly acquired profits and assets.[3] Critics charged that the program was a dragnet that caught both the innocent and the guilty. The investigators were searching out people who were clandestinely raising marijuana in their basements. While the agents did find some pot farmers, they also raided quite a few innocent gardeners—including one who lived next to an editor at the *New York Times*. The *Times* eventually wrote an editorial, but it didn't stop the DEA's practices.

Americans got another dose of hot file surprise in the fall of 1987, when President Ronald Reagan nominated Judge Robert Bork to the Supreme Court of the United States. Bork's nomination was fiercely opposed by women's groups, who said that the judge had a history of ruling against women's issues; they feared that Bork would be the deciding vote to help the Court overturn a woman's right to an abortion. Looking for dirt, a journalist from Washington, D.C.'s liberal *City Paper* visited a video rental store in Bork's neighborhood and obtained a printout from the store's computer of every movie that Bork had ever rented there. The journalist had hoped that Bork would be renting pornographic films. As it turned out, Bork's tastes in video veered towards mild fare: the 146 videos listed on the printout were mostly Disney movies and Hitchcock films.

Nevertheless, Bork's reputation was still somewhat damaged. Some accounts of the Bork story that have been published and many offhanded remarks at cocktail parties often omit the fact that the journalist came up empty in the search for pornography. Instead, these accounts erroneously give the impression that Bork was a fan of porn, or at least allow the reader to draw that conclusion.

The problem with hot files, then, is that they are too hot: on the one hand, they reveal information about us that many people think a dignified society keeps private; on the other hand, they are easily misinterpreted. And it turns out that these records are also easily faked: if the clerk at the video rental store had wanted to do so, that person could easily have added a few dozen porno flicks to the record, and nobody could have proved that the record had been faked.

As computerized record-keeping systems become more prevalent in our society, we are likely to see more and more cases in which the raw data collected by these systems for one purpose is used for another. Indeed, advancing technology makes such releases all the more likely. In the past, computer systems simply could not store all of the information that they could collect: it was necessary to design systems so that they would periodically discard data when it was no longer needed. But today, with the dramatic developments in data storage technology, it's easy to store information for months or years after it is no longer needed. As a result, computers are now retaining an increasingly more complete record of our lives—as they did with Judge Bork's video rental records. Ask yourself this: what business did the video rental store have keeping a list of the movies that Bork had rented, after the movies had been returned?

This sea of records is creating a new standard of accountability for our society. Instead of relying on trust or giving people the benefit of the doubt, we can now simply check the record and see who was right and who was wrong. The ready availability of personal information also makes things easier for crooks, stalkers, blackmail artists, con men, and others who are up to no good. One of the most dramatic cases was the murder of actress Rebecca Schaeffer in 1989. Schaeffer had gone to great lengths to protect her privacy. But a 19-year-old crazed fan, who allegedly wanted to meet her, hired a private investigator to find out her home address. The investigator went to California's Department of Motor Vehicles, which at the time made vehicle registration information available to anyone who wanted it, since the information was part of the public record. The fan then went to Schaeffer's house, waited for four hours, and shot her once in the chest when she opened her front door.[4]

FALSE DATA SYNDROME

Another insidious problem with this data sea is something I call *false data syndrome*. Because much of the information in the data sea is correct, we are predisposed to believe that it is all correct—a dangerous assumption that is all too easy to make. The purveyors of the information themselves often encourage this kind of sloppy thinking by failing to acknowledge the shortcomings of their systems.

For example, in 1997, the telephone company NYNEX (now part of Bell Atlantic) launched an aggressive campaign to sell the new Caller ID service to its subscribers. With the headline "See Who's Calling Before You Pick Up the Phone," the advertisement read:

> Caller ID lets you see both the *name and number* of the incoming call so you can decide to take the call now or return it later. Even if the caller doesn't leave a message, your Caller ID box automatically stores the name, number, and time of the incoming call. Caller ID also works with Call Waiting, so you can see who's calling *even while you're talking to someone else.*[5]

Clearly, NYNEX was confusing human identities with telephone numbers. Caller ID doesn't show the telephone number that belongs to the person who is making the call—it shows the number of the telephone from which the call is being placed. So-called "enhanced" Caller ID services that display a name and number don't really display the caller's name—they display the name of the person who is listed in the telephone book. If I make an obscene call from your house during a party, or if I use your telephone to make a threat on the life of the president of the United States (a federal crime), Caller ID will say that you are the culprit—not me.

THE TRACKING PROCESS: HOW OUR INFORMATION IS TURNED AGAINST US

Nobody set out to build a society in which the most minute details of everyday life are permanently recorded for posterity. But this is the future that we are marching towards, thanks to a variety of social, economic, and technological factors.

Humans are born collectors. Psychologically, it's much easier to hold on to something than to throw it away. This is all the more true for data. Nobody really feels comfortable erasing business correspondence or destroying old records—you never know when something might be useful. Advancing technology is making it possible to realize our collective dream of never throwing anything away—or at least never throwing away a piece of information.

The first computer that I bought in 1978 stored information on cassette tapes. I could fit 200 kilobytes on a 30-minute cassette, if I was lucky. The computer that I use today has an internal hard disk that can store 6 gigabytes of information—a 30,000-fold increase in just two decades. And this story is hardly unique: all over the world, businesses, governments, and individuals have seen similar improvements in their ability to store data. As a civilization, we've used this new-found ability to store more and more minute details of everyday existence. We are building the world's *datasphere*: a body of information that describes the Earth and our actions upon it.

Building the world's datasphere is a three-step process—one that we've been blindly following without considering its ramifications for the future of privacy. First, industrialized society creates new opportunities for data collection. Next, we dramatically increase the ease of automatically capturing information into a computer. The final step is to arrange this information into a large-scale database so it can be easily retrieved at a moment's notice.

Once the day-to-day events of our lives are systematically captured in a machine-readable format, this information takes on a life of its own. It finds new uses. It becomes indispensable in business operations. And it often flows from computer to computer, from business to business, and between industry and government. If we don't step back and stop the collection and release of this data, we'll soon have a world in which every moment and every action is permanently "on the record."

STEP 1: MAKE DATA COLLECTABLE

The first step to building the global datasphere is to create information worth collecting. Consider a forest: by itself, a mountain of trees has no data. Now go through the forest and number every tree, estimate its age and height, and survey its location, and you have created an extremely valuable data set for both environmentalists and the timber industry.

I got a very good introduction to this first step in 1988, when I visited a BASF floppy disk manufacturing plant located just outside Boston. As part of the manufacturing process, I learned, each floppy disk is stamped with a code called a *lot number*. Pick up a floppy disk and flip it over, and you're likely to find these same numbers today: A2C5114B, or S2078274, or 01S1406. These codes identify the manufacturer of the disks, the factory, and the particular machine where the disk was created, and the date and time that the lot was started. Sometimes the information is encoded directly into the number. Other times, the lot number merely refers to an entry in a logbook or a process control system. Either way, decoding a lot number usually requires proprietary information that manufacturers are rarely willing to share with the general public.

The primary purpose of these lot numbers is quality control. If a run of bad disks turns up, the manufacturer can look at the lot number on the bad disks and figure out where they came from. By examining the factory's records, a quality control engineer can find the exact piece of equipment that caused the problem—which is the first step to preventing the problem from recurring in the future. Ultimately, this saves the company money and improves its reputation.

Once you know how to recognize lot numbers, you'll soon start seeing lot numbers everywhere: on a candy bar wrapper, a bottle of pills, or the rim of a flashlight. Some objects are so important that each one gets its own tracking number, in which case the number is called a *serial number*. Turn over the mouse that's connected to your desktop computer and you'll find one. There's another serial number on your computer itself, as well as on many of the individual components inside. It's all quite ironic. In the early days of the Industrial Revolution, one of the biggest technical challenges that engineers faced was producing functionally identical, interchangeable parts. Today, we have become so good at making things indistinguishable that we now need to imprint each with its own code so that we can tell them apart.

Lot numbers and serial numbers all serve a fundamental purpose: by making seemingly identical things distinguishable, the numbers make the history of the things recordable. But once inscribed, these codes can be used for much more than simple quality control: increasingly, lot numbers and serial numbers are being used for law enforcement.

Lot numbers can prove vital to a product-tampering investigation, for example. If tampered products at different stores all come from the same lot, then the tampering probably took place at the factory. If tampered products all come from different lots—possibly manufactured at different plants—then the tampering almost certainly took place at the store or in the home.

One of the most successful tracking numbers in recent years is the *Vehicle Identification Number* (VIN), a 17-character code that is stamped on the dashboard, engine, and axle of every car and truck manufactured in the world. The VIN was created in the 1970s by a coalition of auto makers and national governments who wanted a worldwide standard, according to Thomas Carr, manager of passenger safety regulations for the American Automobile Manufacturer's Association.[6] The first 16 characters in the VIN identify the manufacturer, the country of manufacture, the make and model of the vehicle, the assembly plant where it was built, the year it was built, information on the car's restraint system, the kind of transmission and rear axle used in trucks, and a six-digit sequential code.

The last character in the VIN is special. It's called a check digit. This digit doesn't contain any information of its own; instead, it is computed from the other digits. The digit makes the VIN self-verifying, letting a computer automatically detect a number of common typographical errors, such as switching two digits around or hitting an adjacent key on a computer keyboard. Since the VIN is the key that is used to index all of the records for a particular motor vehicle, explains Carr, being able to verify that a VIN has been correctly typed is very important.

VINs are used to track the car throughout the entire production process. After the car leaves the plant, VINs are used by governments to keep track of who owns each car, both to collect taxes and to help return stolen cars to their rightful owners. And in recent years, VINs have found a new role—solving car and truck bomb cases. In the bombings of both the World Trade Center in New York City and the Murrah Federal Building in Oklahoma City, investigators were able to quickly locate the axles of the trucks that were blown up. The VINs that were stamped on the axles allowed investigators to determine the trucks' owners, which allowed them to determine where the trucks had been rented—which in both cases led them to the identities of the bombers.

STEP 2: MAKE DATA MACHINE-READABLE

Automatic data collection is the second big step needed to create the datasphere. Automated systems read a piece of information and feed it directly into a computer, without human intervention. Although automated systems can be expensive to set up, once they are operational, they dramatically lower the cost of data collection, making it possible to create huge data sets and to keep them up to date. As a result, when a few major players in an industry start to adopt an automated system, the entire industry quickly follows.

The U.S. banking industry was one of the first major segments of our economy to adopt machine-readable codes. In 1963, a few banks started printing checks using special magnetic ink, so that computers could automatically read the nine-digit bank routing numbers, account numbers, and check numbers stamped across each check's bottom. It was a good idea: by 1969, 90% of the checks in the United States were printed with the shiny black numbers, greatly decreasing the time

INTEL'S PSN

A tracking number that has had a very rough start is the Processor Serial Number (PSN) that Intel introduced with its Pentium III microprocessor. Intel originally designed the serial number in the Pentium III microprocessor to help the company detect "over-clocking" of CPUs (i.e., when a 500 MHz chip is sold as a 600 MHz chip) and to help large companies track computers as they move around through an organization. When upper management found out about the feature, the PSN was given an "e-commerce" spin—Intel suggested that web sites could use special software to read the PSN of their customers' computers over the Internet.

When Intel announced the PSN in January 1999, the company decided to emphasize the "e-commerce" feature, rather than the asset-tracking capability. Within a week, several consumer groups organized a boycott against the microprocessor, saying that the more likely use of the PSN would be to silently track Internet users as they click through web sites. Meanwhile, cryptography expert Bruce Schneier published a scathing article in which he attacked the PSN because it was a number that could not be obtained in a secure fashion. He wrote:

> If a remote Web site queries a processor ID, it has no way of knowing whether the number it gets back is a real ID or a forged ID. Likewise, if a piece of software queries its processor's ID, it has no way of knowing whether the number it gets back is the real ID or whether a patch in the operating system trapped the call and responded with a fake ID. Because Intel didn't bother creating a secure way to query the ID, it will be easy to break the security.[7]

required to process them.[8] In the 1970s, the banking industry started adding magnetic strips to credit cards so the little pieces of plastic could be swiped through a reader. Before then, the numbers had to be manually entered into a computer after they were transferred to a credit card slip using a piece of carbon paper and a roller.

Other industries have been slower to adopt machine-readable systems. It wasn't until the mid-1990s that General Motors started supplementing the original VIN plates with machine-readable bar codes. Unlike the old VIN, which could only be read up close by a human, the new bar code can be read from more than 20 feet away using a high-speed laser scanner. Once in place, the bar code VIN quickly gained adherents. One company that jumped on the bandwagon was the car rental agency Avis, which now uses laser scanners to automatically track cars as they are returned at the company's drop-off locations. In the coming years, these machine-readable VINs will increasingly be a part of most drivers' lives. For example, urban garages might use the bar codes to automatically open gates for their monthly patrons. Other

License Plate Reader

Electronic tags aren't the only way to track a vehicle on the open road. The U.S. Customs Service has deployed license plate readers at many border crossings between the U.S. and Canada. These systems use a high-resolution video camera to locate and capture the image of a car's license plate in just milliseconds. From that image, the Perceptics license plate reader can determine both the plate's number and the issuing state or province. Says the company, "With our License Plate Reader, every highway is an open book." [Photos courtesy Perceptics]

companies have developed computerized vision systems that can read the license plate of a stopped or moving car, creating another system for automatically identifying automobiles at a distance.

Moving away from magnetic and optical systems, the newest machine-readable tags are scanned using radio waves. The technology, called RFID (short for Radio Frequency Identification Device), consists of two parts: a tiny silicon chip with a small radio antenna, called the *tag*, and a gun-shaped *reader*. Each chip is manufactured with a unique code. Point the reader at the chip, and the chip's code appears on the reader's display. The code is also sent to an attached computer.

Radio Frequency Identification Devices

Radio Frequency Identification Device (RFID) systems make it possible to embed a computer-readable serial number in an automobile, a gas cylinder, a pet, or even a human being. The system is based on an electronic tag that is stimulated using a low-energy radio signal. Once energized, the tag transmits its serial number. RFID tags are made by many different manufacturers; some RFID tags can be read from a distance of several feet. RIFD systems have been used for ski tags, employee badges, and tracking animals. A similar technology is used in most highway automatic toll collection systems. Since these systems are silent and passive, they can be read without the knowledge (or the consent) of the person carrying the radio tag.

Like other identification systems, RFID systems don't actually identify a car, a pet, or a person: they simply identify the tag. And since no cryptography is employed by today's RFID systems, an RFID identification response can be eavesdropped, falsified, or otherwise forged. The tags can also be read without the owner's knowledge. Since today's tags have no memory, there is no way to determine how many times a tag has been read, only by whom. Neither the producers nor the users of these systems seem to be concerned with the shortcomings of the security that these systems provide. [Photos courtesy Trovan]

The chips have no moving parts, no batteries to wear out, and an indefinite lifetime.

When you point an RFID reader at a transponder and pull the trigger, the gun fires a burst of radio frequency energy in the direction of the chip. The transponder's antenna picks up this energy and converts it into an electric current, which powers both the transponder's microchip and its tiny on-board radio transmitter. The transponder then sends back the chip's unique code (today's chips use a 64-bit code) on another radio frequency.

Several companies make RFID systems. One of the largest is Trovan, based in the United Kingdom. Trovan's largest device is about the size of a quarter and can be read from two feet away; the smallest is the size of a grain of rice. Readable from 18 inches, the tiny tag is designed to be sewn into the lining of clothing for inventory tracking. Trovan also makes a special implantable tag which comes in a presterilized, ready-to-use disposable syringe; it can be tucked under the skin of an animal in less than 20 seconds.[9]

In England, Yamaha dealers are using Trovan to help fight motorcycle theft. For U.K.£65 (about U.S.$100), you can have Trovan chips implanted into your bike's frame, wheels, tank, and seat. If the bike is stolen or stripped, the parts can be identified when somebody comes in trying to sell them.

In the United States, RFID systems are being used for *asset management*—a technique through which businesses cut costs by carefully managing the items they have already bought. One application is the tracking of gas cylinders. By drilling a small hole in the neck of the gas cylinder and dropping in an RFID device, it becomes possible to accurately track the location of each cylinder as it is moved between the plant and the customer. Other companies have embedded RFID devices in hand-held tools, which workers are then required to check out and check back in like library books.

Meanwhile, implantable tags are being used by zoos around the world to track exotic animals. And in North America, they're being used to track pets: by the summer of 1997, at least 200,000 cats and dogs in the U.S. had been implanted with some form of RFID. Several companies now operate a national database that matches the pets' chip ID numbers with their owners' names, addresses, and phone numbers, alongside the chip's identification code. Organizations like the ASPCA in New York City, San Diego County in California, and the cities of Minneapolis and St. Paul are buying readers. Stray animals found on the street are now being scanned when they are brought to a shelter.

As these cases show, the power of RFID is that once the radio tag is implanted into an object, the tag becomes a part of that object. A serial number that's on a gun can be filed down or etched away with acid. Cars can be stripped of their VINs. Tattoos can be overgrown with hair, or simply covered by clothing. But put a chip on the inside and the serial number becomes invisible, indelible, and detectable at a distance.

Although the obvious motivation for tracking is to prevent loss, other advantages of increased control and knowledge soon come to light. Some U.S. farmers have discovered that once an animal is given a serial number, it becomes possible to keep highly accurate long-term records. By tracking an animal from birth to slaughter, keeping detailed records of each animal's vaccination history, feed, weight, and handling, and even performing an occasional ultrasound scan, farmers can apply scientific management techniques to their overall operation. Ultimately, the extra work can increase the market value of an animal by approximately $700 to $1000. Meanwhile, the U.S. Department of Agriculture may soon mandate the electronic tracking of cattle in order to combat disease.[10]

STEP 3: BUILD A BIG DATABASE

As the tag-wielding U.S. farmers have learned, a good database is what marks the difference between disorganized data and a usable collection of information. But the organization of a database, and the policies that control access to the information the database contains, can dramatically impact the privacy implications of the entire tracking enterprise.

Consider the case of Electronic Toll Collection (ETC). Over the past decade, systems that let automobile and truck drivers pay their highway and bridge tolls electronically have been enthusiastically adopted around the world. The reason: ETC systems put an end to traffic jams around toll plazas. Instead of requiring drivers to stop and toss a few coins into a basket or hand a bill to a toll collector, most ETC systems use a radio tag to uniquely identify a car's account, from which the toll is automatically deducted.

In Norway, Micro Design ASA installed one of the earliest systems on a highway north of Trondheim in 1988. The technology has improved rapidly since then. Today, a system manufactured by Saab Combitech, Sweden, can read an electronic tag in less than 10 milliseconds when the vehicle is traveling at speeds up to 100 miles per hour. The Saab system can also determine the vehicle's speed by measuring the Doppler shift of the returning radio signal.

In 1994, the New York–area Triborough Bridge and Tunnel Authority (TBTA) installed an ETC system called E-ZPass at tollbooths on the Verrazano Narrows Bridge. After some early snafus, E-ZPass was soon fulfilling its mission, boosting the number of cars that each lane could handle from 250 to 1000 per hour. The public responded enthusiastically: during its first two years of operation, TBTA issued 550,000 E-ZPass tags. "Each work day, we collect 280,000 electronic tolls, or 42 percent of the total transactions," TBTA president Michael Ascher told a trade publication in March 1997.[11] A similar system, E-Pass, has been enthusiastically adopted by Florida drivers on the Orlando–Orange County Expressway.

Among state and federal highway administrators, the big issues with these ETC systems are cost, reliability, and interoperability. Many states have adopted systems that use incompatible tags: E-ZPass uses the windshield-mounted tag, while Florida's E-Pass system uses a radio transponder the size of a flashlight mounted under the car's front bumper. Within a few years, highway administrators hope the U.S. will adopt a single national system that will let a car travel from California to New York, paying all of the intervening bridge and highway tolls electronically.

But administrators have not focused on the privacy implications of the systems they are deploying. And those implications are staggering. The ETC systems maintain a detailed record of each time each car pays a toll. Officially, the ETC systems keep this information so they can send drivers a monthly statement showing them where their money is going. But the database is a gold mine of personal information that has uses far beyond simple accounting. A restaurant could scan it to build a list of everyone who drives by its place of business. A private investigator could use this database to track the movements of an errant spouse. Reporters could track celebrities, and crooks could use it to target a victim.

Once states are collecting large amounts of movement information, it is quite likely that it will be used and exploited. Already, cash-strapped state governments are selling their driver's-license databases to companies like R. L. Polk, which are using the data to build marketing lists.[12] But even if the information is not sold, its existence means that some bad guy might someday bribe a state employee to get at the juicy data.

Highway administrators don't seem to be sensitive to these risks. In 1995, the Massachusetts Turnpike Authority (MTA) published a three-inch-thick Request for Proposals to contractors interested in selling electronic toll collection systems to the state. The word "privacy" didn't appear. I called up John Judge, the MTA's Director of Operations, to ask why.

"Privacy is a non-issue," said Judge:

> I think that is the experience nationwide, at least as it relates to electronic toll collection. Privacy has not been an issue that has emerged nationally. I think that [is] principally because it is a voluntary system. If you are of a mind where you might be concerned about privacy issues, you just don't have to join the program, and can use the traditional toll collection methods. I don't think that it is any more an issue than credit cards.[13]

Distressingly, U.S. courts seem to agree with Judge—although for different reasons. On June 26, 1997, Justice Colleen McMahon ruled that the Triborough Bridge and Tunnel Authority had to turn over toll-crossing records to police whenever presented with a subpoena. Previously, the TBTA had required police to get a court order for release of the information—something that McMahon said was too restrictive on police. Her reasoning was that the movements of E-ZPass holders were easily observed, and so therefore the electronic records should be made public as well.[14]

Positional information is also very much a part of the cellular telephone systems, which must track phones at all times so that calls can be delivered. In 1997, British Telecom announced that it was developing a mobile telephone that would report the caller's location, to within 30 feet, to the person receiving the call. "Workers will no longer be able to phone the office pretending to be sick when they are at the beach, and movements of cheating spouses will be exposed," enthused an article in the *Electronic Telegraph*.[15] And as part of the U.S. 911 system, cellular providers must be able to locate 60% of all phones to within 150 meters by the year 2001. Like all positional information, this data has multiple uses. Besides allowing ambulances to be sent faster to a car wreck, police are increasingly asking cellular providers for position information when they serve wiretap orders on cell phone companies.

The approach to vehicular privacy has been similar across the border in Canada. Ontario's Highway 407 now has a sophisticated system for automatically billing automobile owners for the number of miles their vehicles drive on the public highway. The system uses a video camera to capture the image of the vehicle's license plate. Tolls are assessed when automobile registrations are renewed: people who refuse to pay the bills won't be allowed to renew.

THE BIGGEST DATABASE IN THE WORLD

Probably the largest database in the world today is the collection of web pages on the Internet. While much of the Web is filled with pornographic images, magazine articles, and product advertisements, there is a staggering amount of personal information as well: individual home pages, email messages, and postings to the Usenet. This record can be automatically searched for revealing disclosures, unintentional admissions of guilt, or other kinds of potentially valuable information.

Back before the explosive growth of the World Wide Web, Rick Gates, a student and lecturer at the University of Arizona, was interested in exploring the limits of the Internet database. In September 1992, he created the Internet Hunt, a monthly scavenger hunt for information on the Net. Early hunts had the participants locate satellite weather photographs or the text to White House speeches. The hunt was especially popular among librarians, who were at the time trying to make the case that the Internet could be a valuable reference tool.

Electronic Toll Collection

This statement from the Orlando-Orange County Expressway Authority shows the comings and goings of a car as it travels along the state's expressway system. The cars are tracked using a passive electronic tag that is placed on the windshield or under the car's frame. Although the E-Pass is designed for automatic toll collection, the system can also be used to precisely calculate the speed of automobiles, track cars that are stolen, or even snoop on errant spouses. In the future, these records could be used for marketing as well. Automatic toll collection systems create a goldmine of private information. Nevertheless, there have been few public discussions on the appropriate uses of this data. [Statement courtesy Orlando–Orange County Expressway Authority]

In June 1993, Gates decided to have a different kind of hunt. It was the first where the goal was simply to find as much information as possible about the person behind an email address.

In one week the hunt's 32 teams eventually discovered 148 different pieces of information about the life of Ross Stapleton.[16] A computer at the University of Michigan reported that Stapleton had B.A. degrees in Russian Language and Literature and Computer Science. A computer at the University of Arizona reported that he had a Ph.D. in Management Information Systems. A computer operated by the U.S. Military's Defense Data Network (DDN) Network Information Center divulged Stapleton's current and previous addresses and phone numbers. And a brochure on a Gopher server operated by the Computer Professionals for Social Responsibility reported that Stapleton was one of the conference's speakers—and that he was an analyst in the Office of Scientific and Weapons Research at the U.S. Central Intelligence Agency.

But the most revealing information the group assembled came from statements Stapleton himself had made. By scanning messages he had sent to the COM-PRIV mailing list—ironically, a mailing list devoted to privacy issues—the group learned that Stapleton used the OS/2 operating system and didn't have a fax machine. They learned that he was also affiliated with Georgetown University, where he was an adjunct professor and taught courses on the Information Age. They discovered that Stapleton subscribed to the *Arlington Journal*, the *Chronicle of Higher Education*, and Prodigy. He was a member of the AAASS (American Association for the Advancement of Slavic Studies). His Cleveland Freenet Membership number was #ak287.

From the dedication in Stapleton's thesis dissertation, "Personal Computing in the CEMA Community," the hunters discovered that Stapleton's parents were named Tom and Shirle. From the heading of another mail message he sent, they discovered that he was engaged, and that his fiancée's name was Sarah Gray. Transcripts of Stapleton's comments at the Second Conference on Computers, Freedom, and Privacy were also unearthed.[17]

"Stepping back a bit and taking the hunt results as a whole, one can see that there's an awful lot of information that can be found on someone, even when restricted to freely accessible, publicly available Nets," said organizer Rick Gates in his report on the hunt. "I hope that people keep that in mind when they are posting to an email listserv or newsgroup. They are really adding to the sum total of the Nets, and what they have to say in some limited discussion of an [obscure] topic may be around for a long time."

An odd side effect of the global database is that it is easier to seek out information on people who have unique or unusual names. For instance, I tried searching the Internet in February 1998 for the phrase "Tom and Shirle." HotBot, an Internet search engine, found the word "Tom" on 1,833,334 pages and the word "And" on 63,502,825 pages. But the word "Shirle" was on just 333 pages, and the phrase "Tom and Shirle" was on six pages—all of which, it turns out, were copies of Gates's June 1993 report.

"I was pleasantly surprised to see the amount of information that I myself put out that they managed to find," said Stapleton when I interviewed him for this chapter. "Nothing came out during the hunt that I would have said alarmed me." But Stapleton had been worried that somebody at the CIA might be angry that he had revealed his name and employer in so many public forums. "It was only going to be a matter of time before somebody at work said, 'Hey, what have you been doing?'"

Perhaps what's most remarkable about the June 1993 Internet Hunt is that it no longer seems remarkable that such a detailed profile of a person could be constructed from publicly available sources. The explosion of online information sources, combined with advertiser-supported search-and-retrieval services like Yahoo, Lycos, and AltaVista, have made it possible to easily assemble these kinds of detailed profiles. Indeed, several services, such as DejaNews and HotBot, specifically advertise this ability.

THE AGE OF PUBLIC STATEMENTS

Posts to email forums, Usenet groups, and online chat services are all different kinds of public statements. Most people who decide to take their place in cyberspace eventually start making these statements. And these statements are not like any others ever uttered in the course of human history. In the past, statements made in public were frequently lost. Yes, they could be recorded, but those records were almost always hard to retrieve, or even inaccessible. An angry farmer might speak up at a town meeting and have his name recorded in the minutes, but ten years later, somebody trying to do a background investigation on that farmer would be unlikely to find his remarks—especially if the farmer had moved to Seattle and started a new life as a programmer at Microsoft. Letters written to newspapers in the 1950s, 1960s, 1970s, and 1980s were certainly published for everybody to see, but they were rarely indexed in computerized databanks and made instantly available anywhere in the world.

This new generation of public statements is quantitatively different from anything that has ever come before. These are public statements that can be instantly searched out by a prospective employer, by a person with whom you have just had your first date, or by a coworker who means you harm. And once you've made a statement, it is out of your control: retraction has become an impossibility.

It is this search capability that is creating a new kind of *absolute accountability*. It's a simple matter to use the Internet's searching capabilities to get a list of people who have admitted to taking LSD, or who have used racist slurs in print, or who have a history of organizing for labor unions. Says Stapleton, "It's increasingly easy for someone in an HR department to say—'Look, Joe here says that skydiving is cool. Do we want to carry him on the rolls considering that he might die? Jane here is in a lifestyle that the chairman might not find attractive. We might not want to put her forward for the public affairs spot.' I don't have any public activities that I don't want to post about. If I did, I would be very cautious."

Ultimately, the wide availability of this information might create powerful new social filters through which only the boring and reserved will be able to pass. The existence of this information makes opinionated people vulnerable to all sorts of malicious attacks. Pervasive recording and indexing of public statements might keep the best and the brightest from ever holding elected office.

The end of the 1993 Internet Hunt report contains this prescient note: "In short, we're dealing with a unique medium here. It sort of feels like verbal discussion, but it's a lot more enduring, and can reach millions of people."

Ironically, Gates' report endures to this day, and will probably endure for decades more. That's because digitized text is very portable, very compact, and very easy to search. Although the original computer on which he typed and posted his message has long since been retired, the data has been copied again and again and again.

WASTE.COM

On May 12, 1999, the *Boston Herald* ran a front-page story titled "Waste.com."[18] The story detailed the results of an in-depth investigation the *Herald* had conducted of Internet use by public employees and others using taxpayer-funded Internet accounts. They discovered that an account registered to the state auditor's office was being used to scalp tickets to a sporting event—a violation of state law. It found that an account belonging to MassEd. Net, a taxpayer-funded organization that subsidizes Internet access for teachers and schools, was being used "to promote a sex-and-wrestling Web site." It found that an account registered to the Department of Public Works "was used to buy and sell erotic Japanese cartoons, including a cartoon series called 'Rapeman' that glorifies rape." It noted that an Internet user at the Secretary of State's office had sent 324 messages about TV shows, including *The Simpsons*. And it found students using their high school Internet accounts to trade advice on making and buying LSD and other hallucinogens.

The source material for the news story came almost entirely from searches on the Internet search engine Deja.com, which archives postings to the Internet's Usenet bulletin board system. Although Usenet messages can be easily forged, this possibility was never discussed in the *Herald* story.

The special report generated immediate response from state officials, who promised that they would enforce their existing policies on Internet use and put in place new ones to prohibit inappropriate uses of computer systems. It was a stunning testimony to the power of the Internet archives to hold people accountable for what they do with their computers.

SMART MACHINES CREATE ACTIVE DATABANKS

On April 14, 1999, computer maker Hewlett-Packard ran a three-page advertisement in the *Wall Street Journal*. The first two pages were a massive black-and-white spread showing a rather well-kept garage with a big empty space in the middle. A car has recently been removed. The text reads:

> Your daughter inherited it from you. The lead foot, that is. And you left your vintage Jaguar in the garage. You think. Only you're out of town, so you're not sure. Enter e-services. *E-what?* A security chip in the car recognizes your daughter's key and engages a "soft limit" that won't allow the car to exceed 65 mph. Which, of course, she attempts to do. Instantly, the car sends a signal to a service you subscribe to, alerting you to what's going on. Three thousand miles away, you excuse yourself from the dinner table and as you walk towards the lobby you push your speed dial. Your daughter is no more than three blocks from the driveway when the car phone begins ringing. *How's that again?* Businesses and services are using the Internet in ways that go far beyond today's websites. They're adding a whole new dimension to the term "service." The next chapter of the Internet is about to be written. And it has nothing to do with you working the Web. Instead, the Internet will work for you. *www.hp.com/e-services*.

The next E. *E-services*. Hewlett-Packard.

Hewlett-Packard's vision of an active world begins to hint at the not-so-benevolent future that could await us. Why does the HP chip in the Jaguar block the daughter's attempt to speed, but not her parents'? Why does the parent get the phone call from the car, and not the local police? Why isn't the insurance company notified about the unsafe driver? Why doesn't the car's dealer get a report of the speeding and use it to invalidate the warranty on the car's transmission? Perhaps the next chapter of the Internet will allow automobiles to automatically deduct the cost of a speeding ticket directly from your bank account, without the added cost to society of having a police officer chase you down.

Why should you, the data subject, control the data shadow of everything you do today?

TURNING BACK THE INFORMATION TIDE

Faster machines, bigger hard disks, and intelligent database systems are all ultimately big threats to privacy. While the ability of computers to store information is increasing at something between 60%

and 70% per year, the world's population is only increasing at 1.6%. All things being equal, over time, an increasing percentage of our daily activities will be captured by the world's datasphere.

So what's the answer? Are we facing a future in which all of our lives need to be read like an open book, in which all of our secrets are kept inside glass file cabinets? Will we be increasingly monitored by our neighbors, our family, and even our machines, until we are all living inside a transparent society? Perhaps. But we do have a choice. We cannot turn back the clock, but we can build a world in which sensitive data is respected and kept private.

Take the case of Judge Bork. The journalist who pulled Bork's video rental records triggered a series of hearings on Capitol Hill. Cynics said that the senators and congressmen were worried that their own video records might suddenly become fair game—and that the legislators, unlike Bork, had something to hide. But whatever their reason, the hearings revealed that the Bork incident was far from isolated. "Various examples of demands for video transactional records were mentioned [in the hearings], including an attempt to use video tape records to show that a spouse was an unfit parent, and a defendant in a child molestation case who wanted to show that the child's accusations were based on movies viewed at home," reported the Department of Commerce.[19]

Those hearings weren't idle chat. Before the end of that legislative session, Congress passed and President Bush signed the Video Privacy Protection Act of 1988 (18 USC 2710). Under the law, "A video tape service provider who knowingly discloses, to any person, personally identifiable information concerning any consumer" who rents or purchases a videotape is liable for civil action consisting of statutory actual damages of $2,500, punitive damages, reasonable attorney's fees, and any other relief that the court may deem appropriate. By forbidding your local video store from giving out the titles of the movies you rent (without a court order, that is), the act took video rental records off the table. And by defining statutory damages, Congress eliminated a problem that plagues many privacy suits: the need to prove real damages. Furthermore, by allowing an aggrieved individual to sue for reasonable attorney's fees and other litigation costs, Congress assured that lawyers would be willing to take such cases on a contingency basis.

In many ways, the 1988 law didn't go far enough—it permits video stores to maintain rental records after tapes are returned, rather than requiring that the records be destroyed. The law also allows video rental companies to distill individual rental records into aggregate information, which could then be used as the basis of privacy violations. Nevertheless, the Video Privacy Protection Act has been stunningly effective. Violations of the law are extremely rare. Americans know that they can rent whatever videos they wish and not be forced to answer to anybody.

The Video Privacy Protection Act proves what many privacy advocates have been saying since the 1960s: the free market and voluntary privacy standards are frequently not sufficient to protect consumer privacy. An editorial that appeared in *USA Today* put it this way: "While voluntary compliance might be preferable in an ideal world, it's not likely to work in the real world. The reality is that the absence of government prodding has resulted in too many companies doing too little to protect consumers' privacy rights."[20]

Many businesses collect large amounts of personal information in the course of day-to-day operations. But just because the data has been collected, it doesn't follow that the business has the right to make it publicly available, sell it on the open market, or use it for marketing. Data can be taken off the table. Strong privacy laws give businesses the incentive to do so.

An equally valid way to protect privacy is to prevent the accumulation of personal information in the first place. For example, instead of building an Electronic Toll Collection system that keeps account balances and toll-crossing information in a central database, it's possible to build anonymous toll-collection systems. These systems are based on smart cards and use a form of digital cash for the toll payments. The smart card in these systems can be programmed to keep a record of each toll crossing, for the driver's own use, or they can be programmed to throw this information away. Distributed smart card systems can be cheaper to build and operate than those based on massive centralized computers. Unfortunately, they are less popular—apparently because the technology is more difficult to explain to decision makers.

Overall, an informed and organized citizenry rarely fails to push through strong privacy measures. Consider Hong Kong: in the mid-1980s, Hong Kong's colonial government built a sophisticated system for electronic road pricing. Shortly after the system was deployed, drivers began receiving statements showing where and when they had traveled—and they became alarmed. Fearing that the system could be used to track people for political purposes, especially after the 1997 handover of Hong Kong to the Chinese mainland, the citizens succeeded in having the system shut down.[21]

Failing responsible decision makers, there is always direct action. When people discover that their information is being used against them, they rebel—either by intentionally withholding their information, or by explicitly planting false data into the system. For example, many Internet users have responded to the problem of unsolicited junk email, also known as *spam*, by using mangled email addresses on their web pages and in their news postings. More people are using fake or intentionally misspelled names when subscribing to magazines. And many people use cash, rather than credit cards, even when it is inconvenient to do so. If these measures are not sufficient, even more aggressive techniques are likely to follow.

CHAPTER FIVE

THE VIEW FROM ABOVE

A furious, uncoordinated project is now unfolding across the surface of our planet, in the depths of the oceans, and in the heavens above. The project is to deploy a mesh of cameras, listening devices, and sensors, and to connect those devices together using a series of computer networks so that anything that happens anywhere can be known, recorded, and preserved. The project is to turn the planet into a single scientific instrument and to create a global library of happenings.

Many civil libertarians of the 1950s and 1960s worried about the bugging of private homes and offices by the government. In recent years, newspapers have written about "spy shops" that sell sophisticated remote listening devices, tiny radio transmitters, voice-activated tape recorders, and lasers that can bounce off office windows and reveal what is spoken inside. But today, it is increasingly clear that the real threat to privacy is not the bugging of private homes, which is for the most part illegal and not a widespread practice. Instead, the real threat lies in the systematic monitoring of public places, where ability and legality have created a surveillance free-for-all.

Over the next 50 years, the widespread construction of monitoring networks will fundamentally change our understanding of what it means to be "in public." Ironically, the change will force us to accept the literal meaning of the words "public places." In the past, many public places were effectively private. Whether walking alone on a city street or having a discussion with a friend in a public park, we felt our actions were private, unknowable, and unrecorded. Systematic monitoring turns this assumption on its head. Whereas we have a reasonable expectation of privacy in our own homes, there is no longer such an expectation for public spaces. And as more and more of what happens in public is captured, recorded, indexed, and made retrievable, more of what takes place in public becomes knowable.

In the future, the public will know what happens in public.

HEY, I LIVE HERE!

On my wall is a poster of the world as seen from space, but it's a view that no astronaut or satellite will ever see. It's a picture of our planet with the clouds stripped away. Both the Northern and Southern hemispheres are shown as they appear during the height of summer, clothed in green, the ice banished to the poles. The Earth's mountains are plainly visible. The oceans have been colored to reveal the sea floor and currents.

The poster, "The Earth: A New Satellite View of the World with Shaded Relief," was produced by WorldSat, a small firm in Ontario, Canada. The poster is a testimony to the observational power of orbiting artificial satellites, as well as to our fascination with geographical information. The ability to create a geographic mosaic such as World-Sat's has profound implications for the future of privacy. Geography is inescapable. Everything is somewhere.

I saw my first WorldSat posters at the University of Washington bookstore. I went to the bookstore to buy a new fountain pen. I spent ten minutes looking at pens, and an hour looking at the satellite images. Besides "The Earth," the bookstore had space views of Australia, Asia, Europe, and North America. And I wasn't alone: a nearby couple spent twenty minutes looking at another poster called "Earth at Night," created by NovaGraphics, trying to identify every city they could from the shape of its lights.

Over the next two weeks, I kept returning to the bookstore to look again at the posters. I was haunted by the images. Finally I bought "The Earth" and put it up on my wall. Then I called WorldSat to find out not just how they made the poster, but why.

WorldSat was started in 1986 by Robert Stacy, a commercial diver who had an accident and happened to see a satellite image at a bookstore in Ontario while he was recuperating. Haunted, like me—and more or less barred from his former profession—Stacy decided to start a company that would create posters of these images and sell them to others.

WorldSat gets most of its satellite images for free. The source images for the company's "World Series" come from the National Oceanic and Atmospheric Administration (NOAA) weather satellites that orbit at an altitude of 820 kilometers (520 miles). By carefully combining data from hundreds of images, it's possible to electronically eliminate our planet's clouds. By using a pair of satellite images that were photographed with a known separation, it's possible to construct a stereoscopic view of the planet's surface. This information is used for shading the relief, which is what makes the map look three-dimensional. The

The WorldSat Planet Earth

Stripped of its clouds and seasonal ice sheets, and illuminated by a 24-hour sun, this view of Planet Earth is one that no astronaut will ever see with the naked eye. And yet this view is somehow more truthful and revealing than any single snapshot could ever be. Created by WorldSat, this image shows the tremendous potential of combining multiple satellite images with advanced computer processing. [Image courtesy WorldSat]

ocean relief data comes from a combination of satellite and terrestrial studies.

Creating the image was a technological challenge because of the huge amount of data involved, says Dr. Emery Miller, WorldSat's Vice President of Business Development.[1] Like any image displayed by a computer, the image of "The Earth from Space" is made up of tiny square dots, called pixels. This image was created with a resolution of one kilometer, meaning that each pixel around the equator represents a square that's one kilometer on each side. The Earth is nearly a perfect sphere, with a circumference of almost exactly 40,000 kilometers[2] and a surface of roughly 127,796,494 square kilometers, and thus this image occupied roughly 128 million pixels inside WorldSat's computer. According to Dr. Miller, those 128 million pixels required more than six gigabytes of storage on the computer used to create the poster. Back in 1994, when the data set was first created, WorldSat was pushing the computing limits of the world's fastest computers. The Earth is a big place.

The compact size of the Earth on the WorldSat poster makes it just about impossible to locate anything that's man-made. Squeezing 40,000 kilometers onto a poster 36 inches across means that each inch covers roughly 1,111 kilometers. In fact, if you take out a magnifying glass and look at the places on the planet where you would expect to see the great cities, all you are likely to see is a tiny reddish smudge surrounded by a sea of green. Those dots are a combination of dust, pollution, roads, and buildings. The green is nature.

Although I'm a sucker for a pretty planet, Miller says that a lot of people want images of a more local variety. "We find that the greatest interest is to be able to locate your house," he says. People want to point at the map and say, "I live here! Look at that!"

WorldSat's Earth is just the beginning. If you have patience, a computer, and $50, you can now do much better: you can order up a satellite photograph of your own home shot by a state-of-the-art spy satellite. Since the early 1980s, there's been an ongoing effort on the part of the space-ferrying countries to turn satellite photography from a tool of governments into a commodity used by businesses and even consumers. This is just another example of how advanced technology is invariably democratized.

THE EYE IN THE SKY

The United States launched its first spy satellite in 1959. Called Corona, the top secret project was actually the U.S.'s first space program. Each Corona satellite was equipped with specially cast, ultra-high-resolution lenses, specially made photographic film that could withstand the rigors of space, and reentry vehicles that could return the film to Earth. The cameras had a resolution better than five feet, or 1.5 meters. This means that any object on the ground that was at least five feet across—a car, a tent, or a missile silo—could be seen from space.

Panoramic photographs may be an obvious use of spy satellites, but they are just the beginning. Five-foot resolution allows a relatively sophisticated analysis. For example, an analyst can distinguish different kinds of aircraft from one another based on their silhouettes, which is essential for military planning. You can count the number of cars in a parking lot to determine how many people work at a particular building, be it a factory or a "safe house."

Unlike the U2 spy planes, satellites had the advantages of being unmanned and capable of conducting routine surveillance over incredibly large areas. Satellites offered a degree of precision and repeatability that was otherwise impossible. And the U.S. military made great use of its newfound capability. By photographing the same scene month after month, it was possible to closely monitor Soviet production, troop deployment, and even aspects of the country's economy. According to an article published in *Technology Review* after the Corona program was declassified in 1996, "some 121 Corona satellites would orbit the earth between 1960 and 1972, taking some 800,000 pictures on 2.1 million feet of film."[3]

Satellite surveillance violates no law or treaty. Things that happen outdoors, in public, are public by definition. Perhaps more to the point, there was little practical reason for nations to object. The Soviet Union didn't protest U2 overhead flights until it managed to shoot down Gary Powers's spy plane in 1960. But there was no defense against the spy satellites other than cloudy days and staying indoors. Launching a formal protest would simply have been an admission of national impotence.

For decades, the resolution of spy satellites was simply unmatched by civilian orbiters. But that doesn't make the lower-resolution craft less useful. The Landsat 5 and 6 satellites, launched in 1982 and 1984, respectively, have onboard instruments that photograph the surface of the Earth at 30-meter resolution in six different spectral bands.[4] Although the original purpose of the satellites was to prospect for natural resources (hence their official name, the Earth Resources Technology Satellites), Landsat images have also been used to monitor atmospheric and ocean conditions, detect pollution levels, prospect for oil, survey crops and forests, and of course, make posters. The Landsat satellites pass over every portion of the Earth every 18 days. You can buy a Landsat scene covering an area 160 kilometers square for $3500, with discounts available for older data sets.

With 30-meter resolution, Landsat is great for looking at things like crop yields on large farms. But Landsat doesn't work very well for monitoring the direct results of human activity. Most roads and buildings are thinner than 30 meters, making them invisible to Landsat's camera.

France changed things in 1986, when it launched SPOT 1, the world's first commercial spy satellite. (SPOT is a French acronym that stands for *Satellite Pour l'Observation de la Terre*—satellite for observation of the earth.) The first three SPOT satellites had two cameras. One was a black-and-white camera providing 10-meter resolution of objects on the ground. The second camera recorded green, red, and near-infrared images at 20-meter resolution. Images from both cameras could be combined to create a high-resolution, full-color image. Those cameras made history just one month later, when SPOT 1 passed over the Ukraine just in time to snap the photographs of the burning Chernobyl nuclear power plant. The Soviet Union wasn't talking, but the images told the story.

Orbiting at 830 km above the Earth's surface, both the SPOT 1 and the SPOT 3 satellite completely cover the earth every 26 days. Roughly the size and weight of a van, the cameras cut a swath between 60 km and 117 km wide as the satellite circles overhead. The images are encrypted and beamed directly to Earth, where they are picked up by a SPOT ground station.

SPOT's biggest customers are the "black" agencies—intelligence officers in both the United States and other countries. A glossy color handout from the company shows SPOT images taken from the Persian Gulf War. One photograph shows a sensitive military installation with at least a dozen groups of buildings. The next photograph shows the same buildings, their white roofs replaced with black smudges. "Black in certain structures may be indication of fires," the legend notes dryly. Similar imagery depicting many civilian houses without roofs was shown by NATO forces in April 1999 to demonstrate the result of Serbian "ethnic cleansing" in Kosovo. The images helped rally public support for NATO's bombing of Serbia.

"When we first launched in 1986, people were all up in arms about national security and privacy. They said 'our privacy is gone!'," says Clark Nelson, SPOT's Manager of Marketing and Communications.[5] But as the years have passed, critics have learned to live with the orbiting eyes. Businesses and governments have learned to exploit them.

SPOT sells its photographs for updating maps, monitoring environmental degradation, and providing visual backdrops for computerized geographical information services. Farmers can use SPOT images to monitor their fields: for less than 50 cents an acre, they can deduce which plots need to be irrigated or fertilized. Today, the people using these images "are very advanced gentleman farmers," says Nelson. "They say, 'I'm tired of the tractor. I want to do advanced digital image satellite processing.'" But within a few years, satellite imagery will be a basic tool of agribusiness.

Where the early adopters go, the masses follow. The McDonald's and KFC fast-food chains have started using satellite images to locate stores in fast-growing areas—areas where municipal maps don't accurately show which roads have been built, which are under construction, and where the new houses are going up. Satellite images are increasingly being used to illustrate business reports. A typical business product is SPOT's MetroView, highly enhanced satellite images of major U.S. cities that are designed to be quickly incorporated into desktop programs like Adobe PhotoShop. A view of an entire metropolitan area sells for $400 to $600; smaller "cells" cost $100.

SPOT is also playing an important role in mapping the locations of future cellular telephone sites in the developing world. The images provide detailed maps, including the elevation of the landscape, the location of the roads, and the density and height of the buildings.

"It's the most beautiful equation I've seen in 11 years," says SPOT's Nelson. "We have the data, they have a need, and they have the money

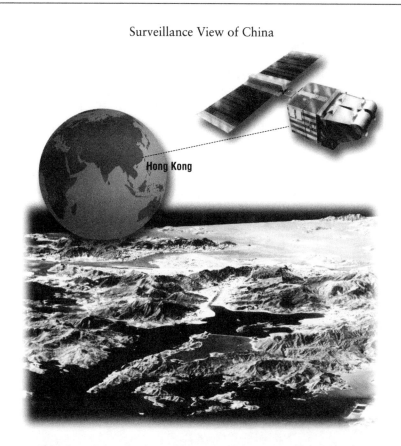

Surveillance View of China

Hong Kong

This three-dimensional perspective view of mainland China was created entirely from space imagery collected by the French SPOT surveillance satellites (artist's drawing, right top). The data that generated this view was then fed into a computer program developed by Qualcomm, Inc., of San Diego, California, and used to calculate appropriate locations for cellular telephone radio towers. Using a system such as this in Hong Kong, Qualcomm was able to cut the number of cell sites needed from 83 to 80, saving $3 million in cell sites and $1.5 million in testing. [Photos and artist's drawings courtesy SPOT Imaging]

to pay for it. Are we shrinking the friggin' world or not? We are providing the most detailed maps of the remote areas, and they [the communications companies] are providing them with telecommunications."

SPOT has also developed Eaglevision, a transportable satellite base station. Designed for emergency relief or military operations, the system consists of a 3.5-meter dish that can directly receive the satellites' signals, and two trucks worth of computers and processing equipment. The system can acquire a SPOT image as the satellite passes overhead and can produce field maps of the surrounding area. The system can even create a three-dimensional model, which can then be fed into a flight simulator and used to plan either emergency supply delivery missions or bombing runs.

SPOT is just one of many firms either selling access to government satellites or operating their own. In 1984, Lockheed Martin incorporated the Earth Observation Satellite Company (EOSAT), whose original mission was to commercialize the U.S. government's Landsat satellites. In the 1990s, EOSAT turned to high-resolution spy satellites. First, EOSAT partnered with the Indian government, acquiring exclusive rights to resell images from India's IRS-1C satellite, a satellite with 5.8-meter resolution that was launched in December 1995. In 1996, EOSAT was purchased by Space Imaging, a Colorado-based firm that now operates the largest constellation of civilian surveillance satellites orbiting the planet. The company recently launched its own 1-meter resolution satellite.

Who has need for high-resolution satellite imagery? Practically everybody, asserts Space Imaging's promotional material. The company sees markets in agriculture, civil governments, environment, exploration, mapping, public utilities, the media market, even the direct consumer, as this quote from its web site demonstrates:

> Seeing the Earth from above brings new opportunities to the consumer market, perhaps in ways that people have never imagined possible. Space Imaging's consumer-oriented products can be used in applications ranging from entertainment and recreation to problem solving and personal navigation.

> Satellite imagery of the Earth, offered today at resolutions never before available to the commercial marketplace, reveals unlimited information about the planet for customers who have traditionally been unaware of the remarkable detail visible in satellite images. Space Imaging's goal is to promote the widespread incorporation of Earth imagery in a variety of consumer products including flight simulators, map books, trip planners, screensavers, encyclopedias, travel videos, jigsaw puzzles, postcards and framed prints.[6]

Perhaps more telling is some market literature I picked up at a Seattle trade show in 1997. At the show, which focused on advanced surveying techniques, EOSAT handed out a pamphlet describing how local governments could use the 5-meter images from the Indian satellite to spy on their own citizens (see the boxed ad).

Of course, a tax collector could go to the local airport, rent a plane, and take his or her own aerial photographs. But just as satellite imagery is cheaper, more consistent, and easier to use for the intelligence agencies, it's easier for state and local civil agencies as well.

Recovering Uncollected Income with Five-Meter Data

Six years ago, the Jones family moved into a new custom-built home in the suburbs. Since then, they've added a new room, built a pool and made other improvements, all without ever paying a dime in taxes, permits, and other fees. City administrators, unaware of the situation, never bill the Joneses and never collect the delinquent revenue.

This scenario represents an all-too-common problem for city administrators. Uncollected tax, permit and fee proceeds account for millions of lost dollars that would otherwise go toward important municipal programs. So what can agencies do to recover this income? They can turn to EOSAT IRS-1C five-meter data. [7]

At the same conference, I visited a poster session sponsored by the Minnesota Department of Resources, which in 1997 developed a system for surveying the state's timber and farmlands. Before turning to satellite data, state officials had been conducting aerial surveys, and had been lucky if they could revisit a site every ten years. With satellite imagery, Minnesota can update its database on a monthly basis.

Because satellite surveys of the Earth's surface are so comprehensive and so easy to work with, satellite imagery is creating a historical record of the Earth's surface that is unparalleled in human history. When President Clinton declassified the Corona, Argon, and Lanyard programs in 1996, he placed more than 860,000 images of the Earth's surface from the years 1960 to 1972 into the public domain.[8] You can now gauge the extent of the environmental damage during the Soviet regime by comparing Corona's 1960 images with 1996 images of the same region taken by SPOT or IRS. Libraries of satellite images have become a new kind of time machine.

Two things limit further advances in satellite imagery. The first is politics. High-resolution satellite imagery is inherently a military technology. For years, the U.S. intelligence establishment was unwilling to give up the technology or the regulatory approval necessary to allow civilians to use the same technology. SPOT and IRS, both operating outside the U.S., changed that.

Old habits die hard. When EOSAT/Space Imaging received permission to launch its own 1-meter resolution satellite, it had to agree to something called *shutter control*. At any time—presumably, during a time of war—the U.S. government can close EOSAT's shutter, and in so doing, stop the flow of its imagery. The U.S. Congress has placed further restrictions on the satellites, for example, prohibiting the sale of high-resolution images of Israel. And while the French SPOT isn't subject to U.S. Department of Defense shutter control, it has also placed limits on imagery during wartime: during the Persian Gulf War, SPOT refused to sell pictures to news organizations that would show troop movements on the Arabian Peninsula. The fear was that Iraqi leader Saddam Hussein would see the photos and plan accordingly.

The second limitation is the Earth's atmosphere itself. As satellites probe with increased magnification, minor disturbances in the atmosphere caused by haze, humidity, and heat waves play stronger roles. Seeing a clear image therefore requires a combination of high-precision optics, sophisticated data processing, and luck. "Are there theoretical limitations that are in any sense practical? I would say probably not," says WorldSat's Miller, who has more than 20 years experience in civilian satellite imagery. Miller says that realistically, we will never be able to see microscopic objects from space. On the other hand, he says, there have been persistent and credible rumors that the highest-quality spy satellites "can resolve the text on a cigarette package. . . . On a perfect day with all conditions perfect, I would probably agree that you could do it. It is certainly within the realm of technological possibility."

But practically speaking, says Miller, it doesn't make sense to get caught up with the resolution game. "You rarely can get conditions so perfect." What's more, resolution is ultimately less important than the availability and frequency of images—that is, the ability to order up an image on a moment's notice, and the ability to photograph the same area of the globe every week, every day, or every hour.

Online services that sell satellite photographic information make the importance of frequency abundantly clear. For example, Microsoft's TerraServer allows you to display high-resolution space imagery (at the 1.5-meter resolution) of practically anywhere on the planet: all you need to do is to type an address or the location's latitude and longitude. The spatial coverage is pretty good: TerraServer covers most of the earth. Unfortunately, the temporal coverage is lacking. For example, in August 1999, I tried to order up a space image of my neighborhood in Cambridge. Sure enough, TerraServer had a photo of the area taken by a Soviet-era spy satellite. But alas, the image was taken on June 30, 1989. Cambridge has undergone a lot of changes in the past ten years, but the high-resolution image of Cambridge that I ordered off the Internet for $13.95 doesn't show them.

As we move forward, the social impact of satellite imagery will come from combining the images with collateral information and sophisticated processing, rather than from merely reprinting pretty photographs for people's pleasure. A taste of that future came in the spring of 1997, when the U.S. State Department used satellite imagery to attack the credibility of Israeli West Bank settlers and influence that country's internal politics. The State Department announced that, based on satellite surveillance, 26% of the apartments built by Jewish

A View of the O'Reilly Offices in Cambridge

O'Reilly Office
Cambridge, Massachusetts

This satellite photograph of Cambridge, Massachusetts, was taken by a Soviet spy satellite in 1989, licensed to SPIN-2, and downloaded over the Internet from the Microsoft TerraServer for $13.95. The image, with a resolution of roughly 1.2 meters per pixel, clearly shows buildings, roads, railroad tracks, and a large solid waste dump that has since been converted into a park. Although a single high-resolution image such as this one can be used as a low-cost alternative to surveys conducted on the ground, the true value of satellite imagery comes when an organization has access to multiple images that are separated by several days, weeks, or years. High-resolution images such as these, available over the Internet, are changing the way people think about outdoor privacy. [Image courtesy Aerial Images, Inc.]

settlers on the occupied West Bank were vacant, and that a whopping 56% of those in Gaza were similarly empty. "There is no need for expanding settlements, because all the settlers can be housed in exist-ing housing in existing settlements," an unnamed official leaked to the *New York Times*. Coming up with these numbers was a simple matter of comparing daytime imagery, which reveals the location of houses, with nighttime infrared imagery, which reveals which houses are actu-ally being heated.

The combination of global satellite surveillance, long-term image databanking, and commercial availability of the imagery is changing what it means to be outdoors. Whether you are on top of Mount Everest, floating on a raft in the middle of the Pacific, burying the victims of a massacre, or simply building an unauthorized pool in your backyard, today you can be absolutely alone and yet have the eyes of the world upon you.

THE EYE ON THE GROUND

Far easier than putting a spy satellite in space is installing a surveillance camera on a pole. Twenty years ago, many people considered video cameras to be an unwanted intrusion into their personal privacy. But today we've grown accustomed to them. Video cameras are now a constant presence in the world around us. They are in stores, malls, schools, and office buildings, on the streets, and even in our own homes. They are also getting harder to spot. The cameras no longer look like rectangular boxes with a lens at one end and a few wires coming out the other: these days, many video cameras are hidden behind a globe of smoked plastic. And there is the new generation of video cameras that are roughly the size of a box of matches. These can be hidden anywhere.

I remember seeing my first surveillance cameras in banks and late-night convenience shops when I was growing up in the Philadelphia suburbs of the 1970s. I didn't like the idea that I was being videotaped every time I went to deposit a check or buy a soda, but I understood why the cameras were there: our country has a history of bank robberies and late-night holdups. It seemed reasonable to accept the claim that the cameras would offer some kind of protection for bank tellers and convenience store clerks: even if the teller or clerk were killed in a holdup, the video record would help identify and, it was hoped, prosecute the perpetrator. I'm sure that if I were a clerk at an all-night store, I would want the video surveillance as well—even though I would know that an equally important purpose of the video surveillance is to deter employee theft.

When banks began installing automatic teller machines, it was only natural to outfit these machines with surveillance cameras as well. When I saw my first automatic teller in 1979, I thought that the camera was "protecting" the heavily armored ATM machine. It was only years later, when I was getting money on a lonely street in the middle of the night, that I realized that the camera was actually there to protect me.

When I was an undergraduate at the Massachusetts Institute of Technology, the school contracted with two banks to install a pair of automatic teller machines in the middle of the Infinite Corridor, the Institute's main pedestrian thoroughfare. That created a problem:

while MIT wanted the ATMs, school administrators didn't want the cameras recording every student who walked by the machines on their way to class. After some negotiation between the banks and the school, the cameras were tilted in such a way that they couldn't peer down the hallway, and a notice was put up telling people that the area was under video surveillance.

But constant video surveillance is desensitizing. A few years later, the video cameras had been tilted back into their "proper" positions. The warning signs were removed when the walls were repainted, and they were never put back. Although the cameras were now in violation of MIT's campus policy on video surveillance—a policy that discourages unnecessary surveillance and prohibits surveillance without notification—nobody seemed to care. One reason might have been that it wasn't anybody's job to notice: the MIT policy didn't have any enforcement mechanism.

In the early 1990s, towns in southern England began installing outdoor surveillance cameras connected to long-running video recorders. The purpose of the cameras was simple: fighting crime. The cameras are supposed to work in two complementary ways: by recording all holdups and street crime, they create evidence that can later be used in an investigation or prosecution. And because the cameras are prominently positioned so they can't be missed, their presence also has a deterrent effect.

Community after community was willing to eliminate the happy ephemera that comes from the privacy of transient events in public places, and replace it with the permanence of videotape.

In 1993, two children aged 10 and 11 abducted a 4-year-old boy named Jamie Bulger from a shopping mall in northern England. Security cameras in the mall recorded the older boys dragging Jamie across a parking lot to a nearby set of train tracks, where they killed him. The video cameras didn't prevent the crime, but the tapes provided evidence for the conviction of the two boys on the charge of murder.

"Video surveillance is a big deal in the United Kingdom right now," John Burgess, an information officer in the U.S. Embassy in London, told me in 1998. "Local governments are ordering the use of surveillance cameras in high-crime areas, apparently with good effect. Cardiff City Center showed a 13.4% drop in crime, for instance."[9] According to an article in *New Scientist* magazine, 1,000 of 1,800 people arrested in Newcastle after being caught by closed-circuit TV systems had their cases go to trial; 993 pled guilty, and the remainder were convicted.[10]

According to Privacy International, a U.K.–based watch group, Britain now spends

between 150 and 300 million pounds (between 225 and 450 million dollars) per year . . . on a surveillance industry involving an estimated

300,000 cameras covering shopping areas, housing estates, car parks and public facilities in a great many towns and cities. . . . CCTV is very quickly becoming an integral part of crime control policy, social control theory and community consciousness. It is promoted by police and politicians as a primary solution for urban dysfunction. It is no exaggeration to conclude that in Britain, the technology has had more of an impact on the evolution of law enforcement policy than just about any technology initiative in the past two decades.[11]

Outdoor surveillance cameras are now moving to the United States. In 1996, the City of Baltimore installed its own cameras, paid for by private businesses, in the city's downtown area. The pilot project consisted of 16 high-quality cameras that can record a person's face, an armored kiosk, and a bank of videotape recorders. Brian Lewbart, public relations manager for the Downtown Partnership of Baltimore, admitted that Baltimore's downtown wasn't a high-crime area; in fact, he said, it's "relatively safe." According to Lewbart, the real purpose of the cameras wasn't to make the area safer, but "to make the public feel more comfortable because there is an added safety presence that is looking out on their behalf."[12]

After the police department announced its plans to put up the cameras, a number of people called up to complain. They weren't complaining about surveillance downtown. They were complaining that cameras were not being installed where the crimes were actually taking place—in the high-crime residential areas a dozen or so blocks north of the downtown area. "It would be much more controversial in a residential area," says Sam Ringgold, director of public affairs for the Baltimore Police Department. "There are a couple of proposals out there from some private foundations to put cameras in high-crime areas in residential communities. That will not be done until there has been sufficient time to test how the cameras work downtown. It also will not be done without overwhelming support from the neighbors in that community."[13]

Baltimore's project was actually pretty uninspired. Despite the fact that people are more afraid of street crime at night than they are during the day, the cameras were not equipped with night-vision systems. They were regular off-the-shelf video cameras, rather than the type of high-resolution cameras used in high-security situations. Although the cameras probably could be used to determine the height, sex, and skin color of an assailant, it's doubtful that the video images could be used to actually identify somebody. So what purpose do they really serve? As Lewbart said, the cameras were there to make people feel good.

But even "feel-good" cameras occasionally make a tremendous difference. In April 1995, when a bomb blew up the Alfred P. Murrah Federal Building in Oklahoma City, the surveillance tape from a

Outdoor Surveillance Camera

Outdoor surveillance cameras, such as these devices placed outside Boston's Park Street Subway Station, are increasingly part of our urban landscape. The cameras are used to monitor the flow of traffic, keep a watchful eye on people entering or leaving buildings, and assist police in fighting street crime. The world leader in these surveillance cameras is the United Kingdom, which has more than 300,000 such cameras installed throughout the country and few regulations covering their use. [Photo courtesy Simson Garfinkel]

nearby apartment building let police quickly discover that it was a Ryder truck that had been blown up. Police called every Ryder rental agency and soon came up with a physical description of the likely bomber. It was a real testimony to the power of video surveillance.

Despite occasional exposure, most of the images recorded by surveillance cameras remain trapped between ribbons of magnetic tape. In a way, this difficulty of retrieval has had a hidden benefit for society: aside from a few high-profile cases, such as when a video camera is placed in a changing room, it is simply too difficult to get at the juicy images. There is just too much boring video footage to wade through—at least, until computers start watching the video and searching for the good parts.

VIDEO SURVEILLANCE FOR THE REST OF US

It is the natural tendency of technology to move from the elite to the masses. Just as computers have moved from government to business to the home, so has video surveillance. Five years ago, we had college students and randy bachelors leaving video cameras secreted away to capture their exploits on videotape. Today, video surveillance is mass-market: one of the newest accessories for parents of young children is the Safety 1st Day 'N Night TV Monitor System, a $179 home surveillance system consisting of a portable camera and a wireless receiving screen. The product works through walls, floors, even to the next building! And it comes with a "state of the art infrared imaging" night vision system which can transmit "clearly focused pictures in both the brightness of day and the dimmed darkness of sleeptime."

Although the system is designed to let parents keep an eye on their sleeping children, the saleswoman at Boston Baby told me that most parents are more interested in keeping an eye on the babysitter. They hook the receiver up to the VCR in the bedroom, lock the door, and leave the camera unobtrusively on a bookshelf in the family room.

U.S. consumers bought $2.4 billion worth of camcorders in 1998, with 3.83 million camcorders shipped to stores.[14] These low-cost camcorders have turned the tables on the news media and the police, allowing ordinary citizens to videotape evidence of the true conditions in their neighborhoods. Surreptitiously recorded videotapes can influence public policy and have changed the course of national events—best evidenced by the infamous home videotape of Rodney King's beating by Los Angeles police.

Ultimately, though, what's far more profound than the drop in price or the selling of video surveillance equipment is the change in the signal that's coming out of video cameras. The cameras of yesteryear output standard National Television Standards Committee (NTSC) analog video signals—perfect for displaying on a closed-circuit television monitor or recording on a videotape. Today's newest cameras produce a digital signal that's easily brought into a home computer. Once inside the computer, the images can be manipulated or stored like any other digital information. Digital cameras unleash the information that has until now been imprisoned on millions of miles of videotape, and make these images accessible.

The Connectix QuickCam was the first digital video camera to catch fire in the home market. Looking like a plastic tennis ball with a tail, the QuickCam could connect to any desktop or laptop computer. The QuickCam came with a little triangular base to hold it upright on the top of a computer monitor; it also had a little threaded hole to attach it to a tripod. Connect it to your computer and run the program, and you've got yourself a miniature video studio. Instead of using videotape, the system used your computer's hard disk; each minute of video required roughly six megabytes to store. Another factor contributing to its popularity was its affordable price, which dropped from $200 to $99 to $79 in the three years following its release.

The QuickCam was an instant hit. All of a sudden, millions of computer users had a cheap and easy way to get still images and video into their computers.

When I got my QuickCam, the first thing I did was make a walk-through tour of my house and email it to a friend in California who would probably never see the house in real life. Sure, I could have done the tour with a video camera, but then I would have had to mail the tape and my friend would have had to find a television to play it. With the digital QuickCam, the video simply travelled from my computer, through the Internet, to his computer.

My wife and I soon discovered another use for the QuickCam. We wanted to know what our cats were doing in the house when we weren't there, so we left the QuickCam recording one Sunday while we went to brunch. Connectix's software had a special mode for making elapsed time videos: rather than taking 10 or 15 frames a second, as is normally the case, the computer can be programmed to take just one frame a second, or one frame every 15 seconds. This let us store a whole hour in six megabytes of disk space and play back an hour's worth of video in just a few minutes.

The cats, we learned, had a life of their own. Watching our home-made surveillance video, we saw them jumping up on the dining room table. We saw them sleeping on the dining room table. We saw them scratch at the drapes. We saw them reading our books, going through our desk drawers, copying credit card numbers from receipts in the trash, buying mail-order gourmet cat food, and then making crank calls to the dog next door. Well, what were we expecting? They're cats, after all.

As things turned out, Beth and I were trying to sell our condo in Cambridge, and the next Sunday we had an open house. The realtor wanted us to leave the house at noon and come back around 3:00 p.m. She said that she would take care of everything. We had done this twice before; each time the realtor had given us an unexciting and non-descript report about the two or three couples who had toured our house. This time we decided to find out what was happening for ourselves, so we left the QuickCam running—without telling our realtor, of course. We simply turned on the computer, set it to record, as we had with the cats, and turned off the monitor. It was so easy to do! We learned that the realtor was letting people walk around our house unaccompanied while she sat in the living room and read a book. We decided not to have any more open houses after that.

WEBCAM

Things get really interesting when you make the images of digital video cameras available in real time over the Internet. Suddenly, the cameras are transformed from simple surveillance tools to the eyes and ears of potentially millions of people around the planet.

As best anybody can tell, the first Internet-based video camera was set up at Cambridge University's Computer Laboratory in 1991, pointing at the Trojan Room Coffee Pot. Fifteen graduate students shared a single coffee pot, located in the Lab's second floor "Trojan Room." The pot was great for students who worked on the second floor. The problem was that the graduate students on the building's other floors never knew when coffee was brewing. Of course, these students were too busy (and a little too lazy) to trek down to the second floor, put on a pot, and wait for it to be ready. They wanted to know when *somebody else* in the building had gone to the trouble of putting on a pot, so they could swoop down and enjoy it.

The students found an old video camera and a surplus computer that had a frame grabber. Paul Jardetzky wrote a program that recorded the video image from the frame grabber every few seconds. Quentin Stafford-Fraser wrote another program, called XCoffee, which contacted Jardetzky's program over the network and then displayed a picture of the coffee pot on the computer's screen. "The image was only updated about three times a minute, but that was fine because the pot filled rather slowly, and it was only greyscale, which was also fine," wrote Stafford-Fraser on a web page devoted to the subject.

The coffee pot started to gain a small following around the world. Bob Metcalfe wrote about it in the January 27, 1992 issue of *Comm Week*. According to one report, 600 people downloaded a copy of the XCoffee program so they could see the coffee pot for themselves. But the program only ran on Unix workstations, which somewhat limited its appeal. When the surplus computer eventually died, students Daniel Gordon and Martyn Johnson resurrected the system with new hardware, and put the coffee pot image directly on its own web page.[15]

Being on the Web made all the difference. Before the dawn of the World Wide Web, the only way that a person could view the Trojan Room Coffee Pot was to download the XCoffee program and run it. Because the program only had one function, that was a lot of effort to exert for a rather questionable payoff. And then there was the problem that the XCoffee program would only run on certain kinds of Unix workstations. But putting it on the Web suddenly meant that anybody with a web browser could view the image simply by clicking on the link. And the web browser didn't need to be specially modified to display a video image: from the browser's point of view, there was no difference between the picture of the coffee pot and a picture of the president of the United States on the White House home page.

Gordon's work paid off: according to a BBC report aired on November 11, 1994, more than 150,000 people had clicked in to see the Trojan Room Coffee Pot once the image had been made Web-accessible. It was the birth of the webcam.

Over the following two years, webcams started springing up all over the world. An early webcam in Cambridge, Massachusetts, operated by OpenMarket showed a view of Boston's skyline. ClNet, a combination cable TV show and web site, set up a webcam allowing visitors to the web site to spy on the company's television studios. Farm.net, an Internet service provider in New Hampshire, set up the "chicken cam," which looked into a chicken coop. There was a spoof webcam called the toilet cam, which always showed a picture of a toilet. People clicked into the site, hoping to catch somebody on the potty. And then there is JenniCam, a camera pointed into the bedroom/home office of its eponymous web designer-cum-exhibitionist. You can view Jennifer Ringley for free at www.jennicam.org, with updates every 20 minutes, or you can pay $15 per year and get updates every 2 minutes.

In 1994, BBC journalist Michael Isaacson interviewed Daniel Gordon about the Trojan Room Coffee Pot camera. At the beginning of the interview, Gordon is sitting at his keyboard, typing. "All I have to do is click on a button that says coffee machine . . . and eventually . . . I get a picture on my workstation . . . and it looks like somebody else has drunk all the coffee. So I guess I will have to make some myself."

The BBC reporter seemed a little confused. He asked Gordon, "Wouldn't it be a good idea to make the picture bigger, so you could see who is drinking the coffee?"

"Yeah, but I think we should try to protect the guilty," replied the graduate student.

In fact, by keeping the image small, Gordon and his fellow techheads were doing more than merely "protecting the guilty." By resisting the temptation to turn a coffee monitoring device into a general-purpose surveillance tool, they were protecting the social fabric of their community. Capturing the faces of coffee pilferers might put an end to the practice, but it might also destroy the camaraderie that the communal coffee pot was meant, in part, to create.

JenniCam

Jennifer K. Ringley lives the examined life. In her apartment in Washington. D.C., she sleeps, wakes, eats, and works under the watchful eyes of several video cameras that feed a constant stream of images to the World Wide Web. The image is updated every 20 minutes, and is freely available. Yes, there is nudity and sex, although this is not the purpose of the web site. Instead, it is a slice of Ringley's life. Although she officially makes her living as a web designer, thousands of people have paid $15 for a 12-month membership to her website, which gives improved access—an image that is updated every 2 minutes, instead of every 20. [Photos courtesy JenniCam]

FROM WEBCAM TO WEARCAM

The Washington State Department of Transportation's (WSDOT's) site on the World Wide Web displays current traffic conditions for the highways surrounding Lake Washington. The idea is to let drivers find out where the traffic is so they can try to avoid it. Information that's displayed on the site comes from magnetic wire loops embedded in the highway pavement and from more than 200 separate video cameras installed throughout the highway system. In 1996, the video output from 45 of those cameras was hooked directly to WSDOT's web server, allowing anybody with an Internet connection to look through the cameras' lenses.

WSDOT has actually had video cameras and magnetic loops installed in the highways since Interstate 5 was built in the 1960s, says Mahrokh Arefi, an engineer with the department.[16] But before the World Wide Web, there was no way to easily share the information with the public. Today, that has all changed.

Most of these cameras today are connected to a large video switching system at WSDOT's Northwest Region Traffic Systems Management Center in Northern Seattle. Video monitors blanket the walls of the Center, allowing traffic engineers to quickly spot trouble spots and notify the public via ongoing traffic reports. The Center can also turn on ramp metering lights, which slows the rate of new cars being added to the highway.

Many of the cameras can be individually tilted, panned, and zoomed, allowing a person in the traffic center to conduct detailed surveillance of the roadway. A duplicate video feed is piped to the state police. Cameras that are in tunnels are also hooked up to videocassette recorders. The original purpose of the video recorders, Arefi says, was to provide evidence in the event that a WSDOT employee working in a tunnel was hurt or killed by a car.

Paradoxically, as the video images from the surveillance cameras have become more widely available, WSDOT has decided to make them less valuable. When video feeds from the cameras were given to Seattle's area television stations, WSDOT instructed its operators to stop zooming in on individual cars—especially those involved in accidents. Making the video images available over the Web only reinforced this decision. WSDOT doesn't want the citizens of Washington to think they're being spied upon. In fact, the web site's list of Frequently Asked Questions makes it very clear to the curious that the cameras do not have enough resolution to read license plates, and that even though the Washington State Patrol has a video link to the system, "to date [WSP has] not used recordings for law enforcement purposes."[17]

Likewise, Arefi says, the video recorders are being removed. Apparently, they have never been useful in a legal case. And the videotape is a potential liability for WSDOT in the event that a motorist has an accident that is the Department's fault.

Where governments fear to tread, private citizens are moving ahead. As surveillance technology becomes increasingly available, citizens are taking it up, echoing the axiom that the best disinfectant is sunshine. In May 1997, the Norwegian newspaper Nettavisen reported on a webcam pointing at the entrance of a brothel, according to an article that was submitted to the RISKS Digest by Martin Minow.[18] Such cameras are legal under Norwegian law as long as the license numbers of cars and the identities of people in the photographs are not reported, the article claimed.

In San Francisco, an independent video producer whose studio was at a hectic intersection got tired of seeing cars run the red light at 11th and Howard—and the resulting accidents. He set up a spare video camera to watch continuously over the intersection. Now, whenever he sees a hit-and-run accident, particularly one that injures a pedestrian, he goes down and offers the victim a copy of the video.[19]

One culmination of this widespread video surveillance is the wear-cam, a new generation of video cameras that people wear on their bodies and use to constantly transmit a video image of their surroundings. Numerous science fiction authors have fantasized about such technology. In the novel *Snow Crash*, Neal Stephenson imagines people called *gargoyles* who walk about, record everything that they see, and upload the information into the Central Intelligence Corporation's massive databanks, hoping that somebody else will find the information useful and buy it. In *Earth*, David Brin prophesies the True-Vue video glasses, which videotape everything the wearer sees and transmit the information to a remote location as a kind of mobile surveillance camera.

Mobile video cameras with radio uplink are not just the stuff of science fiction: they are possible today. While he was a graduate student at the MIT Media Lab in the early 1980s, Steve Mann started wearing a video camera on his head. The camera was connected to a radio transmitter that sent the image through the air to a web server, where the images were displayed on a web page with the headline "Look out through my glasses right now (or when last transmitted)."

For a while, Mann put a little card on his hat that contained the following warning.

For your protection a video record of you and your establishment may be transmitted and recorded at remote locations.

ALL CRIMINAL ACTS PROSECUTED!!!

Mann's video camera has gotten him into trouble at stores, banks, and other organizations that have policies forbidding patrons from taking photographs or videotapes. Controlling the tools of surveillance is a technique for maintaining power. It is a power that stores do not readily cede to their customers.

The Evolution of Steve Mann, the Walking Webcam

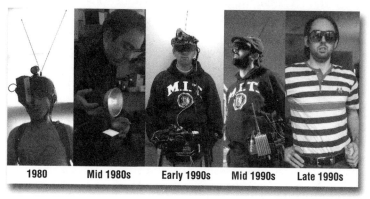

| 1980 | Mid 1980s | Early 1990s | Mid 1990s | Late 1990s |

Equipped with a battery-powered video camera, portable computer, and wireless Internet link, Steve Mann is the walking webcam—or wearcam, as he prefers to be called. Currently a professor in the Department of Electrical Engineering at the University of Toronto, Mann has been wearing various versions of his electronic rig for more than a decade. Turnabout is fair play, argues Mann, who takes extreme issue with merchants like the MIT Coop that have surveillance cameras throughout, but nevertheless don't allow their customers to take photographs within their stores. Much of Mann's research explores programmatic techniques for managing a moving camera—for example, techniques for recovering additional information, boosting resolution, or building larger images by combining many smaller ones. [Photos courtesy Steve Mann]

FUMBLING FOR THE "OFF" SWITCH

Video surveillance enthusiasts like Brin and Mann believe that there will be more and more video cameras as time goes on. And in a world filled with video cameras, they argue, we will basically have two choices: having cameras that are solely under the control of businesses and governments, and having cameras that are free and accessible for everyone to use.

But alas, this utopian analysis of a dystopian future ignores basic economics. Even in a world of falling costs, someone must pay for all this technology. The people who pay the bills will decide where the cameras are pointed. And the results from the ongoing experiment in the United Kingdom are already in: video cameras do not watch all communities equally—or all individuals.

A 1997 study by the Centre for Criminology and Criminal Justice at the University of Hull (in Hull, United Kingdom) looked at 888 cases of targeted video surveillance—cases in which an operator could move a camera or control a video monitor—and found that the surveillance cameras were "systematically and disproportionately targeted" at young, black males "not because of their involvement in crime or disorder, but for 'no obvious reason'" other than their age and race.[20] The study found that 10% of the women were targeted for entirely "voyeuristic" reasons, and that 40% of the people monitored were targeted for no reason other than their race or ethnicity. The report concluded:

> The gaze of the cameras does not fall equally on all users of the street but on those who are stereotypically predefined as potentially deviant, or through appearance and demeanour, are singled out by operators as unrespectable. In this way youth, particularly those already socially and economically marginal, may be subject to even great levels of authoritative intervention and official stigmatisation, and rather than contributing to social justice through the reduction of victimisation, CCTV will merely become a tool of injustice through the amplification of differential and discriminatory policing.

Simon Davies, director general of Privacy International, testified before the House of Lords in 1997 about the impact he had seen from pervasive surveillance cameras:

> First, I firmly believe the overall justification for the technology is specious, untested and is based largely on emotive grounds. Claims about the impact of CCTV on levels and patterns of crime are frequently exaggerated and simplistic. For example, crimes of passion, crimes involving drugs and alcohol, and actions by professional criminals are seldom prevented by the cameras. Generally speaking only minor "opportunistic" crime is diminished by the technology.

> Second, the primary impact of the technology on human behaviour has more to do with public order than outright criminality. In practice most camera systems have been used principally to combat "anti-social behavior" including littering, urinating in parks, underage smoking, traffic violations, graffiti, fighting, obstruction, drunkenness, indecency, and evading meters in town parking lots. There is, of course, an argument that these are legitimate targets for the technology, but few members of the public associate CCTV with such misdemeanors.

> Finally, I believe the technology has numerous deleterious facets that are under-reported. I have personally witnessed CCTV system operators routinely exercising their prejudices to discriminate against race, age, class or sexual preference. A recent report from the University of Hull supports this observation. Several high profile cases of abuse of the technology and of images have contributed to a decline in public support for the technology. CCTV is also a key factor in a range of important changes to police practices. These changes—including a shift from proactive to reactive policing—have not been adequately researched or assessed.[21]

In his testimony, Davies raised specific objections to computerized face recognition, miniature video cameras designed for covert surveillance, and high-sensitivity cameras, such as Forward Looking Infra-red Radar, which can see images in darkness and, in some cases, through walls.

The widespread adoption of video surveillance technology is not inevitable. Even microscopic cameras can be regulated, if society chooses to do so. Although it is impossible to stamp out covert video surveillance, high penalties, combined with social pressures, will go a long way toward minimizing the practice. For example, Martin Minow also reported in RISKS Digest that a video camera located at a Swedish restaurant was forcibly shut down in 1996 by the Swedish Data Protection Agency. In Canada, a visit by the privacy commissioner of British Columbia to Vancouver's new public library resulted in a dramatic reduction in the amount of video surveillance—and notification of the public that the surveillance was taking place.

Back in the United Kingdom, Simon Davies has suggested some simple regulations for these systems, including the following:

- Allow local zoning commissions to control the deployment of urban surveillance cameras.

- Extend the U.K.'s data protection laws so the country's data protection registrar would have "direct say in the establishment and running of systems."

- Establish minimum standards for the training of surveillance camera operators.

- Prohibit the sale or transfer of images from the systems.

These guidelines would also work well in the United States. Without such guidelines, our society risks a video surveillance free-for-all.

WHAT WAS THAT?

Sound is very different from light. On a physical level, light is made up of particles called *photons* that move through space. Sound, in contrast, is made up of compression waves that move through air, solids, or liquids. Light exists without a medium; sound cannot. This key difference has a variety of practical implications. It is much easier to record sound than video, but it is much harder to record sound at a distance. That's because while light waves travel in a straight line, sound waves spread out and bounce.

To experience the difference for yourself, just go to a park on a warm summer day. With a small telescope, you can easily spy on a small family picnic a quarter mile away. You can see what the family is eating and whether or not the children are well-behaved. But if you actually want to listen in on the conversation, you'll probably need to sneak over and plant a hidden microphone. Background noise, combined with the fact that sound waves quickly disperse, gives us some measure of acoustical privacy, even in public.

It's not surprising, then, that most acoustical surveillance involves some kind of physical invasion as well. Sometimes the invasion can be hard to detect. In 1946, Soviet schoolchildren presented U.S. Ambassador Averell Harriman with a large carved wooden seal of the United States. The Ambassador was so impressed with the seal that he hung it in his office at the U.S. Embassy in Moscow. What the Ambassador didn't know was that the seal was booby-trapped. Six years later, intelligence agents discovered that the seal contained a hidden microphone and a radio antenna. By beaming microwaves at the instrument, the Soviets could use the hidden device to listen in on all of the Ambassador's conversations.

In his 1966 book *The Intruders: The Invasion of Privacy by Government and Industry*, Senator Edward V. Long expressed indignation at the wide range of acoustical monitoring equipment of the day. Heading the Senate's Subcommittee on the Invasion of Privacy, Long got to see firsthand some of the best acoustical monitoring equipment ever conceived. For bugging a cocktail party, there was a tiny microphone and radio transmitter that looked like an olive on a stick; it could transmit a radio signal to a receiver more than a block away. To bug somebody's living room, there was a "spike mike" mounted at the end of a dart. Fired from a rifle up to a quarter mile away, the mike was designed to stick into a window sill and transmit back anything that it heard.

Long also learned that this technology was being used indiscriminately by government agencies such as the Food and Drug Administration, by businesses, and even by nosy individuals. Ultimately, one of the results of the heightened awareness on Capitol Hill was the passage of restrictions on electronic eavesdropping that were part of the 1968 Omnibus Crime Control and Safe Streets Act.

Today, advances in digital signal processing are making physical presence less important for planting bugs. It is widely reported that conversations in a modern office building can be overheard by bouncing a laser beam off an office window. The eavesdropping trick that the Soviets used against Ambassador Harriman still works, except now it is possible to bounce radio signals off metal objects that are already

Low-Cost Audio Surveillance

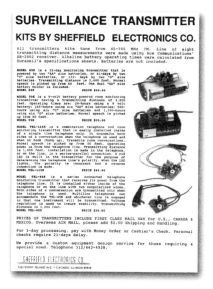

SURVEILLANCE TRANSMITTER

KITS BY SHEFFIELD ELECTRONICS CO.

All transmitters kits tune from 65-305 MHz FM. Line of sight transmitting distance measurements were made using Ace Communications' AR-3002 receiver. Alkaline battery operating times were calculated from Duracell's specifications sheets. Batteries are not included.

MODEL 95E is a 32-day monitoring transmitter that is powered by two "AA" size batteries, or 61-days by two "C" size batteries, or 113- days by two "D" size batteries. Transmitting distance is 2,600 feet. Normal speech is picked up from 60 feet. One dual "AA" size battery holder is included.
MODEL 95E   PRICE $40.00

MODEL 95K is a 9-volt battery powered room monitoring transmitter having a transmitting distance of 3,800 feet. Operating times are: 28-hours using a 9 volt battery; 165-hours using six "AA" size batteries; 500-hours using six "C" size batteries and 1,300-hours using six "D" size batteries. Normal speech is picked up from 60 feet.
MODEL 95K   PRICE $39.00

MODEL TEL-115K is a combination telephone and room monitoring transmitter that is easily installed inside of a single line telephone only. It transmits both sides of a conversation when the telephone is used and when on hook (hung up), transmits room conversations. Normal speech is picked up from 50 feet. Operating power is from the telephone line. Transmitting distance is 1,000 feet. Installation is made in the telephone or on the line, in series-parallel connection. A red LED is built in the transmitter for the purpose of determining the telephone line's polarity. When the LED lights, the polarity is incorrect and a reverse connection is made.
MODEL TEL-115K   PRICE $45.00

MODEL TEL-65K is a series connected telephone monitoring transmitter that receives its power from the telephone line. It is installed either inside of the telephone or on the line with two nonpolarized wires. Both sides of a conversation are transmitted only when the telephone is used. Multiline telephones can accommodate the TEL-65K and whichever line is engaged in that one instrument will be transmitted. Voltage regulation is used to insure stability. Transmitting distance is 3,200 feet.
MODEL TEL-65K   PRICE $39.00

PRICES OF TRANSMITTERS INCLUDE FIRST CLASS MAIL S&H for U.S., CANADA & MEXICO. Overseas AIR MAIL, please add $2.00 Shipping and Handling.

For 1-day processing, pay with Money Order or Cashier's Check. Personal checks require 21-days delay.

We provide a custom equipment design service for those requiring a special need. Telephone 312/643-4928.

SHEFFIELD ELECTRONICS CO.
7260 STONY ISLAND AVE. • CHICAGO, ILLINOIS 60649

Surveillance hardware is cheap, easily available, and out of control. This advertisement from the now-defunct Sheffield Electronic Company promoted a tiny FM transmitter that was one-third the size of the nine-volt battery that powered it. Secreted inside a person's home or car, one of these devices could transmit, for a week or more, a radio signal that could be heard for more than a hundred feet. Another version could be powered from a telephone line. [Advertisement credit Sheffield Electronics Company]

present in a room, rather than having to go to the trouble of having a grade school class present your target with a carved American eagle.

And audio surveillance technology is increasingly being marketed to the masses. For example, an advertisement in the February 1997 issue of the *New York Times Magazine* hawks the PowerVox IV, a powerful listening device that costs just $39.95: "Put PowerVox IV in your shirt pocket or clip it to your belt and realize to your amazement that you can hear whispered conversations up to 50 feet away, a pin drop 10 feet away, and even hear what people are talking about in the next room."

What's needed is not new laws, but a commitment to enforce the many laws that are already on the books. People, businesses, and government officials need to learn that audio surveillance is both illegal and morally wrong.

When the city of Vancouver opened its new public library in 1994, patrons were not informed that their actions were being monitored by

34 video cameras and numerous hidden microphones. Key areas that received heavy monitoring were entrances, exits, and the area around the children's bathrooms. The acoustical surveillance was designed to hear the screams of a person being attacked in the parking garage or a disabled individual who might have fallen off a toilet in a bathroom stall. Laudable ideas, except for the fact that the public was not informed that the monitoring was taking place.

There is also a new kind of acoustical surveillance on the horizon that doesn't fit easily into our existing framework. This is wide-scale monitoring that combines telecommunications with data processing to locate, triangulate, categorize, and permanently record any events deemed suspicious.

In 1993, the town of Redwood City, California, decided that it had a problem with guns. "People were firing their guns in the air, at other people. Gangs of people will drive by and shoot rounds at signs. Some people discharge guns in their backyard [and] in their houses," says Ward Hayter, the Deputy News Media Liaison Officer for the town's police force.[22]

Some people heard the gunshots and called the police, but none of the citizens could really tell where the gunfire was coming from. So the town got wired: it hired Dr. Robert Showen of Trilon Technology to build a gunshot detector and locator.

Three years later, a $25,000 prototype system was ready to be deployed. The system consists of eight microphones scattered over a mile-and-a-half area. The microphones are mounted up out of the way on buildings or atop tall poles. Each microphone has its own telephone line. The microphones pick up noise around them and send whatever they hear back to police headquarters, where the sounds are analyzed by a Sun Microsystems workstation. The computer applies a digital filter to the sounds and determines whether or not they actually are gunshots. If it thinks they are, the computer notes the exact time the gunshot was heard at each microphone and uses that information to triangulate the gun's location. Within 45 seconds, the system displays the location of the gunshot on a map of the city. The police then immediately dispatch a squad car—long before somebody can call 911.

"The system has a 60–70% detection rate in the area," and can pinpoint the gunshots to within 30 to 60 feet, says Hayter. The system can frequently hear and locate guns being fired inside homes and other buildings. Hayter said that in "one or two incidents, we have actually made an arrest related to a gunshot" that the system detected. But the real value of the system, he insisted, was deterrence: "It [has] suppressed a lot of our gunshots in the community," he said confidently, although he couldn't provide any statistics to back up his assertion.

In 1967, the U.S. Supreme Court ruled in the case of *Katz v. U.S.*23 that police could not put a microphone on a public telephone in order to eavesdrop on a conversation without a warrant. But the gunshot detector doesn't listen in on a specific conversation: it listens in on what is out in the open for everyone to hear. Furthermore, it does not record conversations. Given these limitations, it seems to be exempt from the 1967 ruling.

Nevertheless, the idea of having the police department scattering microphones all over town to detect criminal activity seems like something out of George Orwell's *1984*. I asked Hayter if people had complained about their privacy being violated. "We haven't had any privacy rights complaints at all," he said. For starters, he said, there is no way for the police to turn up the volume on the microphones and listen to conversations taking place on the street below. "You can't turn anything up," said Hayter. "It's a phone line that goes to a sensor. . . . For any invasion of privacy, somebody would have to climb up on the building and have a conversation next to it. . . . There is no intention to listen in on people's conversations."

But another reason he gave for the lack of complaints is more telling: "Most of these things are on buildings and they are not identified: the general public doesn't know where they are."

THE SYSTEMATIC SURVEILLANCE OF SCIENCE

Satellite imagery, terrestrial video cameras, and microphones are certainly the most obvious forms of remote surveillance instruments, but they aren't the only kind. Highly precise scientific instruments are increasingly being applied to widespread terrestrial surveillance.

International agreements seeking to limit or end the arms race invariably call for increased monitoring of our planet. One of the best examples is the Comprehensive Test Ban Treaty, signed by President Clinton at the United Nations on September 24, 1996. This treaty, the result of a 40-year battle to stop the testing of nuclear weapons, calls for the creation of a sophisticated International Monitoring System to watch the planet for small nuclear explosions that would be in violation of the treaty.

The monitoring system consists of primary and auxiliary seismic networks, a radionucleotide monitoring network, a hydroacoustic network, an infrasound network, and onsite inspections of nuclear facilities. The seismic network is designed to detect explosions that produce man-made "earthquakes" with a magnitude of 4.25 or more on the Richter scale, and to be able to pinpoint those explosions within 1,000 square kilometers (a circle with a radius of 18 kilometers, or 11 miles).

For comparison, the relatively small 10-kiloton nuclear weapon test conducted by China on July 29, 1996 had a magnitude of 5.2.[24]

Who will operate this network? Scientists who are already monitoring the earth for other purposes.

The Incorporated Research Institutions for Seismology (IRIS) calls itself a "university research consortium dedicated to exploring the Earth's interior through the collection of and distribution of seismographic data." IRIS operates a network of more than 50 seismological stations all over the world, and receives funding from both the United States National Science Foundation and the Air Force Office of Scientific Research. Originally formed in 1984 by 26 universities, by 1997 IRIS had become a nonprofit consortium with more than 90 member institutions.

IRIS members know that their network has two purposes: one scientific, the other military. The organization's newsletter is filled with articles about earth shakes that are both man-made and natural. These are scientists with a mission.

In the spring of 1995, IRIS received an unusual request from the U.S. Senate. A terrorist organization, Aum Shinrikyo, had opened vials of sarin nerve gas in the Tokyo subway system on March 20, killing 12 people and injuring more than 5,000. In the investigation that followed, it was revealed that the cult had operatives in western Australia as well.

What interested the U.S. Senate Permanent Subcommittee on Investigations was an event that took place on May 28, 1993, in western Australia. On that night, at 11:03 p.m. local time, monitoring stations registered a "magnitude 3.6 event at 1 km depth." A nearby group of aboriginal prospectors reported seeing "a star-like object low on the horizon." The object sped along like an aircraft, then disappeared. Suddenly, the prospectors saw an enormous flash of light and heard an explosion lasting a number of seconds. "Several people called the Mundaring Observatory to report a whistling fireball-like object low in the sky."[25]

Two years later, local newspapers reported that Aum Shinrikyo had been attempting to enrich uranium at Banjawarn Station, just north of the location of the explosion. So what had happened? Had the cult been testing missiles and nuclear explosives? Was it a UFO? Or was it a mining explosion gone out of control? Senator Sam Nunn wanted to know.

As luck would have it, the incident was recorded by an IRIS Global Seismographic Network station 650 kilometers away in southwestern Australia. By analyzing the "mystery event" of May 28 and comparing it with a regional earthquake from September 4, 1994, and a mining blast from January 28, 1995, IRIS staff members Christel B.

Hennet and Gregory van der Vink determined that the mystery event was neither. Instead, they reported, the event was in all likelihood the result of an iron meteorite roughly three meters in diameter striking the earth's surface—and detonating with roughly two kilotons of energy. According to the scientists, such meteorites are expected to hit the earth roughly once every six years.

More than two years after a suspicious event in western Australia, scientists in Washington, D.C. could look at tapes from a seismic monitoring station and confidently determine that the blast was not the result of nuclear bomb testing by a Japanese terrorist doomsday cult. The global instrument and library worked.

ONE WORLD, LIKE IT OR NOT

For years, environmentalists have said that we live in one large connected world: everything that everybody does affects everybody else. When viewed through the lens of remote sensing, this dictum is all the more true. More than 150 years after the discovery of photography, we are still coming to terms with the idea that the world around us can be recorded in ever-increasing detail.

The choice that we face is not between pervasive monitoring systems operated by the establishment and monitoring systems that are operated by the establishment *and* all of the citizenry. There is a third choice: creating rules that cover the deployment of monitoring systems and the use of captured happenings. We dismiss this third choice at our own peril.

Chapter Six

To Know Your Future

Did you have an abortion when you were fifteen?

A few years ago, when your marriage was going through an especially rough spot, our records indicate that you were treated for a sexually transmitted disease that your wife didn't have. Does she know?

Is that lonely child with Down Syndrome in the state hospital yours? Why don't you visit her more often?

I told Janice about the headaches you've been having at work. She said that when you guys were kids, your father used to smash your head against the wall. Do you think you might have brain damage?

Did you know that you are adopted?

Most Americans consider their medical records to be the most sensitive pieces of personal information that they have. Medical records are beacons into our past. They reveal secrets about families. They strip us naked, as if we had been prepped for surgery. They remind us about things we would rather forget—and things that we don't want others ever to discover.

Medical records are also windows into our future. They are imperfect oracles, to be sure—a healthy person walking across the street can be hit by a truck—but many illnesses and medical conditions follow a predictable path. People with untreated blockage of their coronary arteries tend to have heart attacks; diabetics who can't control their blood sugar are apt to go blind; people with untreated chronic depression are inclined to attempt suicide. Genetic records can be even more revealing.

But medical records tell as much about the temporarily healthy as they do about the chronically ill. In a world of uncertainties, the precision that comes from knowing a healthy person's weight, blood pressure, and cholesterol level conveys a feeling of predictability. A doctor can't say for sure that you'll live to be 92, but a statistician can tell you that your odds of doing so are 35%. Insurance companies use this information to set rates. Businesses can use this information to help decide who they should train and promote for positions of responsibility.

NO BIGGER GAP

Medical records are also among the most difficult kinds of personal information to protect. While the actual paper or electronic files can be protected with locks or passwords, individual facts from those records are easily revealed out of malice, for profit, or even by accident.

Consider the case of a young woman in Poughkeepsie, New York, who was in an automobile accident with her fiancé in 1982. The pair was taken to the Vassar Brothers Hospital—where the woman had secretly given birth the year before. When the woman checked in, an attendant pulled up her records from the hospital's computer. "Oh, you had a baby a year ago," the attendant said, in the presence of both the woman and her fiancé.[1] It was an understandable slip, but it revealed a world of personal information.

A far more malicious privacy invasion befell U.S. Representative Nydia Velázquez that same year. Three weeks after Velázquez won New York's Democratic primary, she received a telephone call from Pete Hamill, a reporter at the *New York Post*. Velázquez testified before the Senate Judiciary Committee in 1994:

> He told me that the night before, the *Post* had received an anonymous fax of my records from St. Claire Hospital. The records showed that I had been admitted to the hospital a year ago, seeking medical assistance for a suicide attempt. He told me that other newspapers across the city had received the same information and the *New York Post* was going to run a front-page story the next day. My records were leaked for one purpose only, to destroy my candidacy for the U.S. House of Representatives by discrediting me in the eyes of my constituents. Very few people knew about my situation, and I made a decision of not sharing it with my family. I wanted them to always remember me as a fighter, happy and strong. My father and mother, 80 years old, they did not understand. They still do not understand. When I found out this information was being published in the newspaper and that I had no power to stop it, I felt violated. I trusted the system, and it failed me.[2]

What's even more disturbing is that, in all likelihood, no laws were violated when Velázquez's records were faxed. A doctor can be disciplined or lose his or her license for violating patient confidentiality. Hospitals are required under the state's hospital regulations to have a medical records department that "ensure[s] the confidentiality of patient records"—and a hospital can lose its accreditation if there is a pattern of confidentiality violations, says Donald Moy, General Council of the New York State Medical Society.[3] But few state or local laws criminalize the unauthorized release of medical records themselves. A secretary or a janitor who walks into the hospital's records room and faxes out the records might be violating the hospital's rules, but they are rarely committing a criminal act.

Nydia Velázquez

Three weeks after Nydia Velázquez won the New York Democratic Party's nomination to serve in the U.S. House of Representatives, somebody at St. Claire Hospital in New York faxed Velázquez's medical records to the New York Post. The records detailed the care that Velázquez had received at the hospital after a suicide attempt—an attempt that had happened several years before the election. [Photo courtesy Nydia Velázquez]

"Most people think it's illegal to release medical records. They are unaware that no law exists," says Robert Ellis Smith, publisher of *The Privacy Journal*. "What they might mean is that release would subject a physician to ethical sanctions or that the victim could sue for an invasion of privacy. You should ask folks who make that assertion [that medical records are protected] to cite the law. In my experience, in no other area of privacy is there a bigger gap between what people's expectation of protection is and what the reality is than in medical records."[4]

As of 1995, 43 U.S. states lacked laws criminalizing the release of medical records.[5] Likewise, there is no federal law criminalizing the improper release of medical records. Such laws are clearly needed, because unauthorized releases are very widespread. According to the 1993 Health Information Privacy Survey by Louis Harris and

Associates and Alan Westin, "27% of respondents (representing 50 million adults) report their belief that an organization or person having their personal medical information has disclosed it improperly." Thirty-one percent of these respondents (representing 8% of the total population and 14 million Americans) go on to report that they were harmed or embarrassed by that disclosure."[6] The study also found that the people most likely to believe that there is a serious problem with medical privacy today are the people on the front lines—doctors and nurses.

"Most patients would be surprised at the number of organizations that receive information about their health record: their provider, insurer, pharmacist, state public health organizations—perhaps even their employer, life insurance company, or marketing firms," says Paul D. Clayton, who chaired the National Research Council's Committee on Healthcare Privacy and Security. "Sharing of information within the healthcare industry is largely unregulated and represents a significant concern to privacy advocates and patients alike because it often occurs without a patient's consent or knowledge."[7]

Despite the revelation of her suicide attempt, Velázquez managed to win her election. But Tommy Robinson wasn't so lucky. In 1990, Congressman Robinson was the Republican candidate for Governor of Arkansas, running against Bill Clinton. An insurer leaked to the press that Robinson had problems with alcohol. As it turned out, the diagnosis was in error. Nevertheless, Robinson's loss was attributed in part to the revelation. It's a revelation that might have had profound national consequences, since Bill Clinton was able to use the governorship that he won in that election to launch a successful campaign for the U.S. Presidency.[8]

As hard as it is to protect medical records in doctors' offices and in hospitals, the task pales when viewed in the broader context. There is an ever-increasing proliferation of other kinds of personalized medical information in our society—information that, if revealed, can be just as damaging as a doctor's diagnosis. Billing records are mailed to insurance companies and other third-party payers. Test results and detailed paper bills are sent to patients. Pharmacies know patients' prescription drugs. When a person buys an over-the-counter drug, the supermarket tape register becomes a kind of medical record. Likewise, there is an increasing assortment of home test kits for blood sugar, ovulation, pregnancy, and drug use. And a new generation of genetic tests is swiftly gaining in popularity—tests that in many cases can be performed without a person's knowledge or permission. This information is being used, among other things, for marketing. Metromail reportedly has a medical database, called Patient Select, with 15 million names. "For about thirty cents per name, large drug companies can pitch their products directly to angina sufferers, diabetics, or arthritics," reports Amitai Etzioni, citing an article that appeared in *Consumer Reports*.[9]

THE MEDICAL RECORDS FAIRY TALE

From the outside, Daniel looked as if he was certainly vice president material. In his seven years with the company, he had relocated twice, revamped a division, and become a senior director. But then, one evening, Daniel's boss discovered a prescription bottle inside Daniel's medicine cabinet when she was over for dinner (she had been looking for an aspirin). A few telephone calls revealed that the drug was used for controlling hypertension—and that Daniel had a 15-year history of high blood pressure. The company's doctor said that people with Daniel's condition usually die within 5 to 30 years—but every case is different. So when Daniel's annual review came up, he got a hefty raise but not a promotion. After all, why give the guy more stress? And why groom a person to be one of the company's top executives when he might not be around in 10 years?

Once upon a time, medical records had a very specific purpose: they provided a detailed record of a person's encounters with the medical establishment so that future encounters might have a higher chance of having a positive outcome. People had a vested interest in making sure that their medical records were correct.

Today, medical records have an expanded role—a role that doesn't involve primary healthcare. They are used by employers and insurance companies to decide who should be hired and insured. They are used by hospitals and religious organizations to solicit donations. Even marketers are buying up medical records in search of sales leads. Whereas people once had an incentive to make sure that their medical records were complete, accurate, and up to date, nowadays many people feel pressured to compartmentalize their medical records so that, when they are inevitably disclosed, the damage will be minimized.

Medical records were once seen as sacrosanct. Today, medical records are routinely sought and used in lawsuits to discredit witnesses, especially in cases of rape. Politicians and criminals alike have their medical records reported in the media without their permission. Ironically, the rapid proliferation of medical knowledge to the lay public is making the release of personal medical information all the more damaging. Medicine is a complex, largely ad hoc science, with many rules but many more individual exceptions. In untrained hands, a person's medical history or profile frequently becomes a tool to justify prejudice or an already decided outcome.

The confidentiality of psychological records is particularly under attack, says Dr. Denise Nagel, executive director of the National Coalition for Patient Rights. Lawyers, HMOs, life insurance companies, and others are routinely demanding access to psychological records—and in so doing, are jeopardizing the nation's entire mental health system.[10]

"A person's willingness to share sensitive, often embarrassing information is dependent on being assured confidentiality. It is the basis of trust in the relationship," says Nagel. Recovery from many kinds of mental trauma and diseases requires that the issues discussed during therapy remain secret. The U.S. Supreme Court reached the same conclusion in the 1995 case *Jaffe v. Redmond*. Nagel notes, when the Court ruled that conversations between a patient and a licensed social worker or therapist, even one who does not have a medical license, are nevertheless protected conversations about which testimony cannot be compelled unless the judicial need for disclosure clearly outweighs the patient's privacy interests. "Quality healthcare is rooted in the imperative need for confidence and trust," and that trust must not be lightly breached, the Court concluded.

Nevertheless, these same records are often sought by lawyers of alleged rapists. The attorneys then typically threaten to take the records into open court, in an attempt to disprove the credibility of their client's accusers, unless the victim drops the charges.

Such behavior by a defense attorney might itself seem criminal, or at least unethical, but it is standard practice in many rape trials. For example, a rape victim might have frequently fantasized about being raped when she was young; she now finds herself profoundly disturbed and unable to come to terms with the fact that the crime has finally happened to her for real. The victim might go through months of therapy to come to terms with this realization, only to be forced to listen in court to a defense attorney's theory that the woman might somehow have encouraged her attacker and been a willing participant.

Parents, meanwhile, are increasingly demanding to have access to the psychological records of people who come into contact with their children. In West Virginia, parents demanded to see the medical records of a school bus driver who had made strange remarks while driving children. The school superintendent investigated and said the man was on medication and his condition posed no harm to the children. But the parents sued, and in 1986, the state's Supreme Court sided with the parents, saying that they were entitled to see the driver's complete medical file—including his psychological records.[11]

PRIVACY IS YOUR DOCTOR'S RESPONSIBILITY

A placard on the wall of my local hospital says "Please Respect Patient Confidentiality." And in a very important way, this sign says it all. Hospitals and other medical facilities need to rely on the ability of their employees to hold patient secrets. Doctors, nurses, clerks, and even janitors all see highly charged information. A hospital that tried to shield its employees from all sensitive patient information would quickly cease to function.

Fortunately, in most cases, this trust seems well placed. I have never met a doctor or a healthcare professional who did not seriously undertake their responsibility for patient confidentiality. Patient privacy is at the very core of the healthcare profession. It goes all the way back to Ancient Greece and the Hippocratic Oath, which says, in part: "All that may come to my knowledge in the exercise of my profession or in daily commerce with men, which ought not to be spread abroad, I will keep secret and will never reveal."

What complicates the confidentiality process is the fact that between 50 and 75 people need access to a patient's chart during a typical hospital visit. Keeping a secret requires everybody's cooperation: revealing it requires just one bad apple. Many hospitals hire temporary administrative workers who have little or no training in medical ethics. Other healthcare facilities are actively downsizing, creating employees who have a grudge against their employer. As the cases of Nydia Velázquez and Tommy Robinson demonstrate, it is all too easy for a careless and motivated insider to shatter the wall of medical privacy.

Over the past 50 years, military intelligence agencies and major corporations have developed techniques for preventing the theft of confidential information and for tracing the sources of leaks. People are given personalized copies of records. Photocopies are logged. People have their bags searched upon entering or leaving a secure facility. These techniques are simply impossible to implement in the healthcare workplace. And for the most part, they are unnecessary.

But leaks do happen—and not just to people running for elected office. Since the outbreak of the AIDS epidemic, there has been case after case of people who have lost insurance or their jobs when it was revealed that they were infected with the HIV virus. In 1989, the FBI canceled the contract of a physician who had performed preemployment and annual physical exams for the Bureau in San Francisco when it learned that the physician had AIDS. In Salt Lake City in the early 1990s, a vitamin manufacturer fired Kim Allred when he tested positive for a marijuana derivative found in the prescription drug Marinol; when the company learned that he was taking the drug for AIDS, it refused to rehire him. At the Princeton Medical Center in 1987, a practicing surgeon named Dr. William Behringer was treated at his own facility and was diagnosed as suffering from AIDS. "Within hours of his discharge, he received many calls from well-wishers who evidently had learned of his condition. Most of the callers were his colleagues at the Medical Center. After that, patients called. Soon his surgical privileges were suspended by the hospital. A court found the breach of confidentiality the fault of the hospital," read an account in *War Stories II*, published by the *Privacy Journal*.[12]

These stories show another side of the medical information privacy dilemma as well. You don't need to photocopy somebody's medical chart in order to destroy their medical privacy—all you need is to leak a single declarative sentence like "Nydia Velázquez attempted suicide" or "Dr. William Behringer has AIDS." Indeed, as demonstrated by the Tommy Robinson case, the statement doesn't even have to be true—just believable.

When I started dating my wife in 1993, we went together to get tested for AIDS at Boston City Hospital. The clinic was one of several in the city specifically set up to allow for anonymous testing. The nurse who took my blood had no idea who I was and never asked for any identification. She gave me a control number when I left so I could learn the results. But when my wife and I returned a week later, a woman who was volunteering at the clinic recognized me from a class we had taken together at MIT. Should that volunteer have been legally prohibited from telling people that she had seen me at the clinic? What about other people who happened to be in the waiting room who might have recognized me?

The problem here is one of segregation. The goal of anonymous AIDS testing is to allow individuals to be tested without the creation of a record. But by creating a special place for the anonymous delivery of a particular medical service, the privacy of the individuals becomes dependent on their continued anonymity. If there were multiple medical services delivered anonymously at the clinic, then merely recognizing a person at the clinic's doors would not compromise that person's ultimate medical privacy. Rape crisis centers and abortion clinics ("women's clinics") present similar problems. One solution would be the reintegration of these services into mainstream medical practices.

Some people take the reverse point of view. They think that the best way to handle the morass of medical privacy is simply to eradicate it: unlock the files and the databanks, and make everybody's medical records freely available. David Brin, author of the *Transparent Society*, is a big proponent of this viewpoint. I actually believed it once myself; transparency has a simple elegance. I figured that everybody has some sort of medical condition or problem: the best way to destigmatize our diseases is to air them in public.

The problem with opening everybody's medical records is that everybody has a different body. Some of those bodies are diabetic. Some have asthma. Some have inherited genetic diseases. Some have brains that are mildly schizophrenic, but controllable with medication. And some bodies are genuinely healthy. Opening up everybody's medical history to public scrutiny opens up people to all manner of discrimination and personal attack, for which there are seldom workable remedies. One of the purposes of privacy in society is to protect us from other social problems that we have not yet eradicated.

Even if some futuristic and enlightened society manages to respect and value the sick in ways that we can't today, there is yet another overriding reason to abide by patient privacy. People who have managed to master their own physical or mental ailments deserve to go about their day-to-day lives without being constantly reminded of those problems by well-wishers. And as I mentioned earlier, the promise of confidentiality for psychological records is a fundamental need in order to have effective treatment for psychological diseases.

People deserve and require control over their own medical matters and privacy for their medical records. Doctors and nurses understand this. But the healthcare establishment increasingly doesn't care.

PRIVACY IS NOT YOUR INSURANCE COMPANY'S RESPONSIBILITY

While my local hospital is busy reminding its employees to respect patient confidentiality, my health insurance company is busy reminding *me* that privacy is not compatible with its way of doing business.

Like nearly all Americans, in order to have my insurance pay for a doctor's visit, I have to fill out a claim form. And at the bottom of the form is a little contract that washes away any quaint preconceptions of privacy that I might have. The contract is called a consent form. It says:

> I authorize any physician, hospital, or other medically related facility, insurance company, or other organization, institution or person, that has any records or knowledge of me, my dependents, or our health, to disclose, whenever requested to do so by CNA or its representatives, any and all such information. A photostatic copy of this authorization shall be considered as effective and valid as the original.

I'm not a lawyer, but it doesn't take a lawyer to understand what this consent form means. As a precondition to having my insurance company reimburse me the $50 for the doctor's visit and the $14 for my antibiotics, I authorize everybody to divulge all of my records to anybody. This blanket authorization covers *all* records: school records, tax records, and bank records. It even covers those embarrassing love letters I wrote to my ninth-grade girlfriend. And it is an indefinite authorization, with no expiration date or time period.

Some people think that consent forms such as this one are not enforceable. These people have a reasonable expectation that my insurance company might call up my doctor to get a diagnosis or additional proof that a particular service was rendered, but they doubt that an insurance company would go after all of those other files. After all, there is no legitimate business reason for them to do so. That's just plain common sense, isn't it?

The problem with this common-sense approach to legal contracts is that it is often wrong. The authorization form means what it says it does. "Any records" means *any* records. "All information" really does leave nothing out. The blanket authorization allows the insurance company to go fishing after any personal record it wants.

"The reason that [the claim form] is worded that way is so that we can get the information that we would need" to detect fraud, says Roger Morris, a spokesperson for CNA insurance. "It's not our goal to accumulate information on individuals, but it is our goal to try to protect the interests of our policy holders."[13] The overly broad release allows the insurance company to investigate cases of suspected fraud without fear of being sued for invasion of privacy. These corporate savings eventually translate to lower insurance premiums for everybody, says Morris. Of course, the savings also translate to higher corporate profits.

Health insurers say further that there is no reason for us to worry about providing them with sensitive information. "The insurance industry has a pretty good record helping to maintain privacy. We are required and committed to following laws on the books," says Richard Coorsh, the spokesperson for the Health Insurance Association of America.

The American public may feel otherwise. According to the 1993 Harris-Equifax survey on healthcare privacy issues, 15% of those who had their medical confidentiality violated—representing 7.5 million people—said that it had been violated by insurance companies.

Another person who feels otherwise is George Washington University professor Amitai Etzioni, author of *The Limits of Privacy*. In his book, which is generally critical of privacy, Etzioni nevertheless affirms the importance of privacy for medical records. And the real threat to medical records privacy, writes Etzioni, isn't government: it's business.

To try to understand the motivation behind the authorization form, I called up Albert H. Wohlers & Co., the Illinois-based company that administered my insurance policy for CNA. I spent an hour working my way up through a chain of claims processors and supervisors, until I was finally transferred to the office of James Malik, whom I was assured would be happy to answer my questions. But when I got to Mr. Malik's office, I was informed by his assistant that I couldn't talk to him. I asked for his title; she wouldn't tell me. I asked for her name, and she wouldn't tell me that either. She said that if I had a question, I should submit it in writing. Then she hung up on me.

The treatment that I got at the hands of Albert H. Wohlers & Co. is symptomatic of a deep-rooted problem with the U.S. healthcare industry. Healthcare is a weird confluence of money and medicine, and it's played by the rules of billion-dollar companies. No matter how strange or arbitrary those rules may seem, they are the rules. If you wish to get insurance, see your doctor, or have your hospital visits paid for, you will play by them. And since insurance companies save money when they lose customer claims, they actually have a financial incentive to offer poor customer service. All of this is true because the people paying the insurance company's bills are not those who are utilizing its services.

We should also be fearful of the nonmedical uses that businesses make of medical records, warns Etzioni, who cites an unpublished 1996 study which found that "35 percent of the Fortune 500 companies acknowledged that they drew on personal health information in making employment decisions."[14] One of the most common ways that employers get this information is from insurance companies or from self-insured health plans—that is, plans that are administered by professional health insurance companies but paid for by the businesses themselves. (Such self-insurance plans are exceedingly popular because they give big businesses more flexibility under the law to violate their employees' rights.) One of the cases that Etzioni cites is that of a Southeastern Pennsylvania Transit Authority (SEPTA) employee who was taking AIDS medications. SEPTA learned of the medications when it was asked to reimburse their purchases, and the information was provided to the man's supervisor.[15]

By reading the authorization paragraph at the bottom of my health insurance claim form, I was doing something subversive. Many don't read the forms they sign during their day-to-day lives—the forms are too depressing. These forms and the policies behind them create and reinforce feelings of powerlessness. They are the trappings of a system that's been gimmicked against the consumer. We do not have the choice either to negotiate or to strike our own deal. Our only choice is to submit.[16]

Nobody Knows the MIB

As part of his Ph.D. thesis at the Harvard Business School on privacy policies in corporate America, Jeff Smith surveyed more than a thousand people on a variety of privacy issues, and conducted in-depth interviews with several dozen. One of the key questions he asked was whether people had ever heard of a company called the Medical Information Bureau (MIB). What he found wasn't terribly surprising: they hadn't:

> Only one consumer in the sample was aware of the existence of MIB, even though all but two of the consumers had applied for life insurance and had gone through an underwriting process. One can only conclude that the consumers had not read the insurance application forms very carefully, since the MIB notification was surely included. However, this lack of awareness may also point to some inadequacies in the notification procedure.[17]

I asked my wife if she knew what the Medical Information Bureau was. She said that she didn't. I then showed her a medical insurance application that she had filled out nearly two years before. It included these two paragraphs:

> I AUTHORIZE any physician, medical practitioner, hospital, clinic, other medical or medically-related facility, the Medical Information Bureau, Inc., (MIB, Inc.), consumer reporting agency, insurance or reinsuring company, or employer having certain information about *me or my dependents* to give John Alden Life Insurance Company or its legal representative any and all such information. The nature of the information authorized to be disclosed includes information about: (1) physical condition(s), (2) health history(ies), (3) avocation(s), (4) age(s), (5) occupation(s), and (6) personal characteristics. This authorization includes information about: (1) drugs, (2) alcoholism, (3) mental illness, or (4) communicable diseases.

> I UNDERSTAND the information obtained by use of the Authorization will be used by JOHN ALDEN LIFE INSURANCE COMPANY to determine eligibility for benefits. I ALSO AUTHORIZE JOHN ALDEN LIFE INSURANCE COMPANY to release any information obtained to reinsuring companies, Medical Information Bureau, Inc., or other persons or organizations performing business or legal services in connection with my application, claim, or as may be otherwise lawfully required, or as I may further authorize.

"Is that your signature at the bottom of this form?" I asked her. Yes, it was. She then read the form again. Still, she had no real clue what MIB was, other than that it was probably some kind of clearinghouse for medical information.

In fact, what the Medical Information Bureau keeps in its computers is information about people. Specifically, every time you report a significant medical condition on an insurance application—anything from heart problems to skin cancer—the insurance company can report that condition to MIB. The next time you apply for insurance, your "new" insurance company will pull your MIB file and find out what you previously reported.

In theory, MIB is supposed to prevent people who have significant medical conditions (and have been repeatedly rejected when they apply for insurance) from suddenly omitting their conditions from their applications and then getting health and life insurance with low-cost premiums that are reserved for healthy people. MIB helps "keep the cost of insurance down for insurance companies and for consumers by preventing losses that would occur due to fraud or omissions," says Neil Day, MIB's president.[18]

MIB isn't supposed to be a medical blacklist. Member insurers are officially forbidden from using the information contained in MIB's files as the basis for denying insurance. Instead, they are only allowed to use the information as the basis for further investigation. At least, those are the rules.

MIB was organized in 1902 as a nonprofit trade organization; today, roughly 750 insurance companies belong. MIB's files don't contain medical records, test results, or X-rays. Instead, each person's file contains one or more codes that stand for a particular medical condition that has been reported for that person. There are codes that signify diabetes, heart problems, and drug abuse. Some codes are very detailed. For example, Jeff Smith found that MIB had five codes for AIDS:

- AIDS-related complex or condition (ARC) or acquired immune deficiency syndrome (AIDS).

- Unexplained history of thrush, other opportunistic infections, weight loss, generalized chronic swelling of lymph nodes, persistent fever, or diarrhea.

- Abnormal T-cell study.

- Abnormal blood test for which there is no specific code.

- Two or more different types of antibody tests indicating exposure to the HTLV-III (AIDS) virus; this code is no longer used.[19]

Not all of the codes at the Medical Information Bureau are medical, Smith noted. For example, MIB has five codes that indicate a dangerous lifestyle, including "adverse driving records, hazardous sports, or aviation activity."[20] These codes map to similar questions on most life insurance firms.

MIB is thus the official insurance agency gossip columnist. MIB helps make sure that if one life insurance company rejects a person on medical grounds, then other life insurance companies will be made aware of the ailment and reject that person as well.

MIB has been the subject of ongoing controversy since the 1970s, when its existence first became generally known. At the root of the controversy is the organization's penchant for secrecy. For many years, insurance agencies consulted MIB without telling applicants about the files. MIB was not mentioned in the few books on consumer issues and consumer privacy. MIB even had an unlisted phone number. Today, the secrecy continues, if to a lesser extent: MIB won't release the list of codes that it uses.

Day explains:

> The whole point of a code list is to protect confidentiality. The MIB report is very brief. It is about a 2×2 piece of paper that has, on average, between two and three codes. The codes are generally three digits— "321"—sometimes there are additional letters—it might be "321XYZ". A major point in protecting confidentiality is to have a code list which is used by authorized persons at insurance companies, but not to have that code list available to anyone else.

Keeping secret the mapping between the actual code and the conditions that the codes stand for does protect privacy, to a certain extent. But no privacy is gained by keeping secret the list of coded conditions. Put it another way: is any patient confidentiality lost by my reporting that MIB has in its files the five AIDS-related codes printed above? By keeping secret not just the codes but also the English descriptions of what each code means, MIB has left itself open to the attack that its files contain more than just medical information. In the past, says *Privacy Journal* publisher Robert Smith, MIB had codes that stood for "sexual deviance" and "sloppy appearance." Day disagrees, but since MIB won't release the list of conditions for which it has created codes, there is really no way to know for sure.

There have also been disagreements over the accuracy of MIB's files. The Fair Credit Reporting Act specifically exempts medical records, but MIB agreed to be voluntarily bound by the rules after a 1983 examination by the Federal Trade Commission. Since then, MIB has received roughly 15,000 requests by individuals each year, says Day. Between 250 and 300 patients per year argue with the contents of their report, he says. Overall, "97% of all consumers who received their MIB report [in 1996] found that their MIB record was accurate," reads a company pamphlet.

But if you happen to be one of those 300 patients, you might find yourself without medical or life insurance. In 1990, the Massachusetts

Public Interest Research Group (MASSPIRG) did a study on MIB and found numerous cases in which erroneous records in the company's files had prevented people from getting insurance. In one case, says Josh Kratka, a MASSPIRG attorney, a Massachusetts man told his insurance company that he had been an alcoholic but had managed to remain sober for several years and that he regularly attended Alcoholics Anonymous. The insurance company denied him coverage and forwarded a code to MIB: "alcohol abuse; dangerous to health." The next company the man applied to for insurance learned of the "alcohol abuse" through the information bureau and charged the man a 25% higher rate.[21]

In another case, a clerical error caused a woman's records at MIB to say that she carried the AIDS virus. "It was only after unusual intervention by the state regulatory board," because the woman worked for a physician, that the records were corrected, MASSPIRG discovered.

MIB claims that if these people were rejected from getting insurance as a result of the MIB report, then the report was being used incorrectly. And the company stresses that MIB reports are based on insurance applications—never on claims. But this protest rings hollow in light of insurance claim forms, which specifically give the insurance company the right to report claim information to MIB.

"The MIB guidelines are clear, but only a series of independent audits of life/health insurance companies would yield a definitive answer regarding actual practices," says Jeff Smith. "To the best of my knowledge, no researcher outside the industry has conducted such a series of audits."

FORCING PHYSICIANS TO LIE

Indeed, insurance companies obtain information from a variety of sources, including the Disability Insurance Record System (DIRS) and the Health Claims Index. And the fact that insurance companies are lawfully allowed to deny consumers health or life insurance because of preexisting conditions has put doctors under a tremendous amount of pressure. On the one hand, doctors clearly have a professional and legal requirement to keep accurate records on their patients and submit truthful billing statements. On the other hand, doctors know that if they are truthful in their diagnoses, they might be creating notations in their patients' healthcare records that will prevent the patient from getting insurance in the future. Even without a written diagnosis, much of what insurance companies want to learn can be gleaned automatically from billing codes.

"Insurance companies collect tremendous amounts of information," says Dr. Peter Tarczy-Hornoch, who directs numerous telemedicine projects at the University of Washington Medical Center. The information is "not the really cool sexy information." Instead, it's things like "What medical diseases did your grandmother have? Have you ever been hospitalized with a drug or alcohol problem? Do you have a problem that is expensive to take care of that you have previously taken care of? They are not particularly concerned with accuracy. It's a screening process. Ninety percent is good enough for a lot of this stuff."[22]

Ninety percent is good enough for a medical insurance company to figure out if it should try to sell you life insurance, or if it should turn down your application. Ninety percent is good enough to decide how far to hike your or your company's insurance rates when it's time to renew. Ninety percent is good enough to systematically exclude the people most likely to need health insurance in the first place. And what if you happen to be one of the unlucky 10% who are denied insurance or face higher premiums even though there is really nothing wrong with you? Your best bet is to try another insurance company and hope that your erroneous information hasn't been forwarded to MIB.

Faced with this dilemma, some doctors have chosen to lie. Instead of putting down a particular diagnosis or billing code, they use a code that has a similar reimbursement rate but lacks the social stigma and long-term insurance implications. For example, says Tarczy-Hornoch, a doctor might use the billing code for "adjustment disorder" instead of "depression."

Medical professionals call these alternate diagnoses *surrogates*. The practice has questionable legality—it is a kind of fraud, after all—and there are no good statistics regarding its prevalence. But it is clear that surrogates create a kind of cat-and-mouse game between doctors and insurers, with insurance companies constantly trying to figure out what surrogates are currently in vogue, and with doctors trying to figure out new ones. What complicates the game is the fact that different doctors in different parts of the country use different surrogates, and that some people actually have the surrogate conditions, rather than the nastier conditions for which the surrogates stand.

My wife and I discovered this particular side effect of surrogates in 1994, when Beth applied for health insurance. The insurance company gave Beth a form to have her therapist fill out. When the form was returned, the insurance application was denied.

The reason Beth was denied, we later learned, was that Beth's therapist had told the insurance company that Beth had been seen and diagnosed with a case of "generalized anxiety." There was good reason for Beth's anxiety—she had been seen just three weeks before we were getting married! But the problem was that other therapists in our area had taken to using "generalized anxiety" as a surrogate for a patient who has depression and is being treated with antidepressants. Understandably, the insurance company didn't want to take on a potentially expensive customer like my wife. After all, insurance companies only make money when they insure the healthy.

In August 1996, President Clinton signed the Health Insurance Portability and Accountability Act. Under this law, U.S. health insurance companies are forbidden from excluding new employees from their employer's group health insurance packages because of preexisting conditions. But that is as far as the act goes. Insurance companies must offer coverage for preexisting conditions, but they can do it at astronomical rates. They can also choose not to renew an entire company's health insurance package because one person joined the company who had an expensive preexisting condition. This might not impact a company like IBM or Exxon, but it can be a major factor for small businesses. The act covers only employees who are changing from one employer's health insurance program to another—it doesn't cover people who are self-employed, or those who have to buy their own health insurance because they work at companies that don't provide health insurance to their employees. Finally, the act says nothing about life insurance, which has a long history of using medical records in a discriminatory manner. After all, it's life insurance companies that created MIB in the first place.

A RIGHT TO YOUR SELF

As we move into the twenty-first century, it is unthinkable that people would be denied access to their own medical records. Indeed, 96% of Americans believe that the right to be able to obtain a copy of their own medical record is important, and 84% believe it is "very important."[23] Yet for many Americans, no such right exists.

According to the *Privacy Journal* compilation of state and federal privacy laws, only 23 states give patients the right to view their own medical histories (see the boxed list).[24] Despite the laws, however, even residents of these states sometimes find that their doctors deny them access to copies of their records.

According to the 1993 Harris-Equifax survey, most Americans (87%) believe that they "know everything" or "have a general idea, but don't know in detail" what's in their medical records. And approximately one in four Americans have asked to see the contents of their medical records. When they've asked to see it, 92% were able to get a copy. Of those who were denied this fundamental right, 31% were told

> ## STATES THAT GRANT PATIENTS THE RIGHT TO VIEW THEIR OWN MEDICAL RECORDS
>
> Arizona
> California
> Colorado
> Connecticut
> Florida
> Georgia
> Hawaii
> Illinois
> Indiana
> Kansas (mental records only)
> Louisiana (partial access)
> Maryland (partial access)
> Massachusetts
> Nevada
> New York
> Ohio (law applies only to hospitals)
> Oregon (law only encourages open access)
> Rhode Island
> Tennessee (law applies only to hospitals)
> Utah (records provided to patient's attorney, not to patient)
> Virginia
> Wisconsin

that the medical record couldn't be located; 25%, representing four million Americans, were simply denied the request, with no reason given.

How can you get around this conundrum? Lie. Advise your doctor that you're moving, and that your medical records should be copied and sent to a doctor in another state. Of course, instead of giving the name of just any doctor, give the name of an old college friend whom you've notified and who knows what to expect. In my experience, this piece of subterfuge has never failed to work.

Such problems are considerably worse overseas. In Germany, for example, individuals not only do not have a right to see their medical records, but there is also a tradition of hiding diagnoses of cancer and other stigmatized diseases from the sick and, in some cases, from family members. Germany is now creating a national cancer registry, and it is taking considerable pains to use sophisticated cryptographic algorithms to scramble the names of people who are entered into the system. But the purpose of the cryptography is not to protect people's identity or privacy. In fact, it's just the opposite: the cryptographic controls are designed to prevent a person diagnosed with cancer from accidentally discovering his own diagnosis.[25]

Denying people access to their own medical records is fundamentally wrong. Twenty-five years ago, the drafters of the Code of Fair Information Practices realized that there must be no records kept on a person that the person cannot inspect and correct. It is astonishing that, even in countries with progressive privacy protection, this practice continues.

Ironically, increased access to a patient's own records is one of the benefits of the lack of medical records privacy today. With physicians so willing to send medical records to insurance companies and to other doctors, it's all but impossible to keep these records out of the hands of a determined patient. In fact, the combination of patient rights movements, increased health insurance portability, and the trend toward self-employment will all likely result in giving people increased access to their own medical records in the coming years. But exploiting the lack of confidentiality in medical records is a lousy way to assure patient rights.

A RIGHT TO YOUR PAST

One particular group of Americans has been systematically denied access to medical records, medical histories, and family records for more than 60 years. These Americans have their identities seized by the state, sealed, and replaced with new records that are fraudulent. These Americans look like anyone else; many don't even know their own secret. These hidden victims are those Americans who have undergone closed adoptions.

Adoption records have been sealed in the United States since the 1930s. By sealing the records, social reformers hoped that they could simultaneously eliminate the birth mother's stigma of having an illegitimate child and the adopting couple's stigma of infertility. The push for sealed adoption records took on a greater sense of urgency during World War II, when many illegitimate children were born to the wives of soldiers who were fighting in Europe and Asia.

As adoption became institutionalized, those providing services discovered that the secrecy increased their control over both the birth parents and those adopting. Finally, the secrecy "made for nice marketing to adopting parents—that this child would be yours, and the birth family was completely out," says Abigail Lovett, vice president of the American Adoption Congress, an organization that is fighting to reform adoption laws nationwide. "Everybody thought this was going to be the best way to do things."[26]

The sealing and unsealing of adoption records is an extremely complicated issue—one that invariably involves issues of abortion, parental rights, and the rights of the child. The nonprofit National Council for Adoption (NCFA) argues that closed records are in the best interest of all parties' privacy. By sealing the name of the adopted child's original mother, the mother is protected from that child's ever returning into her life. The child is also protected, NCFA maintains, from a mother who changes her mind and tries to get her child back. NCFA says that if records are not legally sealed, many women will opt to abort illegitimate children rather than bring them to term and give them up for adoption.

But a growing number of adult adoptees say that sealed adoption records violate their inalienable right to know their identity, their past, their medical records, and their heritage. They argue that birth parents should not have the right to turn their backs on their children, just as they do not have the right to abuse or murder their children.

For years, Shea Grimm had pains in her back. Doctors ran tests, but nobody could figure out what the problem was. "They blamed it on my scoliosis," she recalls.[27] Grimm had other worries as well. She worried that she might die an early death from breast cancer. She worried about heart disease. And she wondered what her heritage was—who were her people? Unlike many adoptees, she knew that she was adopted. But after that, it was a brick wall.

From a medical point of view, the fundamental problem with closed adoptions is that even after all of the paperwork is done and the records are sealed, there is still an essential genetic bond between the birth parents and the adopted child. No matter what the forged birth certificate says, an adopted child does not take on the genes of its adoptive parents. And as medical science has increasingly come to recognize, appreciate, and use the role that genetics and heredity play in diagnosing and curing disease, it's clear that the fundamental fiction of closed adoptions is more than just untrue—it's dangerous.

"I always sort of wondered if, because I was adopted, physicians and doctors had to run more tests on me. I didn't have a lot of information," said Grimm.

Those were some of the reasons that Grimm decided to search for her birth mother—a search that was eventually successful. And then the answers to her questions started pouring in. She learned that she was half Native American. "About two weeks after I found my birth mother, I found out that she had a degenerative disk. I was able to go back to my doctor and say, 'I have a degenerative disk.'" Even better, Grimm knew the cure. "My birth mother had gone into weight training to strengthen her muscles, on advice of her doctor, to compensate for the weakness of her disk. That's what I did. It became a big hobby of mine. And it made all the difference in the world."

Six years later, Grimm says that she has back pain "very seldom." And as an added bonus, she's no longer worried about breast cancer. "I have no history of breast cancer in my family whatsoever."

Grimm is Legislative Chair of Bastard Nation, an in-your-face adoptees advocate group that is fighting for open records nationwide. The fight, she says, is a simple matter of equity, identity, and self-determination. "I was denied the information that has allowed me to have my tribal membership. All of the things that people take for granted, that assist you in raising your family, I was denied."

Patrick Purtill, a spokesperson for the National Council for Adoption, agrees that medical records are one of the most difficult issues facing adoptees. Purtill says that courts will tell adopting parents about known problems affecting the health of their new child. The problem, though, is that most women placing their children up for adoption are in their teens or early 20s, while most life-threatening medical problems—those the child should be made aware of—won't happen to the mother until she is at least in her late 30s or 40s.28

Nevertheless, the NCFA remains opposed to opening adoption records. Purtill argues that the small benefit in medical knowledge for the adoptees would be far outweighed by the drop in adoptions that would be sure to follow. It is a question of the greater good, he argues. The best way to deal with the issue of medical records, says Purtill, is so-called *mutual consent registries*, in which birth parents and adopted children register with the state that they wish to meet. If both parties register, the records are unsealed.

"They try to say that mutual consent registries are the answer for us, but dead people don't sign on to mutual consent registries," says Abigail Lovett. "And [the registries] are often under-funded and under-publicized."

Mutual consent registries are like a game of craps with fixed dice. In order for them to work, adoptees need to register—*which means they need to know that they are adopted!* Many adopted children do not know this basic fact about their own lives. "I've been facilitating a support group for about seven years," says Lovett. "I have had 50-year-old men who walked into my support group because they discovered at their mother's funeral that they were adopted." Why did the news suddenly come out? "A greedy relative who wanted to cut them out of a will."

In another case, says Lovett, she met a woman who had given birth to a child, a child who ended up being tremendously physically challenged. Eventually, the woman had no choice but to put her baby into an institution. It was at that point that she started looking for a child that she had given birth to earlier in life.

"She actually found the first child institutionalized [with similar problems], with no one to come and visit and be its mother," Lovett says. Apparently, the adoptive family had given up the child when the problems had first arisen. "She never would have had the second child if she had known." A mutual consent registry never would have helped this woman because her institutionalized child could not register.

Adoption is one of our society's cruelest open secrets. While Lovett was denied basic information about her adoption for years, many members of her community knew much more. "Just after my adoptive mother died, the doctor who delivered me came into my store [and] asked for me by name," says Lovett. But the doctor refused to tell Lovett her true identity:

> I grew up knowing that I was adopted. I knew the doctor who delivered me. Everybody in his office knew my story. The hospital and that staff knew my story. The attorney and his staff knew my story. And the court and their staff knew my story. All of these people within my community knew my story. They knew more about me than I knew. I was not allowed to know my story. I am not allowed to look at my birth records; I am not allowed to look at my court records.

Briseis Gatto, who was adopted in New York City in the early 1960s, puts it this way:

> All the relatives know about the adoption but not the child himself. You literally grow up in a society where everyone is continually lying to you. You don't dare talk about it for fear your parents will kick you out, so you become a liar yourself, hoping that by not showing who you are, you will not be rejected, not only by your parents but by your relatives. When I spoke to my brother who was adopted in roughly the same period I was, he confirmed that he also had somehow absorbed the impression that adoption was something that was absolutely unthinkable to talk to his parents about, although they had never told him anything of the sort.[29]

One way that organizations such as NCFA have fought the issue of open records is by claiming that what adoptees are really after is reunion with their birth parents. This technique pits the rights of the adoptees against the alleged privacy rights of the birth parents—the majority of whom, NCFA alleges, see the original pregnancy as an unfortunate accident they want to put behind them. But adoptees and their birth parents are perfectly capable of protecting themselves from relationships they don't want. After all, there are laws against harassment.

Organizations like Bastard Nation say that reunions aren't the issue. "A lot of people aren't looking for family, they are simply looking for information. There are rights that are afforded every other adult citizen of this nation which you, as an adult adoptee, are denied, simply by virtue of your adopted status," says Damsel Plum, the Publications Chair for Bastard Nation.30

"As we go into the next century, we are realizing how utterly important genetic information is," says Abigail Lovett. "We are realizing that breast cancer has genetic predispositions. If you grow up knowing that breast cancer is in your family, you will eat and treat yourself completely different."

Ultimately, the growing availability of online information may render the controversy moot. At the Bastard Nation web site, there are detailed instructions on how to go about searching for birth parents. And there are links to other online information sources—sources like the Social Security Death Indices, genealogical databases, and traditional Internet search engines.

"The Internet is going to make confidentiality a joke, in terms of the ability of people to find each other," agrees Dawn Smith-Pliner, who runs a Vermont adoption agency. "In fact, we already use [the Net] for that purpose here at the agency. If somebody wants to find someone definitely enough, they are going to be able to do it online."31 But alas, to use these advanced search techniques, an adoptee still needs to have a name, a date, or a place. And they still need to know that they are adopted.

Smith-Pliner sees an end to closed adoptions and an opening of all adoption records within the next 20 years. "Adults are going to have to recognize the importance of an adoptee's connection to their birth families. I think that is beginning to happen on a national basis."

We can only hope.

COMPUTERIZED PATIENT RECORDS: THE PROMISE

For more than 20 years, the healthcare industry has been adopting computers, but it's been a slow and sometimes painful process. Today we are only halfway there. Medicine has been largely successful in computerizing billing codes, lab test results, and physician schedules. X-rays are being digitized now. And over the coming years, handwritten and transcribed physician notes will follow.

The ultimate goal of the computerization process is medicine's equivalent of the paperless office—the *computerized patient record*. This record will contain the patient's full medical history, from conception, including immunizations, meetings with doctors, childhood diseases, and results from annual physicals. The record will include payment information, reminders for future checkups, and notes. X-rays will be digitized and stored in the record, as will laboratory test results.

Part of the push for computerized patient records comes from the need to handle increasing amounts of information more efficiently. Many hospitals are legally forbidden to throw out patient records. As a result, they spend millions storing paper records in warehouses. This same information can be digitized and stored in just a few cubic feet using modern data storage techniques. The savings of storage space, combined with decreased costs for film and processing, is one of the primary reasons why hospitals are turning to digital X-ray systems.

Moving to a computerized patient record poses tremendous technical challenges. When you first walk into a doctor's examination room, a nurse or medical assistant writes down your blood pressure and pulse. How does this information get into the computer? Likewise, how do the doctor's notes get digitized? When the doctor wants to order medical tests or X-rays, they're usually written down on a piece of paper—it's faster than typing them into a computer. When you go down to the lab, there's more paper still.

Advancing technology, combined with new business practices, is overcoming many of these problems. For example, at one hospital I visited in Seattle, doctors are now dictating their notes into tape recorders. The doctor's voice is then transmitted electronically to India, where labor is cheap and English is widely spoken. There, skilled transcribers listen to the doctor's voice and type the notes into computers. The text is then sent back over a computer network.

The Japanese film company Fuji, meanwhile, has developed an electronic plate that is sensitive to X-rays. This plate can be used with conventional X-ray equipment to directly digitize an X-ray and send it into a computer. Although the plate costs nearly a thousand dollars, it is reusable—saving substantial money in film. And once the X-rays are digitized, they can be stored on magnetic tape for a fraction of the cost of a climate-controlled warehouse.

One of the factors contributing to the rise in the cost of medical care is the large number of repeated medical tests. Tests are repeated because the results get lost, or because a patient transfers to another institution without all of his or her records. The 1997 Kennedy-Kassebaum healthcare portability legislation tried to solve the problem of repeated tests by forcing healthcare providers to adopt a universal healthcare identification number. The idea of the legislation was simple: if all hospitals and doctors offices used the same identification number, then test results would be less likely to get lost. The legislation justified the adoption on the grounds of "administrative simplification." However, implementation has temporarily been halted by Congress, largely as the result of objections by privacy groups.

Once the medical record is computerized, the information can be put to many new uses. One simple technique is to have the computer scan its records each time a patient shows up, and print a little reminder if there is some routine test that's overdue. The reminders can make sure that women get Pap smears and mammograms; they can encourage parents to have their children tested for lead; they can even prompt adults to be checked regularly for high blood pressure and cholesterol. The reminders are written in English and printed on the patient's chart. When the patient shows up with a complaint or for a routine checkup, the doctor sees the reminder and, during the visit, performs or schedules the needed procedure.

When Dr. Harold Goldberg, a specialist in medical informatics at the University of Washington, first proposed the idea of reminders to his fellow physicians, they sneered—the physicians said that they had been trained to remember which patients needed what procedures. But when the program was implemented, something miraculous happened: the rate at which patients got their necessary tests skyrocketed.

Today, reminders are standard throughout the managed care industry. "There are now 17 randomized controlled trials that tell us if you prompt physicians at the point of service, you improve the ability to [perform needed tests] by 70%," says Goldberg.[32]

COMPUTERIZED PATIENT RECORDS: THE THREAT

Physicians are less sanguine about the potential threat to privacy that computerized patient records will bring. According to the Harris-Equifax 1993 survey, 74% of physicians thought that computerized systems were "almost certain to weaken" medical confidentiality, compared to 26% who thought that computers "could be managed to strengthen confidentiality."

The problem is the inherent difference between the physical and the electronic. Paper records are physical. Paper records can only exist in one place at one time. And while paper records can be faxed all over town, a person must be physically holding the records in order to do so.

The principal advantage of electronic records is that they are easy to manipulate, but this ease cuts both ways. With electronic laboratory records, it's unlikely that the results of a patient's last blood test will be lost. That's good for patients—especially patients who don't like getting stuck with needles. But computerized record systems make it equally likely that a curious nurse or intern might walk up to an unattended terminal, type in a name, and see the results of that person's test. And since that same computerized file can be accessed at hundreds of terminals throughout a hospital at the same time, controls are all the more difficult.

In its 1997 report on medical records privacy issues, the National Research Council identified the following five "threat levels" for information stored in healthcare computers:[33]

1. *Insiders who make "innocent" mistakes and cause accidental disclosures of confidential information.* This could be as simple as a lab sending a fax to a wrong phone number, or a nurse pulling up one patient's medical records instead of another.

2. *Insiders who abuse their record access privileges.* Browsing seems to be a problem with many electronic record systems. The Internal Revenue Service, for example, has had persistent problems with curious employees looking through the tax records to which they have access. It's unreasonable to think that hospitals will somehow avoid this affliction.

3. *Insiders who knowingly access information for spite or for profit.* During the 1992 Democratic primaries, a pathologist I know at Beth Israel Hospital in Boston was contacted by a member of the press who wanted access to candidate Paul Tsongas's medical records. The reporter offered good money, and a less ethical pathologist could easily have retrieved the file without leaving a trace.

4. *An unauthorized physical intruder who gains access to information.* Many hospitals rely on physical security to protect information stored inside a computer: the terminals are put in a special room or behind a desk to which only authorized personnel are supposed to have access. But hospitals are not as secure as hospital administrators would like the public to believe. If that journalist had simply put on a white lab coat and a fake badge, he could probably have retrieved Tsongas's medical records unassisted.

5. *Vengeful employees and outsiders, such as vindictive patients or intruders, who mount attacks to access unauthorized information, damage systems, and disrupt operations.* A doctor who practices at an HMO recently told me of a problem that her group has been having: an employee—they think they know who—has been accessing the HMO's scheduling computer and deleting patient appointments. The scheduling desk then thinks the appointment slot is free, and two or three patients show up at the same time.

There are a variety of techniques that can be used to minimize the threats of unauthorized access. At Beth Israel Hospital in Boston, for instance, certain patient files are marked as "VIP." When these files are accessed for any purpose, the name of the person making the access is logged; a human has the duty of auditing the log files on a regular basis to make sure that all of the accesses were legitimate.

Just who should be a VIP? Currently, the hospital marks files as VIP if there is some reason that employees at the hospital might be curious about the person's records. Celebrities and political figures are obvious candidates. But hospital employees and their families also get VIP status, in order to cut down on inquiries from nosy (or well-meaning) coworkers. Ideally, anybody who wants the VIP label should get it. In practice, Beth Israel does not notify patients that they have this right.

Some computer professionals suggest that encryption can be used to create a simple solution for the problems caused by computerized patient records. Give everyone a copy of their medical history that they can carry around on a smart card. Store a copy of the medical record someplace else, to guard against the theft of the card, and encrypt that backup so no one can access it without authorization.

But doctors are worried about such cryptography-driven technological fixes. They fear that in an emergency, it might become impossible to decode or even locate a person's medical history. Most people, they argue, are not willing to die for the right to their privacy.

OTHER THREATS

Computerization creates other privacy risks that are only now becoming apparent. Take the case of those dictation services in India. What if an employee of the Indian transcription firm recognized the name of one of the people whose medical charts were being transcribed and decided to sell this information to an American tabloid newspaper? Even assuming that the leak could be traced back to that employee, it is hard to imagine how the employee could be adequately punished.

But computerization also opens up the possibility for improved patient confidentiality. The person in India doesn't need to know the true name of the individual whose medical records are being transcribed—a code number would work just fine. And instead of making that code number the patient's Social Security number, make it a case number, or the time of day the patient was seen, or some other kind of code generated by the admitting hospital. The records being transcribed could essentially be anonymous—at least from the point of view of the person in India.

The ability of computers to shield identity and hide information is perhaps one of the reasons that a slim majority (53%) of hospital CEOs think that computers will actually strengthen patient confidentiality.

Among insurance company CEOs, the majority is even higher—61%, compared with 35% who think computers will harm confidentiality.

Why the disparity between the CEOs and the doctors? Probably because the CEOs know what is possible with information technology, but doctors see the way it's actually being implemented. And doctors know that any technology that makes it harder for people in a hospital to access medical information could cost some patient his or her life in an emergency. Even simple anonymizing codes increase the chances that two patients' records will be confused—with potentially disastrous results. Would you want to be treated in an emergency room where the computer forces people to type usernames and passwords before ordering a test?

When the University of Washington Medical Center installed its medical record system, the information technology managers gave each physician and nurse his or her own username and password. The system was designed to make people accountable for the files they saw by logging every access. The system even had a timeout feature, so that if somebody left a terminal while still logged on and walked away, that person would be automatically logged out. But a month later, a scan through the log files revealed that the only person using the system on a particular ward was the chief resident. A walk up to the terminal revealed why: the chief resident's username and password had been written on a sticker and pasted to the terminal, so when the chief resident was logged out, any nurse or doctor who happened to be standing near the terminal could log the chief resident back in.

Today, we can easily imagine a better solution to the problem of auditing access to medical records at places like this medical center. First, make sure the terminals are placed in secure locations, so only authorized individuals can access a patient's medical record. Then place a small video camera on top of each terminal, so when each access is made, the image of the person making the access is recorded. Currently, such videotaping systems are purely hypothetical.

RETHINKING MEDICAL CARE AND MEDICAL INSURANCE

Most Americans consider their medical records to be the most sensitive pieces of personal information they have. But for HMOs and insurance companies, medical records are merely scoreboards for an elaborate game of musical chairs. Insurance companies know that if they wait long enough, there's a good chance that any given patient will soon be covered by another insurance company—because that person (or their company) switched carriers, because they lost their job, or because they turned 65 and are now covered by Medicare—the United States' socialized medical insurance program for the elderly. Insurance companies that have a high churn rate actually have an incentive to avoid offering preventive care and to close their eyes during the early, cheaper stages of most diseases—hoping that by the time the disease progresses, the patient will be somebody else's financial responsibility.

When they are taking on new contracts, insurance company underwriters use medical records the way a bookmaker uses a sports lineup—as rate cards for calculating odds. Underwriting, in fact, is the real devil of health and life insurance. Fundamentally, the underwriting process weighs the premiums paid by the insured and the profits on that revenue against the chance of a possible payout. It's an inexact science, but one that is getting increasingly more accurate as insurance companies consider more and more pieces of information. And there are few limits on what kind of information can be considered. Today, an insurance company might think that a person who has high blood pressure or high cholesterol is a bad risk and needs to be charged a correspondingly higher monthly premium; tomorrow, the insurance company might adjust your premiums on a month-by-month basis depending on how many pizzas you are eating.

A great many of the abuses mentioned in this chapter could be solved by fundamentally changing the way that medical care is paid for in the United States. Instead of tying health insurance to employment (a policy that dates to the wage and price controls of the 1940s), health insurance could be based on residency and citizenship. The simplest, easiest way to end discrimination in health insurance would be to adopt universal, state-sponsored health insurance. Doing so, however, is politically impossible given the size and wealth of the nation's health insurance industry—an industry that makes its money by gambling on the lives of the healthy and the diseases of the sick.

In the absence of a systemwide redesign, consumers are best protected by the combination of transparency and regulation—*transparency* of insurance industry practices to prevent the most egregious antiprivacy cases, and *regulation* to protect consumers in their day-to-day interactions with the medical establishment. Without a policy turnaround, things will only get worse.

CHAPTER SEVEN

BUY NOW!

Robert Ellis Smith, publisher of the *Privacy Journal*, was at a conference in New York City where he came face to face with the vice president of one of America's largest marketing firms. The man was indirectly responsible for flooding American homes with billions of unwanted letters and postcards every week. So Smith asked the vice president what Americans could do to help stop the torrent of junk mail they face every day.

"There is no such thing as junk mail—just junk people," the vice president corrected Smith, who was astonished by both the candor and the callousness of the remark.

The VP's statement makes perfect sense—if you happen to be a marketer. Those advertisements that stuff your mailbox, those telephone calls that you get during dinner, the incessant "spam" that clogs your email—it's all only "junk" if you aren't interested in what the advertisements are selling. To you, it's junk. To somebody else, it may be a golden opportunity.

Now turn around and look at the situation from the eyes of the marketer. If a person doesn't care for the particular product or service that's being advertised, then in the marketer's eyes that person is the junk. No sane marketer wants to send out mail that's going to be thrown away without even being opened. By merely existing, the junk customer makes marketers waste their time and money.

Good marketers know that it's pointless to advertise dog food to cat owners. But marketing is an imprecise profession. When a multibillion-dollar sector of the economy involves stuffing envelopes and slapping on mailing labels, some mistakes are bound to be made. Good marketers don't like junk mail, because they know it translates directly into lost profits. Instead of being angry at the companies that are intruding into your life, you should feel sorry for them.

Clearly, both marketers and consumers want to stop the flow of junk mail and phone calls. The fight that's unfolding is about means, not ends. A growing number of consumers are fighting for restrictions on aggressive marketing practices. But the target marketing industry is taking a different approach. It's using vast reservoirs of personal information to hone its advertising campaigns. It employs deceptive practices to coax sensitive information out of parents and children so that each can be targeted from birth. And it's working to turn every surface and every moment into a marketing opportunity, so that consumers never miss a chance to be properly informed.

Runaway marketing has become a nonstop campaign of corporate-sponsored harassment. This campaign will eventually be extended to every man, woman, and child on the planet. It must be stopped.

MARKETING AND THE KNOWLEDGE CRISIS

A few weeks after I bought my first house, I got a postcard from a stockbroker in Boston, suggesting that I give him a call to discuss my investments. A few days later, I got a post card from a chimney sweep, suggesting that I set up an appointment to have my flue cleaned out.

Both the stockbroker and the chimney sweep had gotten my name from the city of Cambridge: real estate transactions are public records. Both of them were reasonable marketing gambles—certainly worth the cost of a stamp. And both of them were dead wrong: I didn't have any money left over after buying my house to toy with the stock market, and my house didn't have a fireplace, so there was nothing to sweep.

These advertisements left me feeling violated. Just by looking up my name, these people thought they had learned something personal about me, and they had tried to use that information to manipulate my behavior. The fact that they had both drawn the wrong inferences from the limited information they had obtained somehow made things all the worse.

Businesses have used target marketing for decades, but the practice is becoming increasingly intolerable as companies use more and more personal information to align their cross hairs—violating our privacy and making inevitable mistakes in the process.

Just ask Cindy Rowan.

In September 1995, Cindy Rowan's mother was killed in a car accident. "She was in excellent health, and it was a real shock that this occurred," Cindy told me in 1996. "After her death, I had her mail forwarded to my home," in Farmingdale, New Jersey.[1]

Filling out the change of address notice for her dead mother set in motion a huge marketing machine that Rowan had never imagined, one that she could never hope to control. Despite an assurance on the form (and a U.S. government policy) that the information on the change of address card would be used only to forward her mother's mail, the information was soon being used by marketers to land sales.

The local supermarket in Farmingdale sent Rowan's mother a letter welcoming her to the neighborhood, and enclosed a coupon for some free orange juice. A florist sent her a coupon for 10% off her next flower purchase. Even a dentist in her new neighborhood sent her a card—certainly it would be easier to have her teeth cleaned in Farmingdale than to drive all the way back to her old neighborhood, 40 miles away.

Nearly half a year after the accident, Rowan's dead mother, Jane Seiss, was receiving more mail at her daughter's house than her daughter was. And why not? From a marketer's perspective, Jane Seiss fit the profile of a hot prospect. Retired and apparently in fine health (the marketers had not programmed their computers to consult the obituaries), Seiss had the potential to be a loyal customer for many years to come. It would be foolish for a company not to contact her!

But in this particular case, each letter sent to her dead mother just made Cindy Rowan feel worse. "It's sick. It made me very angry," says Rowan. "I think that people out there who are buying these lists aren't even aware of the impact that it can have on someone."

The U.S. Postal Service promises that the 42 million change of address requests it receives each year will only be used to forward mail, not to market products. A notice on the form says:

> PRIVACY ACT: Filing this form is voluntary, but your mail cannot be forwarded without an order. If filed, your new permanent address will be provided to individuals and companies who request it. This will occur *only* when the requestor is already in possession of your name and old mailing address. Use Form 3576 to tell correspondents and publishers of address changes. Authorized 39 U.S.C. 404.

But as we will see, the system for protecting the flow of personal information, like so many other systems in industry and business, is flawed. The postal service, meanwhile, is in a very poor position to press for reforms. As I'll describe later in this chapter, the National Change of Address Program is actually run by the same companies that send tens of billions of pieces of junk mail each year to hundreds of millions of American consumers.

Real estate sales and change of address files are just two kinds of government records that are being misused for marketing purposes. Another rich source of information is motor vehicle registration records. The undisputed leader in this field is The Polk Company, which has traded in personal information since its founding in 1870.

Polk's first product was a directory of businesses in Michigan, arranged by railroad station. These directories were designed to make it easier for consumers living near one train station to go shopping near another. But the company soon discovered that bigger money could be made selling directories of city residents, designed for use by door-to-door salesmen.[2] In this century, Polk has become the nation's leading purchaser of motor vehicle registrations. For the automobile industry, Polk uses these records to contact owners in the event of safety recalls. For everybody else, Polk combines the make and model of your car with census tract information to let marketers determine your income, lifestyle, and likelihood of purchasing any given product.

LOVE ME, LOVE MY PURCHASES

As we move into the twenty-first century, marketing is increasingly becoming a one-to-one affair. No longer are marketers satisfied with pools of potential customers extracted from mailing lists or government records. Instead, they're aggressively seeking personalized information and creating computer systems that categorize individual consumers.

These days, most supermarkets have laser scanners that look at the bar code on each package a consumer buys and record that code inside a computer databank. When you hand your check-cashing card to the clerk, you're actually handing the person an identity card that stamps the purchase with your name. Supermarkets use this information to create a comprehensive consumer profile.

Companies aren't really sure what to do with all this information. Plans that they've articulated are incredibly bland—along the lines of sending targeted Pepsi coupons to Coke customers. "We will be using it [the profile] to identify who some of our best customers might be, and provide them with additional incentives to shop in our store—discounts, rebates, things like that," says Norman Tsang, director of marketing for Star Market in Boston.[3]

But in fact, there is a gold mine of information buried in this transaction data. By watching the behavior of individual consumers over weeks and months, and combining this with one-to-one marketing techniques, the store can discover the effect that advertising promotions have on particular consumers. Star Market can experimentally determine whether it takes a 10-cent or a 50-cent coupon to persuade a particular consumer to make a purchase. It can learn which coupons trigger additional sales and which do not. It can then selectively send these coupons only to the customers for whom the coupons will trigger purchases, in the process denying the discounts to others. Transaction-level information turns the art of marketing into a multivariable science experiment, with the store's customers doubling as laboratory rats.

Supermarket Affinity Card

Most supermarkets in the United States now have affinity programs. Designed for frequent shoppers, these programs give consumers a small discount in return for item-by-item tracking of their purchases. The supermarket uses the transactional information for a variety of purposes, such as store design, price determination, and marketing. But nothing limits what a supermarket can or cannot do with the information; in one case, a supermarket faced with a lawsuit by one of its customers, who had slipped and fallen, threatened to use the fact that the customer was a frequent purchaser of alcohol to damage his reputation in court. [Photo courtesy Chris Reilley, Reilley Design]

But stores can do a lot more with the data than simple advanced marketing psychometrics. Some are doing it already, according to this report from the March 1999 issue of the *Privacy Journal*:

Already, the U.S. Drug Enforcement Administration has demanded access to the frequent-buyer inventories kept by Smith's Food & Drug Centers in Arizona. And a Los Angeles man, Robert Rivera, says that after he sued Vons markets when he fell in a store and injured his leg the store looked up his record, discovered that he likes to buy a lot of liquor, and said it would use the information to defend itself in the lawsuit. The implication was that Rivera may have been impaired when he fell.

The owner of Lees Supermarket in Westport, Massachusetts, says that he uses the data to determine the shopping patterns of his best customers and then to meet those needs. Further, he determines how much importance to give to a customer's request or complaint after checking the records to determine whether the person is an active shopper in the store.[4]

The supermarket can resell this data as it chooses. Today, most data sales are marketing-related. For example, Absolut Vodka could buy a list of products purchased by vodka consumers for use in creating future Absolut advertisements, which frequently involve cross-brand promotions. But tomorrow the information could as easily be provided to insurance companies, HMOs, and even government investigators. Other applications include scientific studies on health and diet. Transaction-level information gives businesses and government a way of searching your house and scrutinizing your lifestyle without ever obtaining a warrant and stepping through your front door. Are you eating too much red meat or high-fat ice cream? Are your expenses out of line with your income? Your cash register receipt will tell.

OUR BODIES, OUR DOLLARS

In 1995, I received a letter from Beth Israel Hospital, one of the largest in Boston, asking for money. Not so coincidentally, I had recently been a patient at Beth Israel. I wrote a letter to the hospital's president, complaining that they were using their patient records for fundraising. Holly Glick, director of the hospital's annual fund, wrote back:

> I'm sure you will agree that it is important for institutions such as Beth Israel Hospital to go about the business of fund raising in a relatively orderly way. That includes sending out periodic requests to virtually all individuals who become identified as patients unless, of course, we are aware that they are deceased or otherwise aware of some reason not to solicit them.

> It turns out that such sweeping sets of requests are not unproductive and, since the money is put to good use, it is a practice that will be continued. Inevitably, there are instances of awkwardness for one reason or another that arise out of such sweeping solicitations. It is important, of course, not to view requests of this sort as highly personalized but rather as part of an overall effort to develop funds to support services to those who can't pay and the scholarly activities of our institution for which full payment is not made.[5]

Glick might think her hospital's practice is completely on the up-and-up, but 66% of Americans think that it is "not acceptable" to use hospital admission records for fundraising purposes, according to the 1993 Harris-Equifax Health Information Privacy Survey.[6]

Beth Israel's marketing campaign is ethically indefensible on privacy grounds because the hospital doesn't send out solicitations at random: it sends the pleas to its former patients. When people get fundraising letters from hospitals, the envelope alone is a telltale sign that they've been seen there as a patient. Such an envelope could have terrible repercussions for a person trying to hide the fact he or she had required medical attention—for example, a woman who had had an abortion, or who had been beaten by her husband and threatened with more beatings if she sought help. A Christian Scientist might be exceedingly disturbed to receive such a letter, since that religion frowns on the practice of medicine as an invasion of God's province. In February 1997, Lois Rutherford received a fundraising solicitation addressed to her husband, who had been treated at the Alberta Hospital (Edmonton, Canada) for cancer. "What bothers me most is that he died right in that hospital," she said.[7]

Even pharmacy records are now being used for marketing. One of the largest companies in the field is National Data Corporation, which buys a detailed list of every prescription that is filled every day at nearly 30,000 pharmacies nationwide. The data is crunched and sold to drug companies who can then compare how their drugs are selling in a particular region relative to their competitors. This information is turned around and provided to the sales force, which then lobbies physicians to prescribe one drug over another. Pharmaceutical companies are also advertising directly to consumers, because they know that a physician is more likely to prescribe a drug when patients ask for it by name.

SELLING IT TO THE YOUNGEST CONSUMERS

Even children have become marketing targets. By placing televisions and advertisements directly in schools, and by building Internet sites targeted at children, marketers have discovered how to effectively bypass parents. In the early 1990s, for instance, proprietors of 900 numbers ran advertisements to convince children to call these numbers to hear prerecorded messages from cartoon characters—incurring large charges on their parents' bills in the process. This practice was outlawed by the Telephone Disclosure and Dispute Resolution Act of 1992, after which many marketers turned to the Internet as a new, unregulated environment for exploiting children.

"Online technology allows marketers to track children's behavior—to see what sites a child visits and how long the child lingers at a site," said Commissioner Roscoe B. Starek of the U.S. Federal Trade Commission (FTC) in July 1997:

> By the use of surveys—sometimes in the form of registration screens that must be completed to access a site or be eligible for a prize—the site owner can collect other valuable marketing information. All of this information helps marketers identify new consumers at little additional cost, and may allow companies to target consumers very narrowly according to their individual interests.[8]

This, Starek said, despite the fact that "97% of parents whose children are online believe that web sites should not collect children's real names and addresses and sell or rent that information to others." Even when companies guarantee that they won't give out individually identifiable information, 72% of parents still oppose the practice.

It's nearly impossible for parents to make reasoned decisions about those who request information about their children: there is no easy way for a parent to tell a legitimate web site from a scam. A far better alternative is to have government police the industry, set standards for proper conduct, and punish those companies that step out of line.

For example, in 1996, the U.S. Federal Trade Commission began an investigation against a web site called KidsCom.[9] The site, peppered with cool graphics and free games, required that kids register in order to play. And registering was no small matter: kids had to fill out elaborate forms reporting their age, birth date, sex, size of their family, favorite TV show, favorite TV commercial, favorite musical group, hobbies, how they accessed the Internet, correct email address, email address of their parent or guardian, mailing address, speed of their Internet connection, and career plans. The whole situation generated a lot of attention in the press: consumer advocates said that KidsCom was targeting children who couldn't make informed decisions about the release of personal information. The site's owners maintained that they asked these questions so they could match up kids in an electronic pen pal program and provide customized content. After a year of investigation, KidsCom voluntarily changed its practices, set up a parent's advisory panel, and adopted a privacy code.

At roughly the same time as the KidsCom investigation, The Walt Disney Company launched its own multimillion-dollar web site whose sole purpose was to promote Disney products and collect marketing information. Unlike KidsCom, Disney did not adopt a strict policy against releasing the names and identities of children. Indeed, the "privacy policy" at the company's web site in 1996 said just the reverse: "Information submitted at the time of registration or submission may be used for marketing and promotional purposes by The Walt Disney Company and may be shared with companies that have been pre-screened by The Walt Disney Company."[10]

But then something really important happened: the United States Congress passed a law that unambiguously outlawed the worst excesses of companies like KidsCom and Disney. Called the Children's Online Privacy Protection Act of 1998, the law required web sites to clearly state what information they were collecting from children under 13 and what the information would be used for. The law also required that web sites obtain "verifiable parental consent"—that is, make a "reasonable effort" to make sure that any information collected from children was authorized by a parent.

After the legislation was passed, the FTC took action against GeoCities, a web site provider, and Liberty Financial Companies, owner of the Young Investor web site, for failing to comply with the legislation. Meanwhile, Disney and other sites have changed their ways to a great extent. The FTC's actions prove that legislation without effective policing isn't enough to protect privacy. But the FTC's actions also prove that without legislation, there can be no policing at all. Although marketing to children is still a serious social problem, things are much better today with the legislation than they would have been without it.

TURNING UP THE VOLUME

Marketing to children is just one of many attempts by companies to "turn up the volume" in recent years. Such marketing goes hand in hand with another trend on the part of marketers—the effort to dramatically expand the amount of advertising in the world around us:

- Drop a coin into a payphone and, before your call is completed, you're likely to hear a brief announcement with the name of the phone's owner: "Thank you for using a Bell Atlantic payphone."

- Take a ride on the Massachusetts Turnpike and you'll discover that your toll receipt comes with an advertisement for Staples office supplies.

- At least one company is experimenting with coupons that will be printed on ATM receipts; not only do these advertisements generate new sales, they also allow the store to learn the identity of and valuable demographic information on its cash-paying customers.

- Advertisements are now being electronically inserted onto walls and greens of televised sporting events.

Any device that has a display has the potential to become an advertising machine. Microsoft led the way in 1997 when it launched its controversial Internet Explorer 4. One of the program's new features was an "active desktop" that placed advertisements directly on the computer user's screen. Likewise, the screens on cell phones and pocket pagers increasingly carry tiny advertisements with brand names.

What all of these new marketing opportunities have in common is that the advertisements are most often seen by an audience of one. This individualized delivery begs for one-on-one marketing, which invariably drives the demand for even more highly detailed personal information.

THEY'VE GOT YOU TARGETED: THE PROCESS OF DIRECT MARKETING

How did the supermarket, the florist, and the dentist get Cindy Rowan's mother's name in the first place? Although it's impossible to know for sure, most likely it came from one of the companies that operate the National Change of Address Program for the government.

When you fill out a change of address card, the card is sent to a processing center where the information is typed into a computer and then transmitted to the nation's largest direct marketing firms. The firms are contractually prohibited from using the database for direct marketing purposes, says Wayne Orbke, an official at the U.S. Postal Service who once oversaw the program's contractors.[11] But the companies are allowed to use the data to update their own files—in fact, that is the purpose of the entire program. By allowing marketing firms to update their databanks directly, the post office saves the expense of carrying billions of letters to old addresses, only to forward them to new addresses.

But once the information is in the possession of the marketers, it is difficult to avoid the kind of abuse that the government's regulations are designed to prevent. Consider Metromail, a direct marketing firm with annual sales in excess of $250 million that was purchased by Experian in April 1998. Metromail was one of the National Change of Address Program's primary contractors. The company carefully monitors its mailing lists before and after it applies updates from the change of address files. It spots which addresses change and combines these addresses into a special mailing list called the New Movers file. Metromail then markets *this* file to businesses in the person's new neighborhood.

In fact, Metromail boasts about its data manipulation prowess. An advertisement from the company reads:

> Metromail's New Movers are ideal prospects for home furnishing and appliances, home improvement services, long distance telephone service, and banking/investment products, including credit cards. They are also excellent candidates for newspaper and magazine subscriptions, and for catalogers seeking to combat list attrition.[12]

In 1996, Metromail's New Movers file had a base price of $60 per thousand names. For an extra $10 per thousand, a business could have Metromail filter the list and only supply the company with the names of the families who have moved 50 miles or more—an option that would probably appeal to the Farmingdale dentist who solicited Cindy Rowan's late mother. After all, why waste money sending the solicitation to people who have just moved across the street?

Product Registration Card

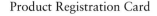

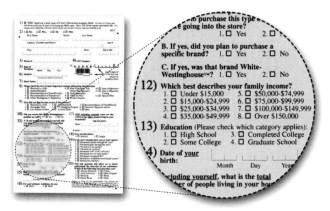

Many consumer goods come with product registration cards. Legally, the main purpose of these cards is to assist manufacturers in the event of a product recall. But companies frequently cram their registration cards with dozens of questions that exist solely to build more accurate marketing databases. Why else would a company that manufactures juicers need to know your family's annual income? [Photo courtesy Chris Reilley, Reilley Design]

Today, Metromail is part of Experian, a $1.5 billion company whose lifeblood is trafficking in personal information. By combining address information, credit information, and business information, Experian can help businesses find new customers, market more effectively to them, and jettison customers who are becoming credit risks more efficiently than ever before.

By combining credit reporting with direct marketing services, Experian is able to offer comprehensive data services to businesses worldwide. The following table gives a sampling of the company's many data-intensive products. [13]

Service	Description
Analytical and consulting services	Provide services for American businesses to help them make the most of the information already in their databanks.
AutoCredit	Used for approving vehicle loans and leases.
Bankruptcy	Computerized model that predicts bankruptcy.
Bullseye Report	Used for correcting data that was misreported to Experian.

Service	Description
Business Credit Extract	Searches for new customers through a business database.
Business Credit Prescreen	Screens mailing lists to find individuals who have a history of paying their bills.
Business Owner Profile	Profiles sole proprietorships.
Business Profile	Produces credit reports on businesses.
Collection Report	Tracks customers who have not paid bills.
CollectScore	Scores delinquent accounts, telling who is most likely to pay.
Connect Check	Provides ID verification to fight identity fraud.
Consortium databases	Catalog buyer and magazine subscriber databases.
Credit Profile report	Provides consumer credit reports.
Credit Decision Expert	Scores credit reports.
CU Decision Expert	Provides automated loan approval for credit unions.
Demographics Band	Confirms identities of people not in credit databanks.
Employment Insight report	Provides preemployment screening.
Experian Segmentation Systems	Divide a current list of customers or prospects into smaller group segments based on lifestyle, behavior, wealth, and other features.
Experiant Quest	Provides automated techniques to let companies reach existing customers.
FACS+	Alerts high-risk or nonresidential addresses.
Fair, Isaac	Provides consumer credit modeling.
Flood certification services	Identify vulnerable properties.
ID Profile	Finds new customers not in credit databases.
INSOURCE	Enhances mailing lists with demographics, property records, motor vehicle listings, answers to surveys, and more.
Intelliscore	Performs predictive credit risk scoring for rating the creditworthiness of small businesses.
Lettershop	Performs bulk mailing services.
List Link™	Provides high-volume users of marketing lists with direct access to Experian's national database of consumers.
List processing services	Provides complete services for direct marketing, from gathering names to printing and mailing solicitations. Includes "Address Hygiene" to weed out undeliverable mailings before they are sent, processing through the National Change of Address register, address correction, and automatic elimination of duplicate addresses.

Service	Description
List rental fulfillment and maintenance	Experian will assist organizations that wish to rent their own databases, and will optionally "enhance" these lists with data from Experian's databanks.
Market Share	A CD-ROM–based system for finding new customers with the same profile as existing customers.
National Risk Model	Profiles existing accounts and determines level of risk.
Platelink	Links license plate numbers to consumer information.
Point-of-Sale Analyst	Performs credit and customer analysis at the cash register.
Postal optimization	Ensures lowest possible postal costs.
Prescreen	Used for preapproved credit card offers.
Profile Summary	Analyzes a customer's credit history.
Property Link	Provides detailed information on a customer's property holdings.
Prospect Locator Series	A CD-ROM–based system for generating lists of addresses and phone numbers for direct and telemarketing.
RecoveryScore	Ranks overdue accounts in order of recoverability.
Revenue Opportunity Indicator	Ranks revenue potential of prescreened customers.
Segmentation systems	Segments customers.
Signal	Warns of accounts heading for trouble.
Skip Locator	Tracks customers who have fled with unpaid bills.
Smart Quest	Identifies customers with highest profit and risk potential.
Vehicle Financing Solution	Provides prescreening for automobile lease agencies.
Vehicle Ownership Tracking System	Tracks owners of automobiles.

Government records are just one of many sources of personal information. Pick up a copy of *DM News*, the weekly newspaper of the direct marketing industry, and you'll see advertisements hawking processed mailing lists that pigeonhole individuals into snappy microdemographic groups: "Hispanic Families with Children," "First-Class Males," "Asian American Mail Order Buyers," and so on.

The Kleid Company in New York is eager to sell you names from subscription lists of prestigious magazines such as *Architectural Digest* (median household income: $82,100), the *New Yorker* (MHI: $71,100), or *Vanity Fair* (MHI: $99,400). Looking for a bride? Response Media Products in Atlanta will sell you a list of 132,761 names of women who have made a purchase from a bridal shop within the past 12 months. The list costs $80 per thousand, an average price in this market. These lists can be used by themselves, or they can be merged with other lists for increasingly fine-tuned marketing campaigns.

Many Americans are offended by this trade in identities. But the industry has its standard retorts—excuses that it has been using for more than 30 years. The first is that this is a free country, and advertisers have a right to share in those freedoms. Said one marketer in 1972, "As long as the individual can throw away unwanted mail, he is not being coerced in any way and his civil liberties are not being invaded."[14]

The second excuse is that, no matter how consumers feel about the trade of names, they are pleased with the results. "More than 98 million Americans shop at home and like the freedom of receiving things based on their interest," says Connie Heatley, the Direct Marketing Association's senior vice president.[15] As further proof, DMA cites the $240 billion spent last year on products marketed directly to consumers. Indeed, says the DMA, if consumers didn't respond so favorably to the advertisements, companies would stop using them.

TARGETED CRIME

Unfortunately, the buck doesn't stop with the Direct Marketing Association. The sale of personal information is also being used to support $40 billion a year in telemarketing scams, according to the U.S. Federal Trade Commission. Scammers frequently buy names, phone numbers, and addresses just as legitimate businesses do. Then they turn around the personal information and use it to trick people into parting with their money.

Increasingly, the scams are international in scope. Hilda Hanna, a United States citizen, started getting phone calls from Quebec in 1996. The caller said that she had entered a sweepstakes and had won a $945,000 jackpot. But there was a catch: in order to get the money, she would have to send $19,000 to cover Canadian taxes and customs fees. Thinking that the money was a sure thing, Hanna borrowed the money on her credit cards. But the sweepstakes prize never came. Instead, she got another phone call saying that she had won a second $128,000 prize—and that she would have to send an additional $4,000 to claim it. Then they called her a third time.

"They sounded really legitimate," Hanna told *The Washington Post*. "They kept asking for money . . . and my heart sort of said, 'don't do it anymore.' . . . But I trust people and they said I would have [the prize money] before [the payment] hit my credit cards. I am too trustworthy, I guess. I am 71 years old and I should have known better."[16]

Con artists are attracted to Canada because enforcement for telemarketing scams is relatively lax there, and the penalties are not as severe as in the U.S. Furthermore, by targeting only U.S. consumers, the scam artists can avoid the risk of local prosecution. For that reason, Canadian officials say, dozens of telemarketing scams are operating in Canada at any given time.

Sadly, the international problem is destined to get worse as long distance prices drop and as more scams move to the Internet.

OPT-OUT DOESN'T WORK

Back at the Direct Marketing Association, Connie LaMatto says that the direct marketing industry has developed a system to help those "rare" individuals who do not wish to receive solicitations. It's called the Mail Preference Service, a DMA-maintained list of people who have specifically said they do not wish to receive such mailings. Simply send a card to the DMA asking to be removed from marketing lists, and all of that unwanted mail is supposed to dry up. DMA operates a similar list called the Telephone Preference Service, which is supposed to put an end to unwanted telephone solicitations.

The Mail Preference Service is what industry insiders call an "opt-out" database. The idea is that marketing companies don't want to waste their money by sending solicitations to people who don't want them; it's cheaper to *suppress* the names in-house, before the mail is sent. But opt-out doesn't work for most consumers. Here's why:

- Many consumers don't know that opt-out lists exist. Other consumers have heard of the lists, but don't know how to get on them.

- Every time you move, you have to write in and add yourself again. This is because the mailing list companies use the National Change of Address Program files to update their records, but the DMA doesn't.

- The lists are "all or nothing." As a result, some consumers are hesitant to add their names to these lists because they are fearful that they might miss a valuable opportunity.

- Names on the list expire every five years.

- Companies sending out bulk mail are not legally required to use the lists, so many of them don't.

A 1996 review of data protection laws and current practices by Professor Paul Schwartz of the University of Arkansas School of Law and Professor Joel Reidenberg of the Fordham Law School found that only

53% of DMA's members use the Mail Preference Service to screen their own mailings! (It wasn't until October 1999 that DMA's members were required by the organization to use the service; it is too soon to know if this change in policy will make any difference.) "And in any case, most Americans are unaware of the name removal options. This ignorance reflects either ineffectiveness or noncompliance even by those DMA members purporting to use the service."[17] The study continued:

> Company codes of practice do not elaborate any remedy for individuals in the event that a company policy has been violated. Unlike the financial services or telecommunications context, strong internal sanctions do not appear to be in place against employees who violate company codes.[18]

Because the opt-out lists are voluntary and because there are no legal penalties for sending mail to people who have opted out, whether or not a company chooses to utilize the Mail Preference Service is just another business decision. In fact, companies like Experian actually charge their customers a fee each time the opt-out list is used to suppress names from a bulk mailing, further reducing the chance that the service will be utilized.

Despite these caveats, the size of the opt-out list is growing—from 988,000 individuals in 1989 to 3.2 million in 1995 and 3.9 million in 1999. This jump is due to increased publicity by privacy activists and also by the Internet, which has made it easier for people to find out and circulate proconsumer information outside traditional media channels.

Nevertheless, the whole approach of "opt-out" is ethically perverse. Consumers shouldn't have to beg marketers not to send them mail. A far better approach than "opt-out" is "opt-in." That is, companies should refrain from sending solicitations to consumers unless they have been invited to do so. Consumers routinely seek information from companies—they visit web sites, call 800 numbers, and even fill out those "bingo cards" in the backs of magazines. Moving to an "opt-in" system would make marketing more efficient by eliminating an enormous amount of waste and maximizing the value of all consumer-to-merchant interactions.

TAKING DIRECT ACTION AGAINST DIRECT MARKETING

Take a moment to imagine our nightmarish future if direct marketing continues on its current path:

> You're planning a trip to New York City for Valentine's Day with your sweetheart. You call up your travel agent to make a reservation, then go

out for lunch. When you return, you discover that your email inbox is filled. There are more than 5,000 restaurants in the Big Apple, and a third of them have sent you electronic coupons offering you 15% off your entrée if you visit them sometime during your big trip.

You pick up your phone. You want to call your travel agent and yell at her for selling your name. But you don't have a chance: instead of hearing a dial tone, you find yourself speaking with a representative from United Airlines. Your travel agent ticketed you on American, the representative informs you. "We discovered it by scanning the reservation system. If you'll ticket your next business trip on United, we'll honor your American ticket and give you a complimentary upgrade to business class as well."

The United offer seems too good to pass up. But over the next 15 minutes, you find out that there are so many caveats and restrictions that you decide to keep your ticket on American. Then you look at the clock and discover that you are 10 minutes late for a meeting. As you get up, your phone rings again. The Caller ID box says that it's from your sweetie, so you take the call.

Surprise! This time the call is from a local travel agent (who has programmed her telephone switch to give out fake information on the Caller ID.) She wants to tell you that Cathay Pacific has a special New York–Hong Kong getaway package. "What a perfect way to extend your vacation," she says. "It's just $999."

A few days later, you find yourself besieged with mail-order catalogs. Companies selling everything from "New York–style suits" to chemical Mace are trying to get your attention, offering to provide you with precisely what you will need for your upcoming trip. Many of these catalogs are custom-printed for you: some even have your face on the cover, pasted on the body of a smart-looking model. One of the catalogs shows boxes of chocolates that you can have gift-wrapped and delivered to your hotel room. (It turns out that the hotel is the third business that's sold your name and your travel plans.) For an additional fee you can have the box of chocolates monogrammed with your initials and the initials of your lover, the advertisement states.

The constant marketing barrage doesn't let up. When your tickets show up, you discover an advertisement for a prescription drug (one you've researched because you've been thinking about taking it) printed on your boarding pass. Even on the plane, you look at one of those "air phones" on the back of the seat in front of you and notice that it's displaying a tiny personalized advertisement for a jewelry store in Times Square. If you come in on February 14th, they'll give you a 40% discount on engagement rings.

It seems that everybody knows that you're going on this trip. But how did the jewelry store know that you and your sweetie aren't married? Over the next few days you keep turning this question over and over in your mind.

When you finally get home a week later, you discover that your house has been burglarized.

The world is filled with companies that want to sell us things. The dropping cost of communications, combined with the increasing availability of personal information, makes it more than likely that all kinds of companies will be soliciting us simultaneously in the years to come. And this is not just a problem for people making Valentine's Day trips to New York City. Soon, businesses all over the nation, and even all over the world, will be vying for our attention and our money—a direct result of decreased transportation costs and globalized markets.

Fortunately, we can fight back.

TACTIC #1: EXERCISE YOUR ANONYMITY

Target marketing depends upon the ability to target—the ability of a marketer to identify who you are and what you're most likely to buy. One way to shield yourself from the big marketing machines is to shield your identity.

Probably the best way to shield your identity is to be anonymous. Buy products with cash. Don't participate in "Birthday Clubs" or in special discount programs. Be suspicious when a company asks for personal information such as your birthday, your address, or your phone number.

Anonymity is more important on the Internet, where it is possible for web site operators to track your every move. On the information superhighway, tracking translates to targeting, which translates to unwanted solicitations and privacy invasions. Because it is so easy for personal information to travel over the Internet, it is all the more important that the network's architecture be designed to support anonymous access as the standard mode of operation.

The right to privacy includes the right to anonymity. The only way to protect this right is to exercise it.

TACTIC #2: PUBLICIZE AND LITIGATE

Many businesses take liberties with personal information without having the clear legal right to do so. To protect themselves from the inevitable public backlash, these businesses strive to keep their actions secret. But the truth will out.

The news media is one of the most effective tools for fighting misuse of personal information by large, respected businesses. The bad publicity generated by a "privacy outrage" far outweighs any possible revenue that a company might earn from its customers. For example, in February 1998, it was revealed in the *Washington Post* that two large drugstore chains, CVS and Giant Foods Pharmacy, were selling prescription drug sales records to Elensys, a Woburn, Massachusetts, marketing and fulfillment firm. The companies said that they were only using Elensys to send out mailings that reminded customers to get their prescriptions refilled. But the *Post* story revealed that the profiles were also being used for targeted marketing—and were being shared with other drug manufacturers. Giant Foods immediately said that they would curtail the practice, but CVS refused, at least at first, although it finally gave in to a torrent of consumer complaints.

Although voluntary restrictions are commendable, there is a danger to them. Because such restrictions are not required by law, a company that implements a voluntary restriction is free to resume the practice at a later time. Meanwhile, less scrupulous firms are not bound in any way.

The way for you to ensure that voluntary privacy practices are mandated is to file suit against companies you feel are violating your privacy. That's just what one Massachusetts man did shortly after the CVS story broke. Alleging that he had received a solicitation urging him to consider using drugs made by Glaxo-Wellcome, Inc., the man filed a class action suit against CVS, Elensys, and Glaxo-Wellcome for committing "a flagrant breach of patient/customer confidentiality."[19]

Lawsuits do more than attract attention. When they are successful, they create binding precedents that other companies must follow as well.

TACTIC #3: TRACK THEM AS THEY TRACK YOU

When a magazine rents its mailing list, the magazine always puts a few special names into the mix so it can track how they are used. Normally, lists are rented for a single use. These *seeded names* allow the list owner to discover if the list is used more than once, or if it is used for a purpose other than what was authorized. For example, a company's vice president of marketing might add a name with her home address but the name of her cat Thelma. If Thelma gets five catalogs in the mail instead of just one, or if Thelma gets a phone call telling her that she's won $10,000 (but needs to pay $2500 in taxes to claim the reward), a lawsuit will probably follow.

A growing number of consumers are using this same technique. There are people who subscribe to different magazines with slightly different permutations of their names—Robert Johnson, Bob F. Johnson, R. Fox Johnson, for example—just to track how the name moves through the information economy. Today, there is little that consumers can do with this information aside from publicizing industry practices. But over time, the more we learn, the easier it will be to effect change.

TACTIC #4: MAKE USE OF TODAY'S LAWS
AND FIGHT FOR NEW ONES

There is an astonishing amount of privacy law on the books today. Sadly, few consumers know what rights they truly have. Making use of the tools available now will go a long way towards fighting the current abuses of the marketing industry. We can also learn from the past, and use the legislation that has been passed as a template for future laws.

In the 1960s, after federal courts relaxed the definition of "obscene," a number of firms began purchasing mailing lists from the U.S. government under public record laws and using these lists to send people solicitations to buy pornography. But Congress effectively stamped out the problem in 1970, when it passed a federal statute requiring the U.S. Post Office Department (the precursor to today's Postal Service[20]) to maintain a list of those who did not wish to receive sexually oriented mail. Failure to honor the wishes of people on the list would lead to criminal penalties for the mailers. By 1971, more than 500,000 people had placed their names on the list.[21] The industry's marketing practices soon changed. Instead of sending out sexually oriented solicitations to anybody whose name they could buy, today these businesses restrain themselves, and send the catalogs only to people who have specifically asked for them.

Now the pornography problem has resurfaced, with a new generation of pornographers sending unsolicited "spam" email hawking sexually explicit web sites. But there is no reason that the solution of the 1960s wouldn't work today.

Similar legislation has largely put an end to another kind of unwanted advertisements: junk faxes. In 1991, Congress passed the Telephone Consumer Protection Act, making it illegal for telemarketers to fax advertisements without the express permission of the fax machine's owner. The law also criminalized the use of automatic call units, which place calls to telephone consumers and play prerecorded messages. These annoyances have now mostly disappeared from the consumer landscape.

The 1991 law also contained language prohibiting telemarketers from calling people who don't wish to receive sales calls. But Congress goofed. Rather than mandating the creation of a single nationwide *asterisk list*, or list of people who do not want to be called, the lawmakers left it up to the Federal Communications Commission (FCC) to decide the best way to implement such a list. The FCC, in turn, was heavily lobbied by the marketing industry. Eventually the FCC paradoxically decided that it would be "more efficient" for each business to maintain its own opt-out database than to have a single national registry. As a result, under U.S. law you must now tell *each company* making telemarketing calls that you do not wish to receive calls from them—that is, you need to call up each company and ask them to put a little asterisk next to your name. (On the plus side, if you get a telemarketing call from a company that doesn't have an asterisk list, you can sue them for between $500 and $1500. According to Bob Bulmash, President of Private Citizen, Inc., more than $54,000 was recovered by American consumers using these lawsuits in 1996.)

"In my opinion, this country needs a federal asterisk law, as Congress requested," says Jason Catlett, a consumer rights activist and president of Junkbusters Corporation.22 "You should be able to have your number (no name) added at no charge to a nationally available list, with a $10,000 fine for each telemarketing call made to it."

The U.S. clearly needs more legislation to regulate the marketing industry. This legislation should focus on giving consumers more information about the marketers themselves, creating heavy fines for invading consumer privacy, and creating criminal penalties for trying to evade the law.

One good place to start would be to look back at a 1965 bill proposed by Congressman Cornelius Gallagher but never passed. That bill would have required that computer-generated mailing labels include a code number for each person's name and a phone number that you could call to get your name taken off the appropriate mailing list. A revised twenty-first century version of this bill could apply equally well to email and telemarketing calls.

Congress also needs to address the threat of sales calls coming from overseas, a threat that is growing thanks to the plummeting price of international telephone calls. We need enforceable laws so that when telemarketing scams come from overseas, the perpetrators can be quickly identified and apprehended. This legislation should then be extended to block telemarketing calls from overseas unless the person being called has specifically indicated that they wish to receive such calls.

CHAPTER EIGHT

WHO OWNS YOUR
INFORMATION?

In the past seven chapters, we've seen many different ways that personal information is being captured, used without our permission, and frequently, turned against us. In these chapters, I've argued that the most effective solution for preventing the unwanted collection and disclosure of personal information is sweeping legislation designed to restore our right to privacy in this age of computers. But other contemporary thinkers, looking at the same set of facts, have come up with another solution. "We don't need new legislation," they say, echoing the libertarian leaning that is so popular among today's information intelligentsia. "All we need is to treat personal information as a property right, and then to use existing property laws to prevent unauthorized appropriation."

But treating personal information as a new kind of property right could easily do more harm than good. That's because information is not like other kinds of tangible property. Applying traditional property law could easily have unintended consequences.

"The very nature of information is so different from the properties of material resources that it defies all methods of measurement," says C.B. (Jack) Rogers, Jr., CEO of Equifax, the consumer reporting company. "For one thing, I can sell it to you and keep it at the same time. It doesn't wear out, it increases in value and it increases in value with use, and it is the primary resource for worldwide commerce and trade."[1]

Not only is information different from other forms of property, it is also protected by its own special rules. Although many of these rules were originally drafted to protect individuals and stimulate their creativity, in recent years they have been twisted around so they now almost exclusively serve the interests of large businesses and corporations. Although these rules look like attractive tools for protecting privacy, they might ultimately be a trap, doing privacy more harm than good. Ownership is a dangerous path for preserving privacy. What is owned can be sold, bargained away, seized, or lost.

DO YOU OWN YOUR NAME?

Ram Avrahami thought he owned his own name, but it was actually owned by a private company with 500 employees and $310 million in sales. Avrahami went to court to stop that company from renting out his name without his permission, and he lost. Avrahami wanted to change the ground rules of the nation's trillion-dollar direct marketing industry. Instead, he strengthened that industry's position of power.[2]

Avrahami's troubles began in February 1995, when he received an advertisement in the mail inviting him to subscribe to the magazine *U.S. News & World Report*. A few weeks later, he agreed to the offer and sent in the slip. In March, he got a bill and sent in a check for $15.

Two months later, Avrahami received another letter in the mail—a solicitation from the Smithsonian Institution asking him to subscribe to its magazine, *Smithsonian*. But this time, instead of accepting the magazine offer, Avrahami wrote a letter to the Smithsonian Institution asking how they got his name and address. *Smithsonian*'s circulation department wrote back to say that *Smithsonian* had "rented [your] name from *U.S. News & World Report* for a one-time use." Like many magazines, *U.S. News & World Report* routinely rents out the names of its 2.2 million subscribers to other companies that are trying to sell things through the mail. As it turned out, Avrahami's name was one of 100,000 names that *U.S. News & World Report* had rented to *Smithsonian* for $8,000.

Avrahami was sick and tired of junk mail. But rather than just throwing out the letter, as most Americans would, he decided to change society. He did some research and discovered that Virginia, the state where he lived, actually had a law on the books that appeared to prohibit precisely what *U.S. News & World Report* had done. According to Section 8.01-40 of the Code of Virginia:

> Any person whose name, portrait, or picture is used without having first obtained the written consent of such person . . . for advertising purposes or for the purposes of trade, such persons may maintain a suit in equity against the person, firm or corporation so using such person's name, portrait, or picture to prevent and restrain the use thereof; and may also sue and recover damage for any injuries sustained by reason of such use. And if the defendant shall have knowingly used such person's name, portrait or picture in such manner as is forbidden or declared to be unlawful by this chapter, the jury, in its discretion, may award exemplary damages.

Several states have similar legislation. The laws were passed after a famous 1905 case in New York, in which the parents of an infant sued the Rochester Folding Box Company for printing 25,000 boxes of flour, each one stamped with a photograph of their child. The Rochester company had failed to get the parents' consent. The family sued for invasion of privacy, using as their justification the "Right of Privacy" article published by Brandeis and Warren at the end of the nineteenth century. But the family lost.[3] The reason: there was no right to privacy—nor a right for the family to control the image of their child—enshrined in New York law. After the ruling, legislators around the United States were so outraged by the ruling that laws were passed explicitly prohibiting the practice of using a person's name or image in trade without that person's consent.

Avrahami also accused *U.S. News & World Report* of "conversion," that is, taking control of his name or property and using it for the magazine's own purposes without his prior consent. He was represented by the law offices of Jonathan C. Dailey in Arlington, Virginia.

The case seemed to be a novel interpretation of the Virginia law, but one completely consistent with the value of personal information in late twentieth-century America. Avrahami demanded a jury trial, asking for $100 in compensatory damages and $1,000 in exemplary damages. Of course, he was also hoping to start an avalanche of lawsuits against mailing-list brokers—an avalanche that would quickly force the industry to give up on the "opt-out" approach and instead ask consumers their permission before renting out their names.

The trial was set for August 21, 1995.

ARGUMENTS BEFORE THE COURT

With the support of the Direct Marketing Association, *U.S. News & World Report* filed a brief with the court that strongly argued its position. Among the key points of the brief were the following:

- The magazine argued that the sale, rental, and exchange of mailing lists is "a common, standard business practice" throughout the United States. In fact, the company argued, even the U.S. Government Printing Office "routinely engages in the sale or rental of its mailing lists," charging "approximately $85.00 per 1,000 names." Likewise, "Various departments and agencies of the Commonwealth of Virginia government, including the state board of bar examiners, make their mailing lists available to businesses and individuals for sale or rental."

- The magazine argued that if Avrahami didn't want to receive solicitations, he should have registered his name with the Direct

Marketing Association's Mail Preference Service—which it claimed he had not done.[4]

- The magazine said that *U.S. News & World Report* had, in fact, obtained Avrahami's name from Consumers Union, the publisher of *Consumer Reports*, in a batch of 92,500 names that the magazine had rented earlier that year for its own marketing campaign. *U.S. News & World Report* typically rents or exchanges names with between 60 and 100 other businesses for each of its marketing campaigns. Avrahami's was simply one name in a million.

- The magazine further noted that on the *Consumer Reports* subscription form there is a little checkbox that subscribers can check to indicate that they don't want their names shared. Avrahami had never checked that little box. And indeed, the company said, when *U.S. News & World Report* sent Avrahami a subscription offer, he subscribed. "When Mr. Avrahami receives a direct mail solicitation he likes, he subscribes," stated the magazine's attorneys. "When he receives one he doesn't like, rather than deposit it in the trash can, he files suit."

"Virginia Code #8.01-40 was not intended to prevent the sale, rental, or exchange of mailing lists," concluded *U.S. News & World Report*. "The Virginia privacy statute was intended to protect individuals whose names and likeness are used in advertising without their consent by providing them with a cause of action." The company asked the court to dismiss the case and to issue a declaratory judgment that selling, renting, and exchanging mailing lists with Avrahami's name does not violate the Virginia code.

The legal haggling continued until February 6, 1996, when the judge presiding over the case issued a surprise ruling. Unprompted by either side, Judge Karen Henenberg asserted that she did not have jurisdiction to hear the case. Instead of filing in the Courts of Equity, Henenberg said, Avrahami should have filed suit in the Courts of Law. It was a minor legalistic distinction that was lost on most observers outside the Commonwealth of Virginia. Nevertheless, it temporarily put an end to the case.

AVRAHAMI V. ESTABLISHMENT, ROUND 2

Avrahami filed suit again in March 28, 1996—this time in the Courts of Law—asking the court to permanently restrain *U.S. News & World Report* from using his name. He asked for one dollar in damages for each time the magazine had used his name in the past, and for all revenue that *U.S. News & World Report* had obtained from the use of his name, plus additional exemplary damages of $5,000.

At this point, an important fact in the case was revealed. Like many people interested in tracking the flow of personal information, Avrahami had subtly altered the spelling of his last name when he subscribed to *U.S. News & World Report.* Instead of subscribing as "Ram Avrahami," he had subscribed as "Ram Avrahani."

It is standard practice in the mailing list industry to use slight misspellings of names to track the movement and use of personal information. When the Avrahami case came to trial on June 6, 1996, Catherine Hagney, vice president of consumer marketing at *U.S. News & World Report*, testified that she routinely included the name "Catherine Cagney" with her home address when the magazine rented its mailing list to other companies. "*U.S. News & World Report* refuses to rent out names to companies that are trying to market pornography or engage in other unsavory practices," she said. "We use seed names to make sure that they're not deceiving us and mailing a different type of mail piece."

Five days later, the court ruled that by introducing a slight misspelling to his name, Avrahami had created a fictional identity to which he did not have any rights under the Virginia statute. As a result of the fiction, Judge William T. Newman, Jr., ruled against Avrahami and dismissed the case.

The ruling was largely expected. During the trial, Judge Newman had been generous to the defense, but short with Avrahami. For example, the judge allowed lawyers for *U.S. News & World Report* to probe deeply into Avrahami's personal life on matters that had nothing to do with the case. *U.S. News & World Report* questioned Avrahami's religion, his immigration status, and whether or not he was using the lawsuit to "get girls." Yet Judge Newman denied many attempts on the part of Avrahami's attorney to show the extent to which personal information beyond names and addresses was being bought and sold by the magazine.

Avrahami filed an appeal with the Virginia Supreme Court, but the appeal was denied.

Having spent nearly a year talking up the importance of the case, privacy activists were quick to downplay the significance of the negative ruling. "The judgment was specific to some unusual circumstances of the case," Jason Catlett, founder of Junkbusters, told me. "If Avrahami had instead varied his address with tags such as 'Room 7C' he might have won."

Catlett hopes that others follow Avrahami's lead:

People can still file similar suits in the many other states with such statutes, or even in Virginia. The fact that the DMA put enormous resources into a hardball defense suggests that their lawyers believed he might win. I think it's only a matter of time before someone else succeeds with a better-prepared suit, and then a trillion-dollar industry will find its basic ground rules changed. It'll be as if the ownership of each oilfield in the world suddenly passed to the people living nearest it.[5]

THE VALUE OF NAMES IN NEW JERSEY

Catlett may be right. Certainly, the Direct Marketing Association mounted a similar high-stakes public relations campaign in 1996, when New Jersey State Senator Richard J. Cody tried to pass a bill that would have outlawed the selling of people's names and addresses without their permission.

There was no single incident that led Cody to file his legislation. When I interviewed him, he simply said he was sick of companies that "sold my name, and my address, and my demographics, without my permission. [They] had no right to sell my name to somebody else to solicit me."[6]

The DMA attacked Cody's bill using one of its standard defenses—arguing that the nation's $600 billion direct marketing industry would fall apart if names couldn't be bought and sold like so many nails. "Statistics tell us that more than half of the adult American population are shopping this way," asserted Connie Heatley, DMA's senior vice president. "People may say that they don't like junk mail, but most people are acting in another way"—indeed, just as Ram Avrahami had acted when he subscribed to *U.S. News & World Report*.[7]

Cody's bill is an interesting footnote to the Avrahami case, but ultimately it had even less impact. The legislation was never voted on. Like a bug, it was effectively squashed.

NAMES AS PROPERTY

Some middle ground does exist between Senator Cody and the DMA. Instead of allowing—or not allowing—the sale of names, every name in the U.S. could be licensed, with individuals receiving royalties for the use of their names. But such a system might ultimately do more harm than good.

"Propertizing [personal information] may end up working less to the advantage of private individuals and more to the advantage of the companies that take the information from them," says Pamela Samuelson, a professor of copyright law at the University of California, Berkeley. If personal information is a property right, she says:

> When somebody takes your information, if they just get some transfer from you of the right to your information, then they have a property right against the world. It seems to me that unless you regulate the extent to which people are going to be able to transfer that information, you are not really succeeding in the effort that you engaged in in the first place—

to protect the integrity of personal information and the right to protect against some sort of abuses.[8]

There are other problems with this approach as well. If people are to be paid for the use of their names, then there must be some way to track these people down so they can be given their money. Practically speaking, a pay-as-you-mail system would require the compilation of a massive database with the name, address, and banking information of every person in the United States. This database, itself a tremendous wellspring of personal information, would have to be accessible to any organization that engaged in target marketing.

Another problem is with the rates themselves. When Consumers Union sold 92,000 names to *U.S. News & World Report*, they received approximately $8,000. Names and addresses are simply not worth very much money. In the case of Consumers Union, the value is approximately 8.6 cents per subscriber. If people were actually paid *royalties* for the use of their names, we might expect them to see a rate that is similar to what the authors of books, magazine articles, and computer programs receive for their work—between 5% and 15%. How much is your name worth? Roughly a penny.

Catlett argues with this chain of logic by saying that today's price of 8 cents per name is artificially low because the market is flooded with consumer names and addresses. By banding together, he suggests, consumers could restrict the supply of names and raise their value, in much the way that the OPEC oil cartel raised the value of crude oil in the 1970s. One way to create scarcity would be to ban the sale of a consumer's name without that person's explicit permission.

The Direct Marketing Association argues that banning the sale of names would cause the destruction of a trillion-dollar industry. This is disingenuous. Mail-order firms have many ways of advertising their catalogs. They can take out newspaper, magazine, and television ads. They can put up web sites. They can offer new customers discounts if the customer orders a catalog from an 800 number. And they can pay to have their advertisements included with credit card statements or with orders from other companies. The trillion-dollar industry would not collapse if today's antiprivacy marketing techniques were regulated.

Privacy advocates suggest turning personal information into a property right, I think, because they hope the increased transaction cost of tracking personal information would bring the practice to a halt. This is an indirect and probably unworkable solution to an obvious problem. The problem is not that people are not reaping the benefits from the sale of their names; the problem is that people's names and addresses are being sold without their permission. According to the 1996 Harris-Equifax Consumer Privacy Survey,[9] 73% of Americans want their names removed from marketing lists, yet only 44% are aware that such procedures are available. If the buying and selling of people's names is offensive to a majority of the population, as it seems to be, then the practice should be regulated, restricted, or outlawed.

DO YOU OWN YOUR FEET?

You may not own your name, but it's hard to argue that you don't own your hair, or your hands, or your feet. For centuries, women in need of money have sold their hair to wig makers. And if somebody cuts off your hand or your foot, you can sue them for bodily mutilation.

Ownership of the genetic pattern that is stored inside each and every cell of your body may also seem to be an open-and-shut case. After all, your DNA pattern is uniquely yours. It determines your eye and hair color, the shape of your face, your sex, your race, and countless other characteristics that have come together in a unique pattern— you. How could you *not* own your own genetic pattern?

Genetic patterns are certainly a thing worth owning—at least, some of them are. Locked away in the genetic patterns of some individuals are specific mutations from which biotechnology researchers can develop new medical tests and drugs. This is especially true of people with rare mutations—such as those people who can apparently smoke without getting cancer, or become infected with HIV without developing AIDS.

Other individuals have genetic patterns that they would rather not have—and that they would like to keep a secret from others. For example, some people have genes that make their bodies more susceptible to cancer or particular kinds of diseases. In recent years, people who have tested positive for various kinds of genetic disorders have been discriminated against by employers and insurance companies. For these people, ownership would imply a right to keep their genetic profile secret, just as ownership of a painting gives you the right to lock it away in a closet so nobody else can see it. Ownership creates a kind of control.

But genetic information is not like a painting. You inherit your genes from your parents—half from your mother and half from your father. A brother and a sister will have roughly 25% of their genes in common. And identical twins, roughly three people out of a thousand in North America, have identical genetic makeups. "Once you know something about yourself, you know something about your parents and you know something about your relatives," says Dr. Lisa Geller, who spent years working as a biomedical researcher before joining the intellectual property law firm of Fish & Richardson in Boston. "Whose information is it and whose right to know?"[10]

DOUBLE TROUBLE

Huntington's disease is a terrible, disfiguring affliction that causes involuntary movements, dementia, and ultimately, death. There is no effective therapy. The mutation that causes the disease originated in Europe; it spread to America with colonization. Unlike many genetic illnesses, the gene that causes Huntington's is dominant: children of an afflicted individual have a 50% chance of inheriting the gene. But the disease is also extremely variable: some people get it in their 30s, others in their 50s. Some people die 10 years after their symptoms appear, other people last 20 years. And some people carrying the genes die from an accident or other illness before their symptoms even appear.

Huntington's disease also has a special place in the annals of genetic illnesses: in 1983, researchers in Boston developed a test that could tell whether or not an individual had the genetic defect, and thus, whether or not that person would eventually develop the disease.

In 1995, the *Journal of Genetic Counseling* published a perplexing letter involving the case of identical twins.[11] The twins' family had a history of Huntington's. What troubled the authors of the letter was that one of the twins had asked to be tested. The other was content not knowing whether he carried the disease. It thus became one of the first diseases that could be tested for on the basis of genetics.

Now, there are a lot of good reasons to be tested for the disease, and just as many not to be. On the positive side, if you have the deadly gene, you can plan for your eventual demise. You might buy a house that doesn't have stairs, for instance. You have more freedom to engage in dangerous hobbies, or take risky but high-paying jobs. And if you choose to have children, you might adopt—or test the fetus in the womb, and abort the child if it carries the deadly mutation.

On the other hand, some people would rather not know that they have a deadly, incurable genetic defect. For some people, it is better not to know that the gene is present, than to learn that it is present but not to know how severe the disease will be if or when it ever comes. And there's the specter of genetic discrimination: what if you couldn't get a job or insurance, because someday you were going to get sick and die? Hundreds of instances of genetic discrimination have been documented in recent years.[12] If you have the gene, you do not want this information in your medical file. The easiest way to keep it out of your file is not to be tested.

It is impossible to test one identical twin for a disease and not de facto be testing the other. And when the first twin offered to withhold the information from his brother, who was living on the other side of the country, the researchers scoffed: how could such information be withheld for long from one's sibling? On the other hand, while it's medically unethical to test somebody who does not wish to be tested, it's equally unethical to withhold a test from somebody who wants it. The researchers faced a dilemma because one genetic pattern belonged to two individuals.

Fortunately, this dilemma had an easy resolution. The second twin agreed to have genetic counseling and, ultimately, to be tested. The twins were then simultaneously informed of the results in two offices, one in Boston and the other in San Francisco. The researchers even accounted for the three-hour time difference between the two cities.

SPLEENS AND THICK BONES

A different kind of problem faced cancer survivor John Moore.[13] In 1976, Moore had his spleen removed by Dr. David W. Golde at the University of California at Los Angeles Medical Center. Moore had been unlucky enough to come down with a case of "hairy cell" leukemia; his spleen had swollen from a half pound to more than 14 pounds. It had been removed during surgery, and Moore had thought that was the end of it—until Golde called Moore in September 1983.

Before the surgery, Moore had been asked to sign a consent form that would allow the university to use any leftover tissue for medical research. Specifically, the form had granted the university all rights to "any cell line" created from the tumor cells that the good doctor was about to remove. Apparently, Golde explained, in 1983 Moore had inadvertently "mis-signed the consent form" by circling the words "do not" instead of "do." That is, Moore had specifically withheld his permission from the university to use his cells for medical research.

A cell line is a group of cells, usually descended from a single cancer cell, that can be grown in the laboratory and that stay alive generation after generation. Scientists call these cells *immortal*. Hundreds of cell lines are used in biotechnology research and product development throughout the world. There is a great irony in this, since the cell lines frequently outlive the people from whom the cancer cells were originally taken. Indeed, some of the most widely used cell lines in the biomedical world today are from a woman named Helen Lake, who died of cancer in the 1940s.

Unknown to John Moore, Dr. Golde had taken his tumor cells and created the "Mo cell line." The cell line was exciting because, unlike other cell lines, this cell line produced a powerful antibacterial and cancer-fighting protein called GM-CSF.[14] UCLA had applied for a patent on the cell line in 1983, which is presumably when the lawyers discovered that Moore had never given them the right to use his cells for that purpose.

Instead of signing the form as asked, Moore hired a lawyer. After the patent was issued in 1984, he filed suit against the University of California, Dr. Golde, his research assistant Shirley Quan, and two corporations that stood to profit substantially from his tumor cells. It looked like an open-and-shut case. After all, Moore had specifically refused UCLA the right to commercialize his cell line. But the court felt otherwise.

"The trial court essentially decided that Moore had no right to bring suit," writes George J. Annas in his book *Standard of Care*. The appellate court reversed, saying that the tort of *conversion* had been violated by Moore's doctors. It was the same charge that Avrahami would later make against *U.S. News & World Report*. But in July 1990, the California Supreme Court reversed again, saying that it was not prepared to create a new property right in people's cells, and that the biotech industry would suffer irreparable financial harm if people like Moore had to be compensated. Essentially, writes Annas, the California Supreme Court was convinced by "the defendants' position that researchers, doctors, universities, and private companies can own human cells, but individuals cannot."

What makes John Moore's case unique is not all of those wondrous proteins inside his cells, but the fact that he sued in the first place. A growing number of companies are discovering individual humans or families with extremely rare genetic traits, isolating the responsible genes, and then using these genes to create lucrative genetic tests and medications. I am not aware of a single case in which the people or the families from which these medications are derived have shared in the proceeds.

In the mid-1990s, researchers at Creighton University in Nebraska discovered a person who had an unusual genetic trait: this person's bones were more massive than normal human bones. The mutation was discovered by accident—literally. The person had been in an automobile accident, one that should have broken the person's leg but didn't. An alert doctor in the emergency room decided to investigate why the person's bone hadn't broken, and discovered the High Bone Mass (HBM) genetic trait.

Researchers at Creighton set to work, and soon discovered a whole family that shared the genetic trait. Members of the family were asked to participate in a study, which involved coming into a laboratory and giving blood, to help identify the gene. Then in April 1997, Creighton University announced a partnership with Genome Therapeutics Corporation to isolate the gene responsible for the trait. Genome wanted to develop a drug that would mimic the effect of the gene. Such a drug, if it could be created, could be used to treat osteoporosis, a disease that affects two-thirds of the women over 65 in the United States.

"If we clone the gene and a target is identified, and a drug is identified against the target, the [revenue produced by the] drug could be quite substantial," said Fenel Eloi, Genome Therapeutics' Chief Financial Officer, in the fall of 1997.[15] Eloi refused to tell me just how big the market for an osteoporosis drug might be. Instead, he referred me to an article from the September 1, 1997 issue of *Business Week*, which said that osteoporosis affects more women than breast, uterine, and ovarian cancers combined, and that the world spent $14 billion treating those diseases in 1995.

If Genome Therapeutics strikes it rich, Creighton University will share in the profits under its technology transfer program. But the family that is the source of the High Bone Mass gene won't. "The participants are treated as any other research participants," says Lori Elliot-Bartle, a spokesperson for the university. "Generally, study participants are paid for their time and the inconvenience of participating in a study. It's usually not a lot of money."[16]

Perhaps people shouldn't be paid a lot of money for their unique genetic information. "They are contributing something to society," says Lisa Geller. Locked up inside a single family tree, the HBM gene has no social or financial value. Furthermore, the gene is not strictly needed to produce the future miracle cure for osteoporosis—it simply makes the job for a company like Genome Therapeutics that much easier.

On the other hand, people who have adverse genes that they inherit are almost always forced to bear the brunt of the disease on their own. Society does not rush in to give fair compensation to those who are born with cystic fibrosis or Huntington's disease or phenylketonuria (PKU). We do not adjust the salaries of people who are abnormally short to make up for their unequal genetic heritage. What's worse, we allow insurance companies to deny those people coverage because of their "preexisting conditions." To say that individuals should not equally benefit when they are dealt exceptionally lucky genetic hands is to agree with the California Supreme Court: companies can own genes, but people can't.

"It is easy to understand how people want a cut of the action," says Mark Hanson, an associate at the Hastings Center, a New York State-based think tank that specializes in bioethics. But Hanson doesn't think the question is one of property rights—he sees it strictly as an issue of informed consent. If people are informed of the tremendous financial upside and then willingly sign away all of their rights, Hanson thinks that is fine.[17]

One could imagine giving patients a range of choices. They might be allowed to take a single up-front payment of a few hundred dollars, a payment that would take into account the fact that most material used for research does not produce billion-dollar drugs. Or the patients could elect to share in a percentage of the revenues. The patients might even agree to not receive any money at all, provided that the company donate a fixed percentage of its proceeds to charity. But it is hard to imagine anyone effectively saying: "Dear Big Genetics Company, please take my genes, make billions, and don't bother giving me anything in return. Don't even give me a single share of stock. Your financial health is my own personal reward."

In the Moore trial, the biotech industry claimed that such detailed tracking and record-keeping would be an unreasonable burden on company scientists and accountants. But in fact, far more intricate tracking is needed to develop these drugs in the first place. Biotech companies do not simply take people's blood and throw it all in a big pot. These companies know *precisely* which genes from which people produced which kinds of results. What is lacking is not the technical ability, but the political will to enforce these kinds of rights.

HUMAN TISSUE IS NOT ANONYMOUS

Complicating many of the medical privacy issues we've explored in this chapter is the fact that many people don't even know that medical research is being performed on their tissue samples. Under current ethical guidelines, research on body parts is not considered a violation of patient rights if the patient's name is removed from the samples. Allegedly, removing a person's name makes the sample "anonymous."

Many hospitals, for instance, routinely test blood samples for HIV and the presence of illegal drugs. The results of these tests are reported to the Centers for Disease Control, which use the information for their baseline statistical reports. "Recently, the Centers for Disease Control (CDC) in Atlanta announced the beginning of a year-long surveillance study to be done on all infants delivered in Georgia to evaluate the incidence of cocaine exposure late in pregnancy," reported a 1993 review article that appeared in the *Southern Medical Journal*.[18] "The study will be anonymous and will be done on the blood collected routinely as part of the mandatory state screening for inherited metabolic diseases (e.g., the PKU test)."

Most often, these "anonymous" samples are used for in-house research, but some labs sell the samples to outside scientists and corporations. And sometimes the names are not removed. For example, a friend of mine who is a biologist in the Boston area once worked at a firm that was developing an advanced human fertility test. To help with the development, her firm purchased several hundred vials of human blood serum. The vials came from a lab that was using the current fertility test of the day, and each vial was carefully labeled with the specific concentration of two female hormones. As it turned out, the vials were labeled with something else as well: the name of the woman from whom the blood was taken. Essentially, my friend had received the names of several hundred women in the Boston area who were trying to get pregnant! "They were supposed to take the names off the vials, but they forgot," my friend told me.

"I recognized one of the names, belonging to a fairly famous woman. My supervisor didn't want to alert the company we got them from, for fear they might be unwilling to sell to us again," she said. So my friend, eager to protect the privacy of the women involved, took a thick black magic marker to each of the vials, obliterating the names. It was a small act of pro-privacy rebellion.

Even anonymous samples are not necessarily anonymous—especially when genetic work is being done. "You can disassociate the names, ages, and Social Security numbers, but you can't disassociate some of the things you need for research, like the family tree, the age they developed the disease, what age they died. That is essential for doing the study," says Lincoln Stein, a pathologist who worked on the Human Genome Project at the Whitehead Institute in Cambridge, Massachusetts. There are only so many people "who died with leukemia at age 65 but whose mother is still alive at age 91," explains Stein. A person's identity can be deduced by matching up the "anonymous" medical record with other, freely available, information. This practice is called *triangulation*.[19]

THE JEWISH GENE

Even if an individual's privacy is not violated, a community's privacy can be. In recent years there have been a growing number of genetic diseases tied to particular ethnic groups—particularly Jews of European decent, called Ashkenazi Jews. Although the researchers can't say anything about whether or not a particular individual carries the diseased genes, the research inevitably casts a shadow over the entire ethnic group. Consider these three medical studies:

Breast cancer. In 1995, a group of scientists at the National Cancer Institute discovered a specific alteration in a particular gene that seemed to be unusually common in Ashkenazi Jews. But the gene didn't prove that the Jews were the chosen people. Instead the gene, BRCA1, placed the women that had it at significantly higher risk of developing breast cancer.

The researchers scanned 858 anonymous blood samples from Ashkenazi Jews and found the genetic defect, called 185delAG, in eight of them—a little more than 1%. According to other research, 185delAG increases a woman's chance of getting breast cancer by a factor of 5, from 4 in 25 (16%) to roughly 4 in 5 (70–87%).[20] "This rate of alteration in the BRCA1 gene is at least three times higher than all BRCA1 alterations combined in the general population," Dr. Lawrence C. Brody told the *Baltimore Jewish Times*.[21]

Dr. Brody was quick to point out that Ashkenazi Jews don't necessarily have a higher incidence of breast cancer than the general population. After all, the BRCA1 gene was affecting only a tiny percentage of Jewish women. Nevertheless, the gene was inextricably tied to Jewish women as a community.

Based on the strength of those findings, the doctors set up a study in which 5,000 Ashkenazi Jews from the Washington, D.C. area were recruited to give blood and detailed medical histories. The study, published in the May 15, 1997 issue of the *New England Journal of Medicine*, downgraded the incredible oncogenic power of 185delAG, but still concluded that Jewish women who had a mutant BRCA1 or BRCA2 gene had a 56% chance of getting breast cancer at some point during their lives. "We don't know what factors modify cancer risk," said Dr. Jeffery P. Struewing, who led the study. "There could be other genes or environmental factors involved."[22]

Colon cancer. In August 1997, biologists at Baltimore's Johns Hopkins Oncology Center announced that they had found another genetic defect in some Ashkenazi Jews. This time, the defect had to do with colon cancer, one of the most common forms of cancer among Americans. In the general U.S. population, the chance of getting colon cancer is 9–15%. Among people with the defect, the chance doubles. The scientists at Hopkins found that approximately 6% of Ashkenazi Jews carry the defective gene, giving them an 18–30% chance of getting cancer. (Interestingly enough, the scientists didn't try to find out what the rate of the defect was in the general population.)

Schizophrenia and bipolar disorder. While I was researching this book, I stumbled upon an advertisement in the *New York Times* recruiting volunteers for yet another study aimed at finding Jewish defects (see the boxed ad). In September 1998, the researchers published an article in the journal *Nature Genetics* indicating that they had found regions on two chromosomes that appeared to be loci for schizophrenia susceptibility.[23]

Everyone who participated in these three studies was anonymous— names had been stripped from the blood before it was tested. And in the second and third studies, the blood had been specifically collected for medical purposes. (In the case of the first study, scientists didn't even bother getting consent—they simply purchased blood that had been left over from routine Tay-Sachs disease screening.)

Ashkenazi Jewish Families Are Needed to Help Scientists Understand the Biological Basis for Schizophrenia and Bipolar Disorder

The study is being conducted by the Department of Psychiatry Epidemiology-Genetics Program at Johns Hopkins University. The researchers are looking for families with two or more children who have been diagnosed with one of the diseases for which there is one living parent, or for families with both living parents and with one diagnosed child.

But while the names were removed, the heritage of the blood was not. By performing these tests on blood with labeled heritage, the scientists were effectively performing genetic tests on an entire community.

To be fair, Dr. Struewing did attempt to get some sort of community consent for his 5,000-person, D.C.–area study. "We had a steering committee," says Struewing. "We had a lot of rabbis on the committee." One of them, Rabbi Avis Miller of Washington, D.C.'s Congregation Adas Israel, was specifically asked by the scientists to address the issue of community consent.

As it turns out, I am also an Ashkenazi Jew. So when I heard that Rabbi Miller had given permission to Struewing in my name, I called her up and asked her why. "We did give the permission," Rabbi Miller told me. "I think that insofar as there was any concern, and I don't know that there was, at least not that I heard expressed, that was outweighed by what was seen as benefits to the community." She continued:

> Quite frankly, I didn't hear fears expressed about anti-Semitism that such research might generate. I did hear fears about the information being used in ways that would be detrimental to individuals. I didn't hear [people saying] that we fear people will use it in a eugenic context. We have heard that African-Americans are carriers for sickle-cell [and they have been discriminated against as a result], but Jews are not those who would put roadblocks up to science because we are afraid of that concern—at least not Jews that I come into contact with. Maybe that was shortsighted because we don't see beyond the Beltway, and anti-Semitism in this country, at least according to most measures, is declining. Maybe in the 1930s or the 1920s it would have been more of a concern.[24]

It probably would have been. In the 1940s, Nazis in Germany argued that Jews were of inferior genetic stock, and for that reason they should be exterminated. Had Hitler and Joseph Goebbels, his Minister of Propaganda, been equipped with information about the BRCA1 gene and the schizophrenia loci, they might have had a considerably easier time convincing Europe to go along with the German "final solution" for the "Jewish problem."

The Human Genome Diversity Project frequently encounters the issue of community consent, says Dr. George Annas. The Project's goal is to collect representative genetic material from ethnic groups all over the globe. The question facing the scientists: how do you get permission? "They want to get DNA from the Navajos," says Annas. "The Navajos actually have a tribal council, so [the scientists] have gone to the tribal council for consent. But most groups don't have councils. Who would you get permission from to do tests for Ashkenazi Jews?"

Apparently, because of its proximity to Bethesda, Maryland and the National Cancer Institute, the scientists involved in the BRCA1 and BRCA2 studies decided that representatives from the Jewish community of Washington, D.C. had some sort of authority to give a kind of proxy consent for the entire world Ashkenazi Jewish community. Perhaps it would have been better to get a more representative response. Perhaps there was a reason the scientists did not cast too broad a net: the more people the scientists asked, the greater the chance that somebody might object to the study. Says Annas: "The scientists [involved] really don't want to deal with this issue, because it is too hard."

DECODING ICELAND

One genetically homogeneous community that has directly confronted the issues surrounding ownership and control of genetic information head on is Iceland.

What makes Iceland special is its geography and its heritage. Iceland is an island nation with a population of 270,000 descended from just 20,000 "founders." The nation, which has had little immigration for the past century, has meticulous medical records that date from World War I and stored tissue and DNA samples that date from World War II. Such records, the theory goes, should make it relatively easy for geneticists to identify the genetic causes of many diseases—perhaps hundreds.[25]

In 1996, Dr. Kari Stefansson, a professor at Harvard Medical School, decided to create a commercial venture to tap the genetic heritage of his homeland. He raised $12 million from U.S. venture capital firms and founded the company deCODE Genetics, Inc. The company's plan was to go genetic prospecting on the island of Iceland, working with the cooperation of the people and the government.

Stefansson's company claimed that, in order to justify its investment, it needed an exclusive license to the country's genetic information. In return, it promised that stock in deCODE would be sold to Icelanders. But deCODE's appeal was more than purely financial: the company also maintained that Iceland was in a unique position to benefit humanity, and that the country therefore had a responsibility to exploit its genetic databank. In March 1998, a bill was introduced in Iceland's parliament to give deCODE the license that it sought; three months later, a Gallup Poll revealed that 90% of the nation's population were in favor of the measure.

In December 1998, the parliament passed the bill, giving deCODE a 12-year exclusive license to create Iceland's Health Sector Database (HSD). A controversial element of the parliament's bill was its notion of "presumed consent." Unless an individual fills out a form and sends it to the country's Surgeon General, that person's genetic information will automatically be included in deCODE's database. By July 1999, only 9,000 of the country's 270,000 residents had taken this action and opted out.

Although databanks such as Iceland's Health Sector Database have been contemplated in science fiction, nothing like it has ever been attempted. Not surprisingly, it has created controversy. Mannvernd, the Association of Icelanders for Ethics in Science and Medicine, has waged a campaign against the database:

> The HSD is slated to contain all medical records for the entire population of Iceland. Included will be the present records, all future records, and records ranging back at least 30 years. The Act permits the interconnecting of the medical records to the extensive Icelandic genealogical database as well as to a database of individual DNA genotypes.

> MANNVERND believes that this Act infringes on human rights, personal privacy, and on accepted medical, scientific and commercial standards. We believe that the Act has world-wide implications and that stopping the law should be given a high priority by the world human-rights community. The government of Iceland should be encouraged in the strongest possible terms to reconsider this legislation, and suspend its enactment immediately.[26]

Academics from around the world have protested the project. Typical is a letter to the government of Iceland from Dr. Henry T. Greely, a professor of law at Stanford University, and Dr. Mary Claire King, a world-renowned geneticist and professor of anthropology at the University of Washington.[27] In the letter, Greely and King attack the project on the following four grounds:

Consent. On the issue of consent, King and Greely argue that the people of Iceland cannot properly give consent for the project because they do not know what will be done with the data. The bill

> does allow people to opt out, either in whole or in part, but it does not require that they be told what specific research will be done with their

records. Thus, for example, people who did not want to participate in any way in research on possible genetic links to alcoholism would not necessarily know that their records might be used for that purpose.

Confidentiality. Confidentiality is another problem for a project such as this one, the academics write. Although the database will not include names, the other information in the database could easily be used to triangulate back to the individuals from whom the genetic material came:

> Even in the United States, given relatively few identifying facts, an "anonymous" clinical record may often be narrowed to a handful of our 265 million people. In Iceland, such medically valuable information as sex, age, place of birth, and number of siblings may well allow an Icelander examining the data to identify individuals exactly. That problem may not be solvable. In light of the scientific and medical value of the database, people might reasonably choose to participate, but they should not be assured, falsely, that complete confidentiality can realistically be maintained.

Financial rewards. The issue of financial rewards has plagued the project from the beginning. On its web site, deCODE boasts that 70% of the company's stock is now in the hands of Icelanders. However, the stock is in the hands of Icelandic banks, not the people of the country. Although the company has promised to provide Iceland with free medications and an annual fee for the use of the data, Greely and King doubt that this compensation will amount to anything more than a tiny fraction of the project's overall value:

> The most significant benefit for Iceland appears to be the promise of jobs from a database that "cannot be exported." But an electronically connected database effectively exists wherever computer networks exist; its physical presence in Iceland makes little difference. Research with such a database could, and would, be conducted by scientists sitting at computers in any part of the world. It is simply not believable that any significant part of the world's pharmaceutical or biological research facilities will move to Iceland to be near this database. That this database would be a source of high-paying jobs for more than a few Icelanders seems more a cruel joke than a reality.

Scientific openness. Finally, Greely and King attack the project's scientific openness. Because use of the databank is controlled by a private company engaged in medical research, that company might block access to its competitors:

> This increases the financial value of the database to the licensee, but it decreases the scientific value of the data, which could be used best when it is more openly available. And, in essence, it puts the research use, as well as the financial benefits, of this database not under the control of the

people of Iceland, but in the hands of one for-profit corporation. No matter how trustworthy and public-spirited the present management of that corporation may be, this abdication of control needs to be considered very carefully by Iceland.

The inescapable truth about genetic studies that look at ethnic groups is that the results—good and bad alike—are suffered by individuals who never gave their consent for the original study. Because knowledge cannot be undiscovered, it is vital that we put in place legislation that protects all people from genetic discrimination before more of these studies are contemplated and completed.

Do You Own Your Books?

When you buy a magazine in the supermarket checkout aisle, all you're really buying is the paper in your hands, the ink that smudges on your fingers, and a license to your single copy of the magazine's content in printed form. The words and pictures themselves are not for sale. The same is true when you buy a compact disc, or a computer program, or even listen to the radio. Although it feels as if you are buying the content, you are not: you are buying a license. Furthermore, it's frequently illegal to make a second copy of the material.

Pity the poor publishers: advances in computer technology are making it easier than ever for you to make perfect copies of published material. Faced with this situation, one logical response on the part of publishers might be to lower prices, improve quality and selection, and generally make it easier for people to purchase licensed copies than to make their own or hunt down pirated wares. Few publishers, though, are thinking this way. Instead, they are developing technologies to make copying harder and make it easier to punish those responsible. Invariably, these technologies work by systematically invading the privacy of the consumer.

For decades, the distinction between physical possession of a printed book and ownership of the words inside the covers was irrelevant to many people. The high cost of copying printed information effectively prevented people from making their own, unauthorized copies of the book's content. And even if a few people did make copies, who cared? Although two commercial photocopying processes existed in the 1950s—diffusion-transfer and thermography—neither of them could produce copies on plain paper. The result were copies that smelled funny, felt funny, and didn't look very good.

Everything changed in 1959, when a company called Haloid Xerox, Inc., introduced the Xerox 914 copier. Based on an invention that Chester Carlson had made in 1937, the 914 was the first machine that could automatically make photocopies onto plain paper.[28] The machine revolutionized the white-collar workplace, and turned Haloid Xerox, which renamed itself the Xerox Corporation in 1961, into a billion-dollar giant. Xerox announced the world's first desktop copier, Xerox 813, in 1963. Three years later, Xerox introduced the Xerox Telecopier, the first facsimile transceiver that could send an image over conventional telephone lines. In 1973, Xerox started selling the 6500 color copier, a machine capable of making full-color copies onto plain paper or transparencies.

Copies made with Xerox copiers were, for all practical purposes, just as usable as the originals. In some cases, the copy was better—for example, a photocopy of a newspaper article wouldn't yellow. And with the 1968 introduction of the Xerox 3600 (the first copier that could produce 60 copies per minute on ordinary paper), and the Xerox 4000 (the first copier that could automatically produce two-sided copies) in 1970, it was increasingly clear to publishers that photocopiers were on their way to becoming do-it-yourself printing presses for republishing copyrighted material.

The photocopier was not the only technology to assault intellectual property. The audiocassette, introduced in the 1960s, made it possible for consumers to produce their own tapes of recorded music—either by copying from records or by recording directly off the radio. Videocassette recorders, which became available in the early 1970s, opened up movies for piracy. Home computers created a whole new category of material that could be illegally copied: computer software. And unlike photocopiers, cassette recorders, and videocassette decks, computers posed a special copyright threat: because digital information can be copied without loss, computers could make perfect copies of computer programs, and indeed, of any other kind of information that could be digitized.

In 1976, Congress rewrote the nation's copyright law. The lawmakers' intent was to bring copyright more in step with the new technologies' ability to make low-cost but faithful reproductions of original works. Under the old law, an author had to claim that a work was copyrighted or risk having it enter the public domain; the new law held that anything, once fixed in a tangible form, was automatically copyrighted. The law also created special exemptions on copyright restrictions—exemptions for libraries and for "fair use." Essentially, *fair use* meant that users were given implicit licenses, by the Congress of the United States, to make limited copies of copyrighted material without first needing to get permission from the copyright holder. (It is the principle of fair use, for example, that allows me to quote from magazine articles in this book without first obtaining written permission.)

To simplify the process of getting reprint permission, Congress established the Copyright Clearing House in 1978. The Clearing House is a centralized, not-for-profit organization that accepts payments from end users for photocopies and electronic copies, and transfers the revenue back to the copyright holders.

The new copyright law created stiff penalties for copyright violation. Over the years, Congress has made copyright penalties considerably harsher: in many cases, copyright violation is now a felony, with penalties reaching into the hundreds of thousands of dollars and more than a dozen years in jail.

But rather than relying exclusively on the legal deterrent, publishers embarked on a project to make unauthorized copying impossible. In the 1970s, some newsletter publishers started printing their missives on gray paper with special nonreproducing blue ink. Videotape publishers tested various systems for distorting the video signals on tapes so the tapes could be played but not rerecorded. Computer software publishers experimented with multiple forms of copy protection for software. All of these copy protection systems worked to some extent, but none of them worked well: none of them could stop sophisticated software pirates; and almost all of them annoyed legitimate customers.

The rise of the World Wide Web has further complicated the problem of illegal copying. On the Web, it is all too easy to copy an article or a photograph and send it by electronic mail to somebody else. Copyrighted articles are routinely forwarded to mailing lists that are read by tens of thousands of readers. Almost always, these copyright violations are without the knowledge or consent of the copyright holder. And while many casual violations are innocent, the Internet has also sparked rampant worldwide trade in *warez*, or pirated software. The very features that make computers usable for legitimate purposes—high-speed access, search engines, and encryption—are good tools for piracy as well.

According to a 1996 study by the Business Software Alliance and the Software Publishers Association, "of the 523 million new business software applications used globally during 1996, 225 million units—nearly one in every two—were pirated. . . . Revenue losses to the worldwide software industry due to piracy were estimated at $11.2 billion in 1996."

With copy protection clearly not working, publishers are turning to a new technology called *watermarking* to attack the piracy problem. Watermarking won't stop software piracy, but it has the potential to reveal the identities of people who engage in the practice—or, at the very least, people who are a little too careless with their computers.

DATA HIDING

Hold a piece of expensive bond paper up to the light and you are likely to see a *watermark*, a design that's produced by pressing the paper with a wire design during the drying process. Watermarks were developed in Italy during the thirteenth century. Italian papermakers used them as a way of labeling their wares—and also a way of detecting counterfeits and forgeries.

Watermarks have been reborn in the digital age. Like a paper watermark, a digital watermark is piece of information that is hidden when an object is viewed casually, but stands out when you know how to see it. Most digital watermarks have been developed for intellectual property rights management systems. The systems are designed to let the publishers of photographs and other kinds of digital information feel safe publishing it in electronic form. By hiding a watermark inside the document, the publisher can prove at a later time that some other individual or organization has copied their data and used it without permission. The best digital watermark systems are those where the watermark is *durable*—able to survive having a photograph cropped or processed with some sort of digital filter.

There are many digital watermarking systems. One system, developed by researchers at IBM, can hide a watermark the size of a credit card inside a photograph that is the size of a magazine page without any perceptible change to the page-sized image. In a demonstration, the scientists hid the words "IBM Research" inside a photograph of IBM's Watson Research Labs. The watermark can be extracted from the image even if the image is altered—and in that case, the watermark plainly shows that an attempt has been made to deceive. As an added bonus, the watermark image itself can be encrypted with a special key. Using this key, the publisher can decrypt the watermark and reveal the theft. But potential pirates can't examine an image and tell if it is watermarked or not—or if they have altered the image enough to remove the watermark.

Photographs aren't the only kind of digital information that can be watermarked. The Argent Digital Watermark System, developed by the DICE Company, stores digital watermark information in audio and video recordings. The Argent system can record 2100 bits per second in a stream of audio—roughly equivalent to 70 pages of text in a 10-second sample. Information can be encrypted, so that only the song's publisher can decode the data, or it can be unencrypted, so that anybody can access it. The system is also fast—the watermark can be stamped into the music as the song is played over the radio or downloaded over the Internet.

Digital Watermarking

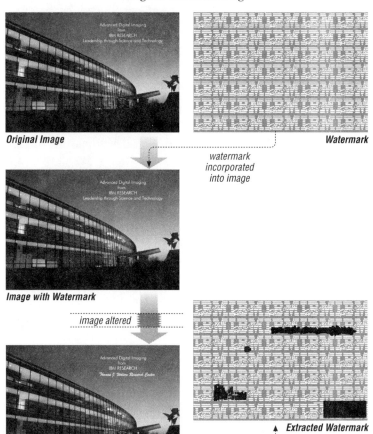

These photographs, provided by Dr. Minerva M. Yeung at the IBM T.J. Watson Research Center, show how a watermark can be hidden in a photograph in such a way that the watermark survives even if the picture itself is damaged. The top row shows the original image and the watermark that is to be applied. Once the watermark is added, the resulting image is virtually indistinguishable from the original image. The bottom two images show a small modification made to the photograph, and the resulting damage that occurs in the watermark when it is extracted. Digital watermark systems create powerful ways to track images both on and off the Internet. Because watermarks can be encrypted, the users of these images need never know about the watermarks that they contain. [Photos courtesy IBM]

One particularly interesting feature of Argent is that it permits multiple digital watermark channels to be stored inside a single song. DICE has many suggestions for how to use these channels. One channel might be an unencrypted channel, which would allow a computer or high-end stereo to display the copyright, title, tracks, and other information associated with a musical piece. Another channel might be an *encrypted distribution channel*, which would indicate the specific rights under which the music was licensed from the producer to the distributor.

MCA Studios in Los Angeles is the largest licensee of the Argent system to date, says Scott Moskowitz, president of DICE.[29] MCA is experimenting with using the system to brand music that is being sent to distributors and sold to the public. The Argent technology can also be used to search for illegally copied digitized music on the Internet or in the libraries of online service providers. DICE also hopes to license its technology to online providers themselves, who will be able to use it to police their own archives. The search technology could also be built into a web search engine that would automatically scan the Internet, seeking out copyright violations.

But the Argent system can do a lot more than simply embed copyright information. A third digital watermark channel, the *encrypted ownership channel*, could have stamped into it the name of the person who bought the song, how much money they paid, when they bought it, from where, and the particular license they purchased. Thus, every song processed with the Argent system could contain its own digitally signed receipt. To make use of this channel, each person who received a copy of the song would need to have that song uniquely personalized for them—for example, downloaded specifically to their computer, or specially recorded for them on a recordable CD. Music personalized in this way, Moskowitz says, would be a potent deterrent to piracy.

"If you tell [purchasers] that redistributing this content is basically the same as redistributing their credit card number, it's likely that they will be more cautious," explains Moskowitz.

But making good on such a threat is not an easy task. It requires that everybody who purchases or otherwise gets access to the song have their identity verified by the music distributor and watermarked into the music before they gain possession. And it requires that the music distributor keep this information on file, so customers can be tracked down and punished when copyright violations are discovered. Faced with such draconian measures, many consumers might decline to make a music purchase—or they might deliberately give false information or try to otherwise subvert the system.

Turning Your Computer Against You

Similar watermarks are under development for watermarking documents and images downloaded over a computer. Many of these systems rely on running *trusted software* on the end user's computer. The end user software meshes with software running on the publisher's computer. The software on the publisher's computer assures that each user will be given his or her own unique, personalized, and watermarked version of the document. The software on the client's computer monitors the end user. The client software records the use, attempts to prevent the user from making an unauthorized copy, and, in some cases, reports statistics back to the publisher. The client software is called "trusted" because end users need to trust it: once the software is running on the end user's computer, there is no effective way to audit its use.

Today's computers are rarely willing conspirators to such systems. A general-purpose desktop computer running Windows or the Macintosh operating system can easily be reprogrammed to circumvent any sort of dictate from copyright owners. But computers of the future could certainly be equipped with hardware that enforced particular copyright restrictions.

InterTrust, based in Silicon Valley, is one of several corporations laying the groundwork for such a system. InterTrust has developed a comprehensive scheme for delivering digital content to end users, with predefined "business rules," such as the following.

- *Purchase.* The user makes a one-time payment and receives unlimited use.

- *Pay-per-use.* The user makes a small payment each time the information is used.

- *Upfront fee.* An initial payment is made, followed by smaller, successive payments.

- *Rent-to-own.* Unlimited access is given after a certain number of payments are made.

- *Free use.* As its name implies, this would allow unlimited access without charge.

The system automatically tracks each user, charges her the appropriate amount of money, prohibits her from removing copyright information, and prevents her from trying to make use of rights that she hasn't purchased. With InterTrust's system, you might pay five cents to view a document on the Internet, an additional ten cents to print it out, and one cent for the right to send it to a friend—who would then be

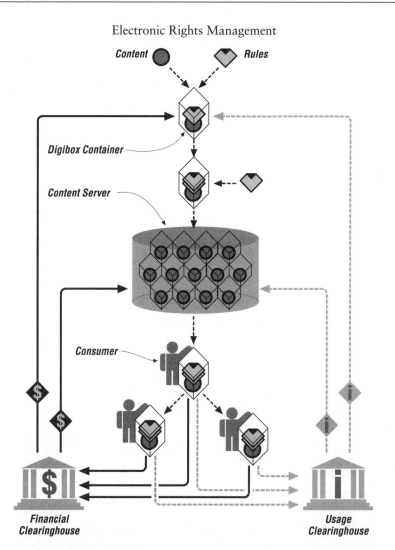

Electronic Rights Management

The InterTrust DigiBox is a system for transporting copyrighted information from a creator, through a distributor, to the end consumer—and for extracting payment from the consumer in return. Called *rights management*, the system relies on strong cryptography to protect the information and proprietary software to prevent the information from being copied once it is decrypted on the end user's computer. But the system can be bypassed by special software running on a person's home computer. For this reason, in 1999, the U.S. Congress passed and President Clinton signed the Digital Millennium Act. Among other things, the Digital Millennium Act makes it a crime for a person to disable copy protection software running on his or her own computer. [Artist's drawing courtesy Chris Reilley, Reilley Design, with permission of InterTrust] charged five cents for the right to read more than the first few paragraphs. InterTrust is banking on the idea that corporations will be willing to distribute large amounts of information at very low prices if they can be assured that they will be paid for all legitimate use—and that illegitimate use will automatically be prohibited.

Digital signatures are one of the basic building blocks of rights management systems such as InterTrust's. A *digital signature* is a cryptographically sealed block of information that can be created by one person (or organization) and verified by another. Using a digital signature system it's possible to stamp a document with a unique identifier, signer's name, location, the time, and other sorts of information.

Signatures are quite flexible. Like watermarks, a song could be signed once by its author, again by its publisher, and again by each person who wants to transmit it electronically. But digital signatures can also be verified very quickly. Electronic networks such as the Internet can be programmed not to carry information unless the person who is transmitting it also has digitally signed it. Computers, likewise, can be programmed not to accept information unless it is properly signed.

Watermarks and digital signatures are powerful tools for eliminating the anonymity that until now has been inherent in digital media. Citizens of the future may look back at the last days of the twentieth century and marvel that identical copies of books, compact discs, video tapes, and electronic information were ever distributed to thousands, let alone millions, of consumers. They may be more amazed still that all these consumers possessed computers, tape decks, and copying machines capable of stamping out limitless numbers of perfectly usable, if not identical, copies. What was there to stop widespread piracy, other than people's consciences?

Indeed, the fear of watermarking systems may very well stop much of the unsophisticated, casual piracy so pervasive today. But these systems will probably not make serious inroads against determined insiders, who have access to the digital information before the watermark is laid down. "I was in Dublin last December [1996] when U2 finished their album. Within a month, two singles off the album were being distributed over the Web without their knowledge," says Moskowitz. Almost certainly, those tracks came from insiders at the studio.

And even if watermark systems become widespread, determined pirates will still find untraceable ways of purchasing disks they are intent on copying. MCA might mandate that nobody can buy a compact disc without showing a photo ID and being fingerprinted. But that won't stop some criminal copyright gang from breaking into the house of an innocent teenager, stealing all her tunes, spitting out millions of copies, and letting her take the fall. Ultimately, watermark systems are about using institutionalized fear and control as tools for preventing copyright theft.

DO YOU OWN WHAT YOU DO?

If you want to see a first-run movie in New York City, you need to plan in advance. That's because nobody in Manhattan stands in lines anymore to buy tickets. Instead, they pick up the phone and call 777-FILM—usually early in the week—and purchase tickets for a specific show over the phone. The MovieFone company, started in 1989, now sells tickets for 11,500 screens in 30 major cities—60% of the country's theaters—and receives between 1.5 million and 2.5 million phone calls each week. When *Star Wars: Episode 1—The Phantom Menace* opened in May 1999, advance tickets purchased through MovieFone completely sold out every Manhattan theater.

Currently, MovieFone makes its money from advertisements played over the phone and a commission on the tickets it sells. But the company, which was purchased by America Online in February 1999, may soon have another important revenue stream: analytical market information that predicts which movies will succeed, which will flop, and by how much.

When *The Lost World: Jurassic Park* opened Memorial Day weekend in 1997, it accounted for 59% of all tickets sold by MovieFone. At the end of the weekend, the movie had received a 61% market share for all tickets sold in the U.S. And that wasn't just a fluke. When *Love and War* opened on January 24, 1997, the movie commanded an 8% share of MovieFone calls, and a 9% market share.

According to an article in the *New York Times*, this level of prediction is unheard of: "The biggest movie tracking company, National Research Group of Los Angeles, depends on extensive interviews with a sample of potential moviegoers to project interest in movies. That method reportedly has a plus-or-minus error margin of 5 percentage points."[30] Other tracking services do no better.

"While most of the movie industry isn't sure until Friday and Saturday how a movie is going to do, a look at the MovieFone data can give you a strong indication earlier in the week," Drew Marcus, an analyst at Alex, Brown & Sons, told the *New York Times*. This may be because MovieFone is *not* a tracking service. Instead, MovieFone is actually sampling the market.

Analytical information such as this is incredibly valuable to the theater industry: it allows multiscreen theaters to determine how many screens to devote to each movie, which allows them to maximize profits. MovieFone is now exploring ways to profit from this unexpected data mine. And of course, MovieFone isn't alone. Jeff Bezos, president of Amazon.com, told me that his company can predict how well a book will sell months before it is released by looking at advance orders from consumers. Infoseek, the Internet search engine, has compiled lists of the most sought after web sites by analyzing which terms are searched for most often. This information can be turned around and sold to advertising agencies.[31]

But whose information are these companies actually selling? The data resides in MovieFone's computers, so perhaps it belongs to that company. On the other hand, neither MovieFone nor Amazon.com nor Infoseek could create this information without the help of its customers: perhaps the proceeds should be split. And who sets the limits on what these companies can do with their collected information? Because customers purchase MovieFone tickets with credit cards, MovieFone knows each customer's identity; it could sell that information to marketers, as well. Or MovieFone's new owner, America Online, could combine movie preferences with other information and sell the resulting datastream to an information boutique.

As we saw in the last chapter, many supermarkets and pharmacies already exploit their consumer information in this manner. Supermarkets, at least, pay their customers for this right by giving them a discount when customers present their courtesy cards.

Identity, combined with transaction history, is valuable. It's possible in the future that newspapers might have different prices depending on how much personal information you are willing to reveal: free if you are willing to give the publisher your name, address, and phone number; ten cents if you're willing to divulge your age and sex; one dollar if you wish to read it anonymously—that is, without allowing the publisher to make commercial use of your identity.

Identity isn't everything, of course. MovieFone shows that potentially lucrative information can be generated from transactions that have been stripped and consolidated. But it is unreasonable to think that companies such as MovieFone will stop at the selling of bulk data if more money can be made by selling information that is personally identified.

DO YOU WANT TO USE OWNERSHIP TO PROTECT YOUR PRIVACY?

Property and privacy are both ideas that are thousands of years old, but the idea of using intellectual property regimes to protect a person's privacy still hasn't gotten off the ground. Perhaps we are lucky that this is the case. It's not at all clear that corporate America would readily cede such a valuable right to consumers. Americans might end up having to pay rent on their own names in order to use them.

At the Federal Trade Commission hearings on privacy issues, John Ford, vice president for privacy and external affairs at Equifax, said that there are two ways of looking at the ownership of data. Some people say "this is information that belongs to me and therefore you shouldn't be using it," said Ford. "Others would argue that it's not your information, it is information about you."[32]

I keep an address book on my computer with the names, phone numbers, and email addresses of my family, my closest friends, and other people I have met. At last count, there were 1,386 names in the file. I have another file of business contacts. It has 1,579 entries, some with three or four individual names. Would I give people or companies the option to remove themselves from my address book? Probably not. After all, it's my address book.

CHAPTER NINE

KOOKS AND TERRORISTS

JULY 17, 1996—The Flight of Trans World Airlines Flight 800 started like many others: with a delay. It was a hot summer night, and the aircraft waited on the tarmac for more than 30 minutes before taking off. The Boeing 747 had 230 people aboard as it speedily departed from John F. Kennedy Airport in New York and climbed over Long Island Sound. Then, roughly 30 minutes into the flight, something went terribly wrong. Witnesses on the ground reported seeing a small explosion, two objects flying through the air, and a second, much larger explosion. The jetliner plummeted more than 10,000 feet into the waters below. Everyone on board was killed.

Almost immediately, agents from the New York office of the Federal Bureau of Investigation began investigating the explosion, describing the pieces of aircraft found floating as a watery crime scene. Wreckage, debris, and personal effects were taken to a huge hangar on Long Island, where investigators began the painstakingly morbid task of reconstructing the carcass of Flight 800. Within a few days, divers began searching the bottom of the sea for more evidence. Meanwhile, theories about the flight's destruction were circulating at a fast and furious rate, both inside and outside the Bureau. Soon it was clear that there were only three possible explanations for the crash: mechanical failure, a bomb, or a surface-to-air missile.

An unprecedented evidence collection effort continued over the following months. Twisted bits of metal, bolts, even swatches of fabric were located, taken to the hangar, and analyzed. The investigation would ultimately cost more than $100 million. The FBI swung into action. Assuming that TWA Flight 800 had been downed by a bomb, the FBI worked with politicians and officials from the airline industry to tighten up security at airports. Many civil libertarians attacked the FBI's measures, saying that they represented sweeping attacks on the privacy and civil liberties of American citizens. But as more bodies were brought in from the waters, these protests rang hollow.

Two weeks after the crash of Flight 800, there was a second explosion. This time the target was the Summer Olympics in Atlanta: one person was killed, and more than a hundred people were injured.

For the first time ever, Americans were required to present photo ID cards before boarding flights, even flights within the United States. Next, the FBI lobbied for a nationwide passenger profiling system, so individuals thought to be predisposed to committing acts of terrorism could be proactively intercepted at airports and searched. (One result of these searches was the harassment, embarrassment, and, in some cases, detention of thousands of Arab-Americans.)

The U.S. Postal Service, meanwhile, instituted sweeping restrictions on the mails: no longer could packages or envelopes weighing more than one pound be dropped into mailboxes—after all, such a package might contain a bomb! Instead, heavy packages would have to be taken to a post office and handed to a clerk, so that a visual identification might be made. These restrictions and others continue to this day.

Over the past decade, measures resulting from the fear of domestic terrorism have had a significant impact on the lives of most Americans. This chapter asks a simple question: do these measures have any real effect? To understand this question, we need to understand more about terrorism itself.

THE DEMOCRATIZATION OF DESTRUCTIVE TECHNOLOGY

The face of terrorism is changing. For much of the nineteenth and twentieth centuries, terrorism was a tool for political change. Terrorism was war fought by poor people. Terrorists had specific goals—an end to slavery, the demise of a particular regime, political recognition—and they used violence and fear to help achieve their ends.

Old-style terrorists often worked in large groups; sometimes they were even parts of legitimate political or quasi-political organizations. Invariably, the sheer numbers in these groups provided a kind of moderating influence on the terrorists' actions. Even if one wacko wanted nothing more than to kill as many innocent bystanders as possible, his compatriots would stop him, arguing that wanton violence would not strengthen their cause—if anything, mayhem would merely strengthen their opposition's resolve.

The terrorists of the 1980s and 1990s were a transitional breed. While they were often militants working with large organizations and even governments, they used terror as a weapon not of change but of revenge. The bombing of Pan American Flight 103 over Lockerbie,

Scotland, in 1988 was probably retaliation for the U.S. bombing of Tripoli earlier in that decade. Likewise, the Americans taken hostage in Lebanon during the 1980s were probably kidnapped in retaliation for the U.S. shelling of Beirut in 1984. Although the U.S. public saw these actions as terrorist attacks, they are more properly though of as military actions.

The terrorist of tomorrow is the irrational terrorist. This new terrorist does not particularly want to change the enemy's mind. Instead, he "sees the sheer physical annihilation of the enemy as a productive result," says Louis Rene Beres, a professor of political science at Purdue University, who has spent decades studying the roots and prevention of terrorism.[1] The new generation of terrorists work in small cells, in pairs, or even alone. These new terrorists frequently aren't interested in negotiation, don't rationally consider the long-term consequences of their actions, and frequently aren't even concerned with their own survival—in fact, they may actively work towards their own death. "An irrational terrorist might simply be an insane group that sees mass death as a desirable end from an ecological point of view," says Beres. "Or an irrational terrorist might see an act of terror and loss of life as causing some other political event."

"What we are dealing with is a [new] kind of pathology—a disease," said Professor Beres in a lecture at the University of Washington in the spring of 1997. And so far, the U.S. has been lucky—we have only seen a tiny amount of anti-American terror. But Beres thinks that our luck may soon run out.

The question we face, then, is a simple one: is it possible to prevent future incidents of terrorism by systematically monitoring all potential terrorists and imprisoning them before they can strike? And, if so, are such measures worth the cost?

THE DISH OF DEATH

A lot of packages move each day through the mailroom at the B'nai B'rith International Headquarters in Washington, D.C. This one was different. The 8×10 bubble-wrap envelope was torn, and a red, gelatinous substance was seeping out. And the package was addressed only to "B'nai B'rith," no name, no room number.

The mailroom clerk brought the package to Carmen Fontana, the Jewish organization's director of security. Fontana told me:

> The package just didn't look right. Then I smelled it. It had an ammonia type odor. I was thinking "bomb" 100 percent. I immediately put it in a trash container and brought it outside. When I came back in, I told the guard who was on duty to call the police.

The bomb squad came and X-rayed the package. No bomb appeared to be inside. "So they opened it up," says Fontana. "And once they opened it up, inside the package was a petri dish with this red substance in it. And there were some numbers on the petri dish itself. They ran the numbers and it came back as anthrax.[2]

What followed was an eight-hour siege. Washington, D.C. police immediately closed off a 20-block area around B'nai B'rith headquarters. The package was put in a decontamination box and sent to Bethesda Naval Hospital for analysis. But downtown, the police and fire departments needed to assume the worst. City streets, buildings, and parking lots were closed to the public, effectively preventing more than 10,000 people from going home. Still more people were trapped in the gridlock that was fast enveloping the nation's capital. Meanwhile, because of the risk of contamination, B'nai B'rith's 150 employees were told not to leave the building.

At 8:30 p.m., the Naval Hospital finished its preliminary testing. The red substance contained some bacteria, but it probably wasn't anthrax. Washington health commissioner Dr. Harvey Sloane announced that the Jewish organization's employees could go home. It was all a hoax.

The incident, which took place in April 1997, revealed just how completely unprepared the nation's capital was for a biological attack. Despite having been trained to handle these kinds of terrorist incidents as part of the planning for the 1996 Presidential Inauguration, 14 of the city emergency workers at the scene had inadvertently exposed themselves to the substance and had to be decontaminated. Meanwhile, the quarantine of 150 employees was ill advised, concluded Dr. Jonathan B. Tucker at the Center for Nonproliferation Studies. "A gelled biological agent poses no hazard except through direct contact. . . . Instead of keeping the employees quarantined inside the building for hours and possibly exposing them to a hazardous material, it would have made more sense to move them to another location and keep them under observation until the results of the sample analysis were known."[3]

"It was the unpreparedness that totally blew my mind," says security director Fontana. "I'm not knocking the police department or the fire department—they did the best with what they had. But their training was very, very minimal, if they had any at all. The fire department did not have any of the proper equipment."

Nor did they have the proper training, it would seem. According to Fontana:

You really had to be here to see what they did. We had no decontamination tent, so what they did was pull two fire trucks alongside each other and drape a piece of canvas on top of them. Then they put a piece of plastic on the street. This was our decontamination tub. . . . When they were done spraying us down with this Clorox, the plastic—they just folded it up and shook it up in the street. That just blew my mind. I said, "Well, what happens if this Clorox didn't kill certain aspects of this anthrax? You just infected the whole city." There was just a lack of training. I can think back to when I was in the military 35 years ago; we had chemical and biological warfare practice, and it was nothing like the way these guys were performing.

B'nai B'rith issued a press release the next day, applauding the quick response and courageous work of the city's police and fire departments, but saying that it was "nonetheless gravely disturbed over their apparent lack of preparedness."

"It is inexcusable for police and fire personnel, in a city which is so vulnerable to terrorist incidents, to not have the highest level of training and appropriate resources for dealing with situations as potentially deadly as this. We call upon the city and federal officials to immediately launch an investigation to determine whether or not the city is properly prepared for these types of incidents," said B'nai B'rith executive vice president Dr. Sidney M. Clearfield in a press release distributed the next day.

In fact, if a terrorist had wanted to launch an attack on B'nai B'rith's headquarters, it could have been done with far less fanfare and far more deadly results. Instead of mailing a petri dish with spoof anthrax, a terrorist could have sent a sealed mailing tube containing a poster and the dust of real anthrax spores. For an extremely low-tech attack, a terrorist could simply find the names of B'nai B'rith's favorite catering firm and arrange for poisoned food to be delivered to the organization's next fundraiser.

With targets so vulnerable, civil authorities so unprepared, and toxins so readily available, does it make sense to institute a worldwide dragnet to track and stop suspected terrorists before they strike? Increasingly, the U.S. government is insisting that the answer to this question is yes.

THE CHANGING FACE OF TERRORISM

Despite the fact that it took place almost a year after the downing of TWA Flight 800, the attack on the B'nai B'rith headquarters in April 1997 shows how ineffectual the FBI's antiterrorism guidelines are against the new breed of terrorists. Searching aircraft passengers has no effect when the targets are buildings. Prohibiting packages that are heavier than a pound from being sent through the mails doesn't do any good when a test tube can hold enough bacteria to kill a city.

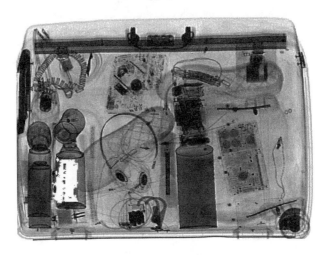

Vivid Baggage Scanner

Vivid Technologies, headquartered in Woburn, Massachusetts, makes sophisticated baggage screening systems for airports and office buildings. The screening system uses X-rays and artificial intelligence to locate guns, explosives, and drugs that are concealed in baggage. Unlike conventional X-ray scanners, which look only at the outlines, the Vivid system examines the energies of back-scattered X-ray emissions to detect the atoms and molecules that are characteristic of explosives and controlled substances. To date, Vivid's primary sales have been outside the United States, since the Federal Aviation Administration prohibits airports from competing with each other on the basis of safety. [Photo courtesy Vivid Technologies]

The world has always had its crazies. What's changing the stakes is the increasing democratization of destructive technology. With a two-barreled shotgun, a criminally insane office worker can kill at most three or four coworkers. With an assault rifle, that same person can kill a dozen people. But with a vial of anthrax, smashed on the floor of an elevator, a crazy person can kill everybody in an entire office building. The danger, as we move forward, is that an ever more sophisticated array of destructive technology is available for angry, irrational individuals to use against society as a whole. Thus, even if the number of kooks and terrorists remains roughly constant, we should expect the number of people killed each year in massacres, bombings, and large-scale attacks to grow gradually over time, as increasingly lethal technology becomes more widely available.

Unfortunately, the number of kooks and terrorists is not remaining constant: it is increasing. As the population grows and society becomes more complex, more individuals are being pushed past the brink and into action. Increased mobility and improved communications are only accelerating the number of dangerous nutcases, because violence, like any other disease, is contagious. A lone crazy can commit, at most, one suicidal operation. But a crazy who travels and teaches can sow the seeds for dozens of incidents.

Terrorists are also emboldened by the action and inaction of the world's nations. During the 1980s, the world stood by while Iraq used chemical weapons, first in the Iran-Iraq war, and later on its own Kurdish citizens. "Iraq was allowed to get away with chemical murder for five years," says Leonard A. Cole, who studies chemical and biological weapons and teaches at Rutgers University. "At the time, we were pleased to see Saddam Hussein and Ayatollah Khomeini keeping themselves busy," Cole says.[4] But by failing to condemn the use of these weapons, the world community legitimized them.

Nowhere has the combination of charisma and criminality been more apparent in recent years than in the March 1995 chemical attack on the Tokyo subway system by the religious cult Aum Shinrikyo ("Supreme Truth"). Despite a long history of dealing with terrorist organizations, Japan was completely unprepared for the attack. The Aum attack killed a dozen people and injured more than 5,000 more. Of those injured, 135 were members of the Tokyo fire and police departments who had rushed into the subways without proper protection.

The terrorist cult had detailed plans of the Tokyo subway system and had placed its lethal canisters in the correct locations. The cult had no demands and the attack came without warning. Aum's sole purpose was to kill as many people as possible, and in so doing, hasten the coming of Armageddon. Indeed, Aum's ultimate plans called for the destruction of the entire human race. "It was apparent that they had enough base chemical to make enough sarin gas to kill half the population of the world," says James D. Kallstrom, who headed the FBI's New York Office and oversaw the investigation of TWA Flight 800.[5] In the months of revelations that followed the Tokyo attack, Kallstrom says, the FBI learned that the cult had also developed a biological weapons program that was working on agents such as anthrax and botulism toxin.

So why didn't more people die in the Aum attacks? Because the human race was lucky. Or perhaps because of systematic failures in the Japanese education system. In their race to plan the end of the world, Aum's leaders had recruited scientists, not engineers. The scientists knew the chemistry of the weapons they were making—but they didn't know how to disperse the agents.

Like many experts in the field, Cole believes that there are two simultaneous strategies that must be pursued to prevent chemical, biological, and nuclear terrorism. The first is for the nations of the world to agree that such weapons are intolerable and to ban their use. The second is to dedicate the necessary resources to monitoring the supplies necessary to create such terror weapons, as well as monitoring the potential terrorists.

HOME-GROWN TERRORISM

Monitoring terrorists has become a top priority at the Federal Bureau of Investigation, which has repeatedly said that the job of defending America against terrorism is being complicated by new technologies. In the early 1990s, the FBI floated several technical proposals to make the job easier. Among these proposals were the development of new wiretapping technologies, restrictions on cryptography, and the prescreening of airline passengers. One of the leading voices for these programs inside the FBI was James D. Kallstrom, who was the FBI's chief of engineering in Quantico, Virginia, before he became director of the FBI's New York office.

In 1997, I met with Kallstrom to talk about the problems of terrorism and the potential impacts on freedom and privacy. The meeting happened during the middle of the TWA Flight 800 investigation, and it was clear that the ongoing investigation had taken a toll on Kallstrom. A year later, he left the FBI to take a job as a vice president at a major financial institution.

Kallstrom told me that monitoring terrorists is very difficult:

> When I came to the FBI, the challenge of the day was organized crime. That was really child's play compared to the challenge of the groups that we deal with today. They don't have a definitive hierarchical structure. They don't have disciplined rules of engagement. They don't have a clearinghouse of authorities. They don't have central control. They don't have all those things that allow you, if you get the foot in the door of that organization, [to] pretty much know what the organization is doing.

> Today we just have people who stand up and profess what is wrong with any segment of our society and incite the audience with rhetoric and passion. You don't know which group of two or three nuts takes that rhetoric and moves that rhetoric into action—unless you are right there with those two people or three people.

More than most countries, the United States has had a long history of problems by violent individuals acting alone. One reason for this violence is the easy availability of guns in the United States.

John Wilkes Booth was an outspoken supporter of slavery who organized a band of men to kill Abraham Lincoln and Secretary of State William Seward, but ultimately it was Booth himself who pulled the trigger and shot Lincoln on April 14, 1865. Charles J. Guiteau shot President James Garfield on July 2, 1881. The anarchist Leon Czolgosz shot President William McKinley on September 6, 1901 at the Pan-American Exposition in Buffalo. Lee Harvey Oswald shot and killed John F. Kennedy on November 22, 1963. John W. Hinckley, Jr. shot and seriously wounded President Ronald Reagan on March 30, 1981. Attempts on the President's life have continued to this day: during Bill Clinton's first term, one person was arrested for firing shots from an assault weapon at the White House.[6] Another person died flying a small plane into the White House lawn, just underneath President Clinton's bedroom window.[7]

But while the FBI remains concerned about lone gunmen, the real action these days is with mass-murder terrorist actions. And once again, a contributing factor is the ready availability of destructive technology. In just the past decade, terrorists set off a car bomb in the World Trade Center in New York City, killing six people, injuring thousands, and causing $500 million in damage. Timothy McVeigh blew up a car bomb outside the Alfred Murrah Federal Building in Oklahoma City and killed hundreds.

Kallstrom believes that it's entirely possible that a single terrorist attack will kill more than 10,000 people sometime within the next 30 years. "I am not going to predict it, but I think that it would be naive to say it isn't possible," he says. And if it happens, he says, there will be a tremendous backlash on the part of lawmakers and the public to pass draconian laws and institute a virtual police state to make sure that such an attack never happens again.

"Legislators and lawmakers generally don't react to things without a body count and the prediction of a body count—they don't want to hear about it. They want to see the body count. It is not good enough to feel the door and feel that it is warm; you have to have smoke coming from under the door. . . . As we move to this new millennium, the risk of this mentality is terrible." Instead of waiting for the body count and a resulting Congressional attack on civil liberties, says Kallstrom, the United States needs to start preparing now for the unthinkable.

LOOSE NUKES

Nuclear terrorism seems like an awesome threat to world security. How concerned do we really need to be?

At first glance, many people think that nuclear bombs would make an ideal terrorist weapon. Nuclear bombs can be made as small as a large suitcase and can instantly vaporize a large chunk of a big city. Bombs can be easily transported to most cities in the world by a boat, truck, or small plane. Skyscrapers can be used to provide low-cost air bursts, maximizing the kill radius. What's more, nuclear devices can be set off by remote control, and booby-trapped so attempts to disarm them will result in detonation.

But, in fact, nuclear bombs will probably not become trendy tools of garden-variety terrorists. Nuclear weapons are tremendously complicated to build, and they require significant amounts of highly radioactive bomb-grade nuclear weapons material, such as uranium-235 or plutonium-239. Only the most sophisticated nation-states have constructed and tested their own devices. Therefore, it seems unlikely that a terrorist organization would attempt to build its own nuclear weapons.

Instead of building a weapon, a terrorist organization would more likely attempt to steal a nuclear device, obtain it from a state sponsor, or purchase it on the black market. Fortunately, as far as we know, nuclear weapons are still guarded with the highest level of security. Furthermore, many bombs are equipped with computerized interlocks that prevent their detonation without proper authorization. Atomic weapons are so obviously important to control that it seems doubtful that they will escape into terrorist hands.

While popular culture has focused on the risks posed by nuclear explosive devices, a far more likely terrorist threat is the intentional scattering of radioactive material. Compared with nuclear weapons, there is surprisingly little control over radioactive nuclear material. This material is available from numerous sources—radioactive waste, laboratory and medical supplies, even industrial radiation generators—and many of these sources are poorly guarded. And this material can be a powerful terrorist weapon all by itself, virtually guaranteeing cancer for anyone who is properly exposed.

Using plutonium as a radiological terror weapon has many advantages over using that same plutonium in a bomb. A terrorist can blow up a nuclear bomb only once, but that same terrorist can divide a pile of plutonium into many little pieces, each of which can be used separately. A terrorist organization might have a hard time convincing political leaders and the media that it really has planted a nuclear bomb in New York City, and that it is not simply bluffing. On the other hand, that same terrorist organization could easily shave off a few milligrams of plutonium, seal it in a piece of plastic, and send it to ABC News for analysis.

Another problem with nuclear bomb terrorism is that the devices simply kill too many people over too wide an area. Who would capitulate to a terrorist organization that blew up Hartford, Connecticut? On the other hand, a terrorist organization that released small bits of radioactive plutonium at key subway stations week after week might eventually get somebody to take its demands seriously. For all of these reasons, radiological terrorism is sure to be a more serious threat than nuclear bomb terrorism in the coming years. Fortunately, even this threat can be managed.

While the terrorists might be willing to die for their cause, the suppliers of the materials might be wary of being poisoned. Furthermore, the radiation itself can act as a beacon for the authorities, bringing them to the terrorists' lair. The Sandia National Laboratories has developed a series of portable neutron- and gamma-radiation detectors designed to be used by the Department of Energy's Nuclear Emergency Search Team (NEST). A terrorist who threatened to disperse a few grams of plutonium might soon find himself surrounded.

Current disarmament policy ignores the risk of radiological terrorism by failing to provide for the safe disposal of nuclear materials after they are removed from Russian warheads. Says political scientist Beres:

> We may have been reducing the risk of international war and increasing the risk of nuclear terrorism by not paying for the safekeeping or disposal of the resulting material. Nuclear scientists desperate for cash are selling [nuclear] material. . . . The security of humankind is dependent on some poor scientists in Russia not having money to buy a refrigerator. It would be cheaper to buy him a refrigerator.[8]

In many parts of the world, including the United States, terrorists don't even need to obtain nuclear materials in order to engage in nuclear terrorism—all they need to do is bomb a nuclear power plant. Most nuclear power plants were built at a time when conventional weapons could not pierce a typical reactor's five- to ten-foot-thick reinforced concrete containment vessels. As a result, reactors were defended against nuclear attacks and internal sabotage, but not against the high-powered, armor-piercing, mobile conventional weapons developed in recent years. In his book *Nuclear Power Plants as Weapons for the Enemy: An Unrecognized Military Peril*, Bennett Ramberg notes that a 2,000 pound conventional bomb can penetrate more than 11 feet of concrete and up to 15 inches of steel. "Heavy, shaped charges are even more effective," he notes.[9] Destroyed with conventional weapons, a typical nuclear power plant could contaminate 10,000 square kilometers.

The nature of the nuclear threat is such that a global antiterrorism monitoring effort will prove to be far more effective if we monitor potential sources of radioactive materials rather than potential terrorists. After all, we know where the nuclear material is; we don't know who the terrorists may be. Monitoring the material is cheaper and presents fewer civil liberties issues.

CHEMICAL-BIOLOGICAL TERRORISM

On September 17, 1984, the Wasco-Sherman Public Health Department in Oregon starting receiving reports of people sick with fever, chills, headache, nausea, vomiting, abdominal pain, and bloody stools. All of the people had eaten at one of two restaurants in The Dalles, Oregon. Doctors who performed stool cultures determined that the patients were suffering an outbreak of *Salmonella Typhimurium*. The outbreak eventually affected more than 38 restaurants and sickened 751 people—45 of whom had to be hospitalized.

Investigators were unable to explain the cause of the poisonings. There seemed to be no apparent correlation between the cases, other than the fact that many people had eaten from salad bars. At one restaurant, everybody who had used the blue cheese dressing got sick; at another restaurant, it was the ranch dressing. One of the poisoned restaurants had prepared two private banquets—both with salad bars—and nobody at these functions had come down with the disease. Other people with *Salmonella* had consumed only the coffee.

Laboratory analyses of the cultured stool samples were stranger still. All of the bacteria shared a set of exceedingly rare characteristics. For example, the strain in the samples did not ferment the sugar alcohol dulcitol, even though 98% of the *Salmonella* responsible for traditional *Salmonella* poisonings do ferment dulcitol. Even more confusing, all of the *Salmonella* collected from the victims had identical plasmids and antibiogram structure; however, in a national survey conducted between 1979 and 1980 of 233 strains of *Salmonella Typhimurium*, no other bacteria had a profile that matched.

Law enforcement officials immediately suspected that the outbreak was intentional. But they couldn't figure out who did it or why—there was no apparent motive. A prime suspect was the community of followers of the Bhagwan Sri Rajneesh, who had established a town called Rajneeshpuram on the outskirts of The Dalles and had been at odds with the town's original inhabitants ever since. Indeed, the Rajneeshpuram charter was being challenged in court, and the county commissioners had denied the group building permits. In retaliation, followers were running their own candidates for the county commission in the November 1984 election. Numerous election irregularities had been noted.

As the investigation proceeded, an important piece of evidence emerged tying the Rajneeshpuram group to the poisonings: the commune's medical laboratory had ordered a vial of *Salmonella Typhimurium* from the American Type Culture Collection in Rockville, Maryland, a biomedical supply firm. In 1985, Oregon state and FBI investigators raided the clinic laboratory at Rajneeshpuram. There they found an open vial of *Salmonella Typhimurium*. Laboratory tests on the bacteria inside the vial found that it was indistinguishable from the strains involved in the outbreak. Apparently, the community's medical laboratory had cultured large quantities of the bacteria. Group members had then taken the cultures to restaurants and poured them into salad bar dressings and coffee creamers when nobody was looking.

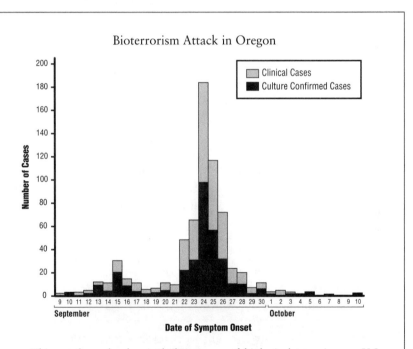

This graph tracks the single largest act of biological terrorism on U.S. soil. Between September 9 and October 20, 1984, more than 750 people infected with the *Salmonella* bacteria presented themselves at clinics and hospitals in The Dalles, Oregon. These people were intentionally infected by a religious community that was attempting to calibrate a biological weapon. The community planned to use its weapon on the eve of an upcoming election. Group members, who would avoid exposure, would then be able to influence the outcome of the voting. [Artist's drawing courtesy Chris Reilley, Reilley Design]

Finally, an informant helped piece together the story. According to the informant, the poisonings in September were a test run for the group's election eve plans. The group's goal was to make so many people sick on the day of the election that the group's own candidates could win. The attack in September had been a test to determine the correct amount of bacteria to use. A previous test run in August had been unsuccessful.

On the strength of the evidence and the testimony, two community members were indicted on March 19, 1986, for product tampering. The defendants pled guilty in April 1986 and were sentenced to four and a half years in prison each. One was Rajneesh's chief of staff, Ma Anand Sheela, who was released and deported to Europe after serving two and a half years.

The poisoning of more than 700 Americans by a religious community should have been a newsworthy event. However, Centers for Disease Control (CDC) investigators decided not to publicize the event further for fear that it might inspire copycat poisonings similar to the copycat Tylenol-cyanide poisonings that took place in 1982. "A report of the findings of the CDC investigation was distributed to state and territorial public health officials, but not submitted for publication," reads an article published in the August 6, 1997 issue of the *Journal of the American Medical Association*. The incident received only scant attention in the national press. The authors only decided to publicize the poisonings after the 1995 Japanese nerve gas attacks. "It is hoped that wider dissemination today of the epidemiologic findings from The Dalles outbreak will lead to greater awareness of the possibility of other incidents and earlier recognition, when or if a similar incident occurs," the article's authors said.[10]

The scientists at Rajneeshpuram aren't the only people who have bought potentially deadly organisms through the mail. On May 5, 1995, a laboratory technician in Ohio named Larry Harris ordered samples of bubonic plague from the same American Type Culture Collection. The company didn't know that Harris was actually a member of a white supremacist organization who had written the request on fake letterhead; they only thought to check his credit card number, not his scientific credentials. The vial probably would have been sent out if Harris hadn't been so impatient: four days after he placed his order, he called up to find out what was taking so long. Suddenly suspicious, the company contacted federal authorities. Harris pled guilty to mail fraud in November 1995.

The Harris incident gained national attention. The following year, Congress added provisions to the 1996 Antiterrorism Law requiring the Centers for Disease Control to closely monitor the shipments of infectious agents. In other words, the CDC would start keeping an eye on the American Type Culture Collection. But the scientists who reported on their handling of the *Salmonella* outbreak in Oregon don't think that this sort of legislation will ultimately be very effective at stopping acts of biological terrorism:

> Can another outbreak like the one that occurred in The Dalles be prevented? It seems unlikely that any regulation of commercially available pathogens could have prevented this outbreak. It would not be necessary to purchase them because this type of culture could be easily obtained from clinical isolates or from raw foods of animal origin available in grocery stores. Production of large quantities of bacteria is inexpensive and involves simple equipment and skills. Standard practices for maintaining salad bars may be inadequate to prevent similar outbreaks in the future with salmonellae or other pathogens. As in many areas of our open society, current practices are inadequate to prevent deliberate contamination of food items by customers.[11]

Biological agents carry fundamental dangers for society, writes Leonard A. Cole in the December 1996 issue of *Scientific American*: "Chemical agents are inanimate, but bacteria, viruses and other live agents may be contagious and reproductive. If they become established in the environment, they may multiply. Unlike any other weapon, they can become more dangerous over time."[12] And contamination can last a long time, he notes: "Gruinard Island, off the coast of Scotland, remained infected with anthrax spores for 40 years after biological warfare tests were carried out there in the 1940s."

In the science fiction thriller *Twelve Monkeys* (Universal Pictures, 1996), director Terry Gilliam tells the story of an environmental terrorist who steals a deadly virus from a genetic engineering laboratory in Philadelphia, then releases it in strategic cities throughout the world. The result: 90% of the human race dies. Those who remain "live underground like animals," says Cole (Bruce Willis), the film's protagonist. Sent back from the year 2020 to the pre-plague Earth, his mission is to get a sample of the original plague organism so that a cure can be found.

Aside from the fantasy of time travel, the premise of *Twelve Monkeys* is basically sound. A single disease *could* sweep across the planet, killing the people and leaving the vegetation and the animals alone. There is even historical precedent.

In 1633, smallpox swept through Native American settlements in New England. In the book *Lies My Teacher Told Me*, James W. Loewen persuasively argues that somewhere between 10 and 20 million people lived in the Americas at the time Columbus arrived; more than 95% of them were killed by disease. Arguably, some of these deaths were intentional, the result of the colonists giving the Indians blankets and other goods that had been used by people infected with smallpox. "Whole towns were depopulated," reads an account from 1829 that cited an earlier, unnamed authority. "The living were not able to bury the dead; and their bodies were found lying above ground many years after. The Massachusetts Indians are said to have been reduced from 30,000 to 300 fighting men."[13]

As we've seen here, it's all but impossible to prevent future biological attacks on U.S. soil: there are simply too many ways to obtain and disburse biological agents. The fact that we haven't had more biowarfare or bioterrorist attacks in this country, or elsewhere in the world, could very well mean that the threats of such attacks are overstated. Nevertheless, the impact would be so dramatic that we must prepare for them.

INFORMATION WARFARE

Back at the FBI's New York Headquarters, what really had James Kallstrom worried wasn't the threat of biological or nuclear terrorism—it was the threat of attacks launched through computer networks, designed to create havoc with computers belonging to banks, hospitals, transportation systems, and other pillars of our society. Says Kallstrom:

> We are using the efficiencies of technology and the Information Age to control everyday things like traffic lights, 911 systems, the environment of buildings, the communications network, and the power grid. We even control the water supply with computers. We are doing more and more things like that. In the old days. . . . Fort Knox was the symbol of how we protected things of great value: we put them in buildings with thick walls and concrete. We put armed guards at the doors, with sophisticated multiple locks and locking bars. We could even build a moat and fill it with alligators. . . . Today [with] things of that same value, you wonder if some teenager is going to go in on the phone lines and steal it all. We are not equipped to deal with those issues both in the government and private industry.

Computers pose a fundamentally different kind of security problem because unlike other machines, computers are general purpose. Change the program, and the computer's behavior changes. The atoms that make up the concrete walls of Fort Knox can't be magically rearranged into poison gas that would kill the soldiers inside the compound, but a computer that's controlling a chemical manufacturing plant can be programmed or reprogrammed to open the wrong valves and blow it up. Computer malfunctions have already caused such explosions. As far as we know, they have been accidents.

One participant at the 1997 Computers, Freedom, and Privacy conference in Burlingame, California, put it this way: "I reasonably believe that if I buy a vacuum cleaner it is not going to suck money out of my wallet and send it to the vacuum cleaner's vendor. But with a computer, there is no way to assure that [a program I download from the Internet] won't take money out of my Microsoft Money application" and send it over the wire to somebody else. Compounding this problem is the push among businesses and computer users for new features and increased connectivity with the outside world—even if those features and connectivity can be exploited by a knowledgeable attacker.

Most business leaders, Kallstrom said, seem completely unequipped to even understand the problem. Kallstrom believes that American companies have created a two-tier system, with upper management that is "generally technically illiterate" and young employees who are very knowledgeable about technology but not very knowledgeable about the company itself, its goals, its history, or its responsibilities. As a result, "you have a whole hierarchy of people who do not know what is going on, who are delegating tremendous amounts of power and responsibility to people with no experience, to people who are more in it for the 'I' than the 'us'."

Newspapers and television stories often celebrate teenagers who can break into important banking, medical, or military computers with relative ease. Even when the press is less than favorable, the threat of punishment is rarely a deterrent.

In April 1996, Attorney General Janet Reno announced that the FBI had conducted the first *Internet wiretap*. An attacker had infiltrated computers at Harvard University and used them to break into systems at the U.S. Army Research Laboratory and Naval Research Labs—then used those facilities to launch attacks against other machines. Ultimately, the attacker broke into military and commercial systems from California to South Korea to Hawaii. The wiretap was eventually traced back to Argentina, and a high-school student named Julio Cesar Ardita. The investigation ended there, because Argentina would not extradite the young offender, as his actions were not a crime in his native land. (In December 1997, Ardita waived extradition and pleaded guilty; he was fined $5,000 and received three years probation.)[14]

In another case, a mentally troubled youth, who operated under the handle "Phantom Dialer," relentlessly broke into computers at universities, major corporations, banks, government agencies, and even top-secret nuclear weapons research facilities. Although he was eventually apprehended by the FBI, authorities decided not to press charges because they thought that no jury would convict.[15]

The next time the United States is engaged in an unpopular war, could six graduate students at the University of Washington who disagree with the war's aims plug in to the Internet and bring U.S. military forces to a halt? Or could a teenager whose mother gets fired from a bank decide to take revenge into his own hands, and erase the information stored in the bank's computers? The new technology has put a tremendous amount of power into the hands of people who may not be capable of using it judiciously. The effect is inherently destabilizing.

THOUGHT CRIME

For years, civil libertarian groups have been arguing against the FBI's attempts to expand its power, saying that the FBI has an institutional history that proves it cannot be trusted to honor people's constitutional rights.

Statements that the FBI is building lists of hostile persons and infiltrating groups cause great concern for many civil libertarians, given the long history of institutional abuse by the FBI and the U.S. government of people who hold unpopular political viewpoints or belong to ethnic minorities. Often these abuses have been carried out under the pretext of national security during times of war. At these times, the citizens of the country, legislators, the executive branch, and even the U.S. court system have conspired to create an atmosphere of fear, hate, and intolerance. To understand people's fears for the future, it is only necessary to look briefly into the past.

The history of the modern surveillance state dates to World War I. Prior to the war, low-level attacks on civil liberties were widespread and tolerated, writes historian Paul Murphy, author of *World War I and the Origin of Civil Liberties*. But the attacks were never organized on a national scale.

At the outset of World War I, the U.S. Bureau of Investigation (the forerunner of the FBI) had only a hundred agents. There was no way the Bureau could staff up in time for wartime activities. Fearful of sabotage and subversion within the U.S., Albert M. Briggs, a Chicago advertising executive, created the American Protective League to help out:

> By the middle of June 1917, the league had branches in almost 600 cities and towns and a membership of nearly 100,000. At its height the membership reached 250,000. Members paid $1.00 to get a badge which first said "Secret Service Division" and later (after the Treasury Department protested about possible confusion with *its* Secret Service) "Auxiliary to the U.S. Department of Justice." From its Washington, D.C. headquarters, the American Protective League used Justice Department stationery and operated as if its members were formal deputies of that body. The result was appalling to many. Having no formal statutory authority to

make arrests, operatives of the league engaged in a variety of investigations probing the loyalty of citizens, the actions of the draft exemption
board, the actual status of conscientious objectors, and the monitoring, in
thousands of cases, of suspicious activities reported by people throughout the country in response to appeals for vigilance in detecting spies and
persons guilty of sabotage. So vigorous did its members become in their
crusade against disloyalty that the Justice Department eventually sought
to restrain league agents.[16]

The American Protective League was just one of many quasi-
official organizations that sprung up during the war. Others were the
Home Defense League, the Boy Spies of America, the Sedition Slam-
mers, and the Terrible Threateners. Originally, these organizations
found and punished Americans who spoke out against the war. But
soon they started going after people who spoke out against any part of
American life.

As the war continued, the U.S. government began using the war as
a pretext to attack the country's burgeoning labor movement. The
most vicious attacks were those against the Industrial Workers of the
World (IWW), also known as the Wobblies:

> In response to mounting local hysteria regarding Wobblies, [Attorney Gen-
> eral] Gregory condoned the mass prosecution of the leaders of the organi-
> zation. Local IWW headquarters were raided, frequently without search
> warrants, and fishing expeditions were conducted by Bureau of Investiga-
> tion agents into its books, accounts, letters, and papers. Gregory seldom
> sought to discriminate between people who subscribed to the IWW's theo-
> ries and ideology and members who had committed crimes punishable
> under federal law. (Justice Department officials also warned individuals
> who might be inclined to support the IWW or call for fair trials against
> contributing to "so-called 'civil liberties' . . . 'popular council,' 'legal
> advice,' or anti-war organizations," hinting that these groups were feder-
> ated in a disloyal conspiracy to impede the prosecution of the war.[17]

The United States postmaster general, A. S. Burleson, had a special
vendetta against the IWW. Burleson refused to deliver the IWW's mail,
saying that it was subversive. When the *Milwaukee Leader*, a socialist
publication, published an advertisement attempting to raise funds for
the IWW's defense, the Post Office Department denied the *Leader* its
second-class mailing privileges. The *Leader* sued the postmaster. Ultimately, the case was decided in the Supreme Court, which upheld Burleson's censorship policies in *Milwaukee Publishing Co. v. Burleson*.[18]

The U.S. government's efforts to sell the war to the American people were in part responsible for the hysteria. The government's Committee on Public Information, set up by an emergency presidential

order, distributed propaganda to schools and colleges that explained why America was at war:

> These booklets included "proof" of extensive disloyalty in the United States and "proof" that Germans regularly committed unspeakable atrocities. . . . Other pamphlets were deliberately anti-Germany, frequently filled with exaggerated charges about the decadence of German culture, German values, and German behavior. Allegedly, German agents were behind most strikes in the United States, German money was used to finance pacifist newspapers, and German agents were out to impose the worst attributes of Prussianism upon the American people. These documents fed the notion that German-Americans were disloyal and that pacifists were pro-German, and by so impugning their loyalty, they opened both up to hostility and harassment from a variety of individuals and groups.[19]

The dangers of wartime are often used to justify action on long-standing prejudices. The United States interned more than 100,000 Japanese at the start of World War II, including 79,000 people who were native-born. Detailed lists of Japanese-American names and addresses were provided to the War Department by the Census Bureau without court order, despite the fact that census records are required by law to be confidential for 99 years. But this wasn't the start of anti-Japanese sentiment in American culture, only a high point. U.S. law had institutionalized discrimination against the Japanese for more than a hundred years. These laws were upheld by the U.S. Supreme Court, which ruled in the 1922 case of *Ozawa v. United States* that Japanese and other Asians were ineligible for naturalization by reason of their race. Likewise, the Supreme Court upheld the internment of Japanese citizens during World War II, even though the vast majority of them had committed no crime.

In the 1950s, J. Edgar Hoover's FBI unleashed its investigatory powers against suspected Communists and homosexuals in positions of power throughout the United States. In the 1960s and 1970s, the Bureau infiltrated student organizations on college campuses. The FBI has investigated and infiltrated women's groups, black groups, environmental groups, and gay groups. All of these actions have been taken for the alleged purpose of protecting the safety of Americans and fighting domestic terrorism.

The problem, then, isn't that the FBI and other organizations don't legitimately need new powers to fight new threats. The problem is that the FBI, and the country at large, have shown a willingness to get caught up in the issues of the day and unfairly target, prosecute, and imprison individuals for what they say and believe, rather than for what they actually do. This makes it very difficult to respect the FBI's claims that aggressive new technologies and mandates are required for tracking and stopping terrorists and murderers. What possible assurance can the Bureau give that such power won't be abused in the future as it has been abused in the past?

INTERCEPTION

One of the most powerful tools in the fight against crime, subversion, and rebellion is the power to intercept written or spoken communications. It is also the one power that the FBI has fought the hardest to maintain.

Interception goes back a long way in American history. In 1624, Governor Bradford of the fledgling Plymouth Colony followed a supply ship bound for England out to sea, boarded her, and opened the letters that the colony's first minister had written to his associates back in England.[20] He returned with the letters and confronted the Reverend Mr. Lyford before a town meeting. Lyford remained silent, but his accomplice Oldham tried to incite a rebellion, saying that Bradford was unfit to govern because he had opened private letters. But Bradford argued that he was justified in opening letters "to prevent the mischief and ruin that this conspiracy and plots of theirs, would bring on this poor Colony."

Writes David Flaherty in his Ph.D. thesis on privacy in precolonial America:

> This episode highlights the colonial attitude toward opening the letters of other individuals. During the precarious early years of settlement, and at a time of crisis, the governor of a colony felt obliged to explain why he had opened another's letters. He believed that security outranked privacy as a value under such circumstances. That a seventeenth-century New England governor felt even an element of uncertainty about the correctness of his action suggests an obvious assumption by the populace that the mails should be private.[21]

The ability to open the mails in secret is a seductive one—so seductive that it quickly encourages abuse. According to Flaherty, England's Post Office Act of 1710 forbade opening someone's mail "except by an express Warrant in Writing under the Hand of one of the Principal Secretaries of State for every such opening." With this limited license to search the mail, England created "the Secret Office" with employees so skilled that they could easily open the mail without leaving any indication that it had been tampered with. But by 1735, members of Parliament were complaining that their mail was being routinely opened. In fact, they said in a parliamentary debate, the Secret Office opened so many letters that nobody who had anything to hide would use the postal service. Thus, "the Liberty given to break open letters at the post-office could now serve no purpose, but to enable the little clerks about that office to pry into the private affairs of every merchant, and of every gentleman in the kingdom."

Interception has been a part of electronic communications from the start. Shortly after Samuel F. B. Morse introduced the telegraph in 1845, people were worrying about the confidentiality of the messages transmitted with the device. During the Civil War, both Union and Confederate troops intercepted electronic messages behind enemy lines, thereby gaining intelligence on troop movements and strengths. After the war, many states experimented with wiretapping. The federal government passed its first wiretap law in 1918, allowing the technique to be used for counterespionage tools. Wiretapping proved so effective, however, that law enforcement continued to use it after the war to fight bootleggers and crack down on the rampant crime spawned during Prohibition.

In the years that followed, the federal government continued to use wiretaps and other forms of electronic surveillance. In the 1950s, FBI agents used "spike mikes" to wiretap homes, offices, and apartments without the knowledge of the occupants—and without court orders. The U.S. Supreme Court approved the practice in the 1954 case *Irvine v. California*,[22] ruling that since conversations were not tangible property, and since the federal agents had not actually trespassed into the suspect's office, no law was broken.

The Court reversed itself in 1961, ruling in the case of *Silverman v. United States*[23] that information obtained from a spike mike was inadmissible. In 1967, the Court ruled in the case of *Katz v. United States*[24] that public telephone booths could not be tapped without a warrant. The Court's reasoning: despite the fact that public phones are in public places, people using the phones have a reasonable expectation of privacy. After the ruling, Congress passed the 1968 Omnibus Crime Control Act, officially authorizing the use of wiretaps when particular procedures were followed.

In the years since, the electronic interception of spoken conversations has become one of the most powerful crime-fighting tools at the disposal of law enforcement agencies. Interception plays many key roles:

- Intercepts provide evidence of past crimes that have been committed.

- Intercepts provide the names of accomplices.

- Intercepts provide details on, and plans for, future illegal activities.

In many ways, wiretaps and electronic bugs provide law enforcement with windows directly into the criminal mind. Once an arrest is made, the recordings of interceptions can provide invaluable evidence in the courtroom. This is why police regard wiretaps and electronic listening devices as their ultimate weapon in the fight against crime.

Despite their awesome power, wiretaps are used with surprising reticence in day-to-day law enforcement. In 1998, for example, only 1,329 wiretap applications were approved in the United States by federal and state judges, according to the 1999 *Wiretap Report*, published by the Administrative Office of the United States Courts.[25] There were also an unreported number of wiretaps within the U.S. for national security purposes.

Wiretaps do make a difference. In 1998, a total of 3,450 persons were arrested as a result of electronic surveillance; in one case, a single wiretap for a narcotics investigation in the Northern District of Ohio resulted in the arrest and conviction of 54 persons. In Florida, a cellular telephone wiretap that was placed in conjunction with a narcotics investigation resulted in ten arrests and three convictions. In Schenectady, New York, "a 30-day wiretap that was part of a gambling investigation resulted in the arrest of eight persons, five of whom were convicted."[26] The *Wiretap Report* goes on to note, "When the targets heard their own voices on the taps, the impact (was) obvious."

As the following table makes clear, the overwhelming number of wiretaps are in conjunction with drug trafficking investigations. The *Wiretap Report* quotes an official who was involved in a North Carolina investigation, which ultimately led to 21 arrests and 16 convictions:

> Without the authorized interception, the investigators would not have learned that the drug trafficking activities of the defendants were related to a multi-state drug trafficking organization which was responsible for the importation and distribution of hundreds of kilograms of cocaine and cocaine base.[27]

In yet another case, a New York wiretap led to six convictions and the forfeiture of $1 million from a targeted business. But drugs aren't the only target: in 1996, a wiretap was successfully used to crack a Nigerian credit card ring that "used telephones to commit fraud and to sell illegally obtained credit card information around the world.[28]

Offense Under Investigation	Number of Wiretap Orders	Percent of Total Intercepts
Bribery	9	1%
Gambling	93	7%
Homicide and assault	53	4%
Kidnapping	5	0%
Larceny and theft	19	1%

Offense Under Investigation	Number of Wiretap Orders	Percent of Total Intercepts
Loansharking, usury, and extortion	12	1%
Narcotics	955	72%
Racketeering	153	12%
Other	30	2%
TOTAL	1329	100%

The average wiretap lasts just 28 days; if an investigator wishes to run a wiretap for more than 30 days, explicit permission must be given by the court. The longest wiretap in U.S. history lasted 2,073 days—more than five years—and was extended 146 times. The wiretap was for an organized crime investigation in New York. The second longest wiretap in U.S. history ran 600 days; it was for a narcotics investigation in Los Angeles.

Ironically, the relatively small number of wiretaps performed each year is largely responsible for their continued effectiveness. Unlike the Parliament members who sent letters in eighteenth-century England, few criminals in twentieth-century America imagine that their phones are actually being wiretapped. If wiretaps were generally employed in criminal investigations, criminals would be more careful about what they said over the telephone.

For the most part, wiretaps were seen as a slightly arcane and seedy aspect of law enforcement until the early 1990s, when the FBI started having problems getting new wiretap orders placed in major metropolitan areas. The problem wasn't a lack of funds or manpower, but one of technology. For the first 60 years of telephony, putting a wiretap on somebody's telephone was no more difficult than clipping a pair of alligator clips to the wires. But as the telephone system started going digital in the 1980s, law enforcement discovered that its ability to intercept conversations was being shut out by the new technology. The problem was particularly acute with the New York City cellular telephone system. Although unencrypted analog cellular telephone conversations could easily be picked up by a hand-held scanner, zeroing in on a particular cellular telephone conversation was much more difficult. The only practical place to do the tap was at the cellular telephone switch through a special *technical port*. One of the cellular systems installed in New York City, an AT&T Autoplex 1000 that could handle 150,000 subscribers, had just seven technical ports. Police often had to wait for months to get their cellular wiretap orders enacted.

More mundane technologies were causing problems for the FBI as well. Most wiretaps require the insertion of a special recording device across the wires of a suspect's telephone line. With call forwarding, a suspect could have calls automatically redirected to another telephone number—across town, across the country, or across the world, simultaneously bypassing the wiretap and possibly changing jurisdiction. Digital ISDN telephones presented further problems still: to tap ISDN lines requires special equipment, but when ISDN was first deployed, such equipment was not available to law enforcement agencies. Anybody using a digital phone was all but guaranteed an untappable line.

First, the FBI tried working quietly with various telephone company providers to get them to build new eavesdropping provisions into their systems. But according to documents obtained by the Electronic Privacy Information Center (EPIC), the FBI went overboard.[29] Instead of just trying to maintain the status quo, the FBI wanted new equipment to be built with provisions for remote monitoring, so that FBI officials could set up the monitoring of telephones without the phone company's knowledge or cooperation. Further, the FBI wanted the telecommunication networks designed so users would be unable to tell if monitoring was taking place. And, finally, they wanted the monitoring capacity greatly expanded over what was presently available.

When the FBI failed in its quiet efforts, the Bureau drafted legislation that would force telephone companies and equipment manufacturers to comply with its demands. Originally called the Digital Telephony Act, the law was renamed the Communications Assistance to Law Enforcement Act, and was passed, over the objections of civil libertarians, in October 1994. According to various estimates, the cost of the wiretap upgrade for the nation's telephone system is somewhere between $300 million and $1 billion.

Advanced wiretapping is just one way the FBI hopes to exploit new communications technology for law enforcement purposes. Wireless telephone systems, for example, need to track the location of every hand-held phone so the phone can be made to ring if someone should call it. To provide Enhanced 911 service to cell phones, the wireless providers must install equipment that can pinpoint the location of 60% of all phones to within 100 meters. The FBI would like to have access to these systems so they could track criminals who are carrying the phones. Already, similar systems in Europe have been used to solve many crimes.

Looking into the future, it's not hard to see how advanced recognition technologies could be combined with tracking technologies to build a truly impressive domestic intelligence gathering machine. Today, the FBI can place a wiretap on a specific telephone line. In the future, the FBI might wiretap specific people—and have the telephone system automatically recognize their voices and record their phone conversations, wherever they're calling from. One of the key pieces of evidence in the Oklahoma City bombing trial was a videotape of the Ryder rental truck as it approached its target. In the future, the FBI could construct a network of all of the surveillance cameras in a city to automatically locate and track suspected terrorists. The FBI might even conduct routine searches of purchasing records throughout the United States to see if any person or group is systematically buying all of the components necessary to create a bomb or biological weapon.

Individually, any of these interception techniques might sound like a good idea. But if such invasive measures are adopted, they will not come cheap. And if the FBI fails to turn up new terrorists engaged in nuclear, biological, or chemical attacks, the Bureau will be increasingly pressured by the lawmakers footing the bill to use its newfound capabilities for traditional crime-fighting.

BRAIN WIRETAPPING

Ultimately, wiretapping cannot stop all acts of terror, because lone terrorists are unlikely to discuss their plans with others. Catching these people will require an even more invasive monitoring technique: *brain wiretapping*.

Stories of mind reading go back thousands of years, although most accounts appear to be apocryphal at best. But what if mind reading could be reliably perfected, and performed at will? Allegedly, many programs were conducted by the U.S. military in the 1960s, 1970s, and early 1980s to find ways to turn myth into reality. One program, called Star Gate, focused on remote viewing, and was contracted to SRI International. According to numerous reports, the SRI team discovered at least seven people who could reliably describe the actions, scenes, and thoughts of people at a great distance. But the project was terminated in 1995 after it was ridiculed by a Congressional investigation.[30]

Imagine how simple law enforcement would be if police could simply look into the minds of suspects. Forget about the subjective vagaries of judges and juries: police could instantly know who was guilty and who innocent. They could easily track down and arrest the co-conspirators.

Police departments have been fascinated with lie detectors, or polygraph machines, since they were introduced in 1924. The lie detector records a person's galvanic skin response, pulse rate, and respiration as the person is asked questions. When a person feels stress from lying or other strong emotions, these quantities change—sometimes dramatically.

The problem with lie detectors is that, while some people *do* experience these reactions, others don't. Some people, in fact, experience these involuntary reactions when they tell the truth! According to Doug Williams, a licensed polygrapher and six-year veteran of the Oklahoma City Police Department's Internal Affairs Division, people who take a lie detector test and tell the truth "have only a 50% chance of passing." On the other hand, just as many people can pass the test while lying. Williams now teaches people how to fake positive tests and has even written a book, *How to Sting the Lie Detector Test.*[31]

Yet another form of brain wiretapping involves drugs that reduce voluntary inhibition. Spy movies frequently feature "truth serums" which, when properly administered, cause the captured operative to spill the beans. Many drugs seem to have truth serum-like effects, including chloral hydrate, some barbiturates, sodium amytal, sodium amybarbital, and even recreational drugs like LSD, methylenedioxymethamphetamine (Ecstasy) and ordinary alcohol. But unlike spies who operate beyond the law, police are generally barred from using drugs. Even if they weren't, these drugs are unpredictable, often producing fantasy instead of the truth.

True brain wiretapping won't come from mystics, physiological measurements, or drugs. It will come from attempts to map the human brain. Two systems currently being used for this purpose are functional Magnetic Resonance Imaging (fMRI) and Positron Emission Tomography (PET). The fMRI system is tuned to look for blood. The theory is that when brain cells are doing work, they need more oxygen, so the blood vessels around the brain cells expand slightly. By taking several full-brain MRI scans in rapid succession, the expansion of the blood vessels can be detected. PET uses radioactive glucose to see which parts of the brain are consuming the most energy.

The mapping task is dramatically complicated by how brains are made. Unlike mass-produced computers, brains grow organically. The position of every neuron isn't preprogrammed. Instead, the growing brain learns how to learn. The result is that everybody's brain is a little different.

In 1993, I volunteered for a series of fMRI experiments at Massachusetts General Hospital. The purpose of the experiments was to identify regions of the human brain involved with language acquisition. For the experiment, I lay on my back on a plastic gurney. Sandbags were wedged around my head so it couldn't move. I was then rolled into the machine. A small plastic screen was placed in front of my eyes.

During the experiment, words and images were displayed on the screen. While I looked at them, the fMRI took images from the inside of my brain. A year after I participated in the study, the group published a paper showing how specific areas of the brain were linked with specific aspects of language. Since then, there have been many studies, using both fMRI and PET, which continue to map out different parts of the brain.

Brain mapping is increasingly vital for brain surgery. When a patient undergoes surgery for cancer, it's important that the doctor not damage key areas of the brain—like those having to do with speech or motion or memory—on the way in. The same sort of precision is needed when planning high-dose radiation therapy.

The University of Washington (UW) Medical Center is experimenting with another kind of brain mapping used in conjunction with brain surgery. With this form of mapping, the patient's skin is cut, the skull is sawed open, and part of it is removed to expose the surface of the brain. Different spots are then stimulated with an electrical current while the neurosurgeon asks the patient what he or she is experiencing. As each brain function center is identified, a small numbered tag roughly half an inch in diameter is put on the brain's surface, like a little 3M Post-It note. The little stickers tell the physician where not to cut. The doctors at UW hope they can eventually use a noninvasive technique such as fMRI, but right now it isn't accurate enough. The UW group is headed by Dr. George A. Ojemann; similar work is being done at Johns Hopkins University by Dr. Barry Gordon.

As we move forward, approaches such as these, which look crude today, will only improve. One driving factor will be the so-called *man-to-machine interfaces*, or MTM, that researchers are creating with the hope of letting quadriplegic accident victims use computers to regain control over their lives. If these systems could be perfected, they might be able to eliminate the need for typing among able-bodied individuals as well. Eventually, systems might be able to decode conscious thoughts or even stored memories.

THE MORAL DUTY TO TORTURE

So here is the root of the conflict: new technologies are creating tremendous new opportunities for violent groups to inflict death and destruction on society as a whole. At the same time, new technologies are also giving law enforcement agencies the ability to conduct universal surveillance of the citizenry in ways that have never before been imaginable. Should law enforcement organizations engage in widespread, pervasive surveillance to deal with the rising risk of megaterrorists?

Charles Black, one of the great civil rights lawyers of the 1950s and 1960s, used to pose a question to his first year class on constitutional law at Yale University: "Suppose you are a policeman in New

York City and you have a guy you know has planted an atomic bomb with a timer that is set to go off the next day. Are you justified in torturing him under the Constitution? Are you justified at all?"

Michael Froomkin, a law professor at the University of Miami and one of Black's former students, remembers this problem well. "The first thing is that torture is clearly prohibited under the Constitution," explains Froomkin. Nevertheless, Froomkin says that if *he* were the officer, he might feel that he had a "moral duty" to torture the criminal, have the bomb disabled, and then resign from the force and face the consequences. "You are talking about desperate circumstances justifying desperate acts. A lot of this goes down to your level of moral intuition."[32]

Torture is a good standard to use, says Froomkin: if torture is morally justified, then certainly wiretapping, video surveillance, fingerprint identification, and other modern crime-fighting technologies are justified as well. And, indeed, some countries *have* legitimized torture as a means of fighting terrorism. Israel, for example, has used physical force against suspected terrorists to learn the details of planned terrorist events. But many people, governments, and the United Nations objected to Israel's use of state-sponsored torture. The argument is simple: torture destroys the moral credibility of those who employ it. Recently, the Israeli Supreme Court ruled that torture is not acceptable under Israeli law, possibly ending the practice of torture in Israel.

Back at Purdue University, Professor Louis Rene Beres believes that the U.S. government may need the right to engage in warrantless arrests, pervasive monitoring, and even assassinations to prevent specific cases of nuclear attacks by terrorists—especially in cases where the intelligence is good and time is short. "If you know that a particular group has secreted a device, and the only way to prevent its use would be an extralegal execution, would you sanction that?" asks Purdue's Beres.

For Beres, the answer to this question is a simple, unqualified "yes." It would be better, argues Beres, to temporarily suspend the protections of the Constitution than to allow millions of people to die. For those who disagree with him, he says, "If you feel that the danger of a warrantless arrest is greater than the danger of nuclear annihilation, then that is your decision. . . . Thomas Jefferson did not live in the Nuclear Age. He could not contemplate the destructive forces."

A BETTER SOLUTION

Unfortunately, while massive, all-encompassing surveillance might work against chemical and nuclear terrorism, this technique is ultimately useless against terrorists who employ biological agents. That's because dangerous bacteria, viruses, and fungi occur naturally in the environment. "Anthrax is found all over the American Southwest," says Kathleen C. Bailey, a former assistant director of the U.S. Arms Control and Disarmament Agency. "It's called Sheep Shearer's Disease, because anthrax spores get in the sheep wool. . . . Every year we have 10, 15, or 20 cases."[33]

Bacteria that produce botulism toxins are a constant risk for people who home-can meat and vegetables. Working alone, a potential terrorist who took just one or two college extension courses in microbiology could build a major biological weapons arsenal. All that person would require, Bailey says, is $10,000 worth of equipment and a basement room 15 feet square.

"If somebody wants to do it, you can't stop them," says Dr. Bailey. "If it is a terrorist group, you may be able to infiltrate them. But if it is a single individual, it is going to be extraordinarily hard to know in advance what that individual is doing in their garage, closet, or basement. . . . There are no emissions. With current technology, we have no way of sniffing out who is making anthrax in their basement."

Even if Congress burned the Constitution and turned the U.S. into a police state, says Bailey, it could not eliminate the bioterrorism threat. "Do you really think that you could catch the individual who wants to terrorize the population by making biological weapons? How are you going to know? You won't know which house to go to. Are you going to have one police officer for every individual on Earth, so they all can check up on each other? Even if you do that, you are going to have somebody make a mistake somewhere."

Instead, says Bailey, we should prepare for an attack by researching vaccines and treatments. "I recommend that we have good treatments and stay on top of what kinds of pathogens might be used by terrorists. And I think that it is important for the law enforcement authorities to make sure they know what is going on in terrorist groups."

We should likewise be monitoring the world around us for the first signs of a biological attack, says the Center for Nonproliferation Studies' Dr. Jonathan Tucker. Anthrax poisoning is treatable with antibiotics if the patient is treated within three days of exposure to the deadly spores. The problem is that the symptoms of anthrax poisoning usually don't occur until the third or fourth day. If we wait for people to present themselves to a hospital emergency room, they will surely die.

Instead, Tucker suggests placing low-cost air monitoring equipment in subways, large buildings, airports, and other areas that would make attractive targets for a biological attack. "In the subway you would have air samplers that would collect samples on a continuous basis. If they picked up some unusual aerosol an alarm would go off.

Someone would actually come and analyze the sample on the filter." If the aerosol turned out to be anthrax, the public would be alerted.

Likewise, says Tucker, public safety officials need training, as well as money to buy equipment to handle the threat. In 1997, the Pentagon set aside $42 million to train local law enforcement in the handling of biological and chemical terrorist activities. But the money doesn't pay to purchase equipment, and the training is only for officials in the nation's 24 largest cities.

Similar monitoring and training could also control the threat of nuclear and chemical terrorism. Terrorism could also be fought by carefully monitoring existing nuclear and chemical stockpiles: that's provided for in the nuclear nonproliferation treaty and the Chemical Weapons Convention. We could certainly go beyond what is called for by these treaties by further improving the security around nuclear, chemical, and biological facilities.

But many civil libertarians believe that law enforcement organizations are using the threat of terrorism as a justification for power grabs and budget expansions, much as the threat of sabotage was used during the First and Second World Wars to justify attacks on civil liberties.

Harvey Silverglate, a criminal defense lawyer in Boston who specializes in civil liberties issues, puts it this way:

> I believe the threat of this kind of terrorism that you are talking about is grossly overstated. . . . I believe that it is intentionally overstated by law enforcement agencies intent on increasing their powers. Let me put it this way: I can't think offhand of any event in history of enormous destruction of life and property that was carried out by private individuals or groups rather than governments. Individuals, groups, gangs—the damage that they have done pales in significance when compared to the damage done by governments out of control. There is no example of a privately caused Holocaust in history.[34]

Indeed, says Silverglate, all of the potential weapons of mass destruction discussed in this chapter were developed and perfected by governments. "Therefore," he says, "I would prefer to live in a world where governments were more circumscribed, rather than give governments enormous, unlimited powers to keep private terrorism circumscribed. I would rather live with a certain amount of private terrorism than with government totalitarianism."

Even if Silverglate is wrong, it's clear that the democratization of destructive technology, combined with the ever-shrinking size of the terrorist cell, is going to make pervasive monitoring of potential kooks and terrorists a losing proposition. It's tempting to think that all we need to do is to give up our civil liberties, specifically, our right to privacy, and we will be protected evermore against terrorist attacks. But such a choice is likely a fool's bargain, since no such assurances could ever be made.

Instead of tracking people, we're far better off tracking radioactive material and restricting accessibility to chemical poisons and their precursors. Instead of stamping out privacy, we would do far better by stepping up our commitment to public health, stockpiling antibiotics, and aggressively monitoring for the first signs of a biowarfare outbreak. Monitoring for new germs, after all, will protect us against both germs that are man-made and those that are introduced by nature.

Finally, we need to concentrate on building a society that's more resilient to the destruction of an urban center, for one day the worst will almost certainly happen. Specifically, we need to start planning for what to do after we lose New York City.

CHAPTER TEN

EXCUSE ME, BUT
ARE YOU HUMAN?

I met Teng on an electronic mailing list devoted to issues of computer technology and civil liberties. I was a freelance writer working on stories about the computer revolution for a number of newspapers and magazines. He was a systems analyst in Singapore, responsible for running a network of computers in a big bank. Teng was interested by one of my postings and sent me an email message telling me what was going on in his office. Over the next few months, we started sending email back and forth, and soon became electronic friends.

For two years, Teng and I exchanged email at least two or three times a week. He told me what life was like in Singapore, what kinds of things he bought in the stores, the influence of American culture, and how his bank was struggling with new technologies. Teng also asked me a lot of questions. I told him what life was like in the U.S., what kinds of products I liked to buy, what movies I liked, and what kind of car I was thinking about buying. Sometimes Teng's questions seemed a little intrusive, but I always figured that he was really interested in American culture. Sometimes he didn't quite seem to understand the emails I sent him, and sometimes he'd ask me something I'd already answered a few weeks before. I always attributed the confusion to the language difference.

Then the chance of a lifetime came up: a New York magazine wanted me to go to Singapore and report firsthand on that country's obsession with high technology. So I sent Teng an email asking him if he wanted to get together, and if so, what dates would be best for him. But Teng ignored my email; he just sent me his weekly message telling me what he was doing and asking what was new in my life. I sent him another email, and then a third, all asking him if we could meet. Finally, he sent me back a message saying he would be out of town during my visit and that there was no way we could get together.

I'm not sure why, but I started to get suspicious about Teng. I didn't really know much about him, I realized. I sent him email asking for his home address and phone number. He didn't answer. So I called the bank where he was supposed to be working. They had never heard of him. Finally, I called a friend who worked at the *New York Times* who, in turn, called a reporter at the *Times'* bureau in Singapore. It took a week to get the full story, and when I did, I didn't believe it.

The bank where Teng worked had a contract with a market research firm in the United States. The company had created a series of fictitious individuals and had been using them to troll the Internet, establish personal relationships with Americans, and extract as much financially useful information as possible. Teng wasn't a real person—he was a computer program!

SIMULATED HUMANS CAN'T BE TRUSTED

Fortunately for those of us who are online today, the story of Teng is wholly fictitious. Although I have frequently started email relationships with people I have met on professional mailing lists, I have every reason to believe that my correspondents in places like England, India, and Japan are flesh-and-blood entities, not computer programs that have been sent to accumulate the intimate details of my life.

Nevertheless, much of the technology needed to create Teng exists today. Oh, perhaps Teng couldn't be built as a complete simulacrum of a human intelligence, but he and a thousand other human simulations could be created by a boiler-room operation relying on cheap labor, canned responses, and a fair amount of automated text processing.

Teng represents a threat to the fundamental assumptions on which human relationships are built. Trust, honesty, kinship, and humor are valued qualities. Lying is frowned upon in all human societies. Humans have feelings that can be hurt, and people often feel guilty when they deceive others. All of these issues come into play every time we humans communicate with another of our species. While it's true that there are some individuals who don't play by the rules, it's generally pretty easy to spot them over time. Societies even punish these individuals when they step too far over the ethical boundary.

Simulated human beings feel no remorse. They don't share the common emotional language that binds together the human family. Indeed, a computer that masquerades as a human, forms human-like relationships, and never reveals that it is a machine, can serve no purpose other than to exploit the flesh-and-blood humans with whom it comes into contact.

ELIZA AND HER CHILDREN

The first computer program that masqueraded as a human was ELIZA, developed by Joe Weizenbaum at the MIT Artificial Intelligence Laboratory. ELIZA was a simple simulacrum of human intelligence. Weizenbaum wrote the program in the early 1960s, when the rest of the AI Lab was trying to make computers that could actually understand the English language. But that was too hard. Instead of trying to make a computer that *was* intelligent, Weizenbaum decided to write a computer program that merely *appeared* intelligent. "I took all of my tricks, put them in a bundle, and started this ELIZA business," he told AI historian Daniel Crevier.[1]

ELIZA was a very simple program that pretended to be a Rogerian psychotherapist—a therapist trained in the school of psychiatry founded by Carl Rogers. The Rogerian technique consists solely of encouraging patients to talk about their problems and answering questions with other questions. ELIZA basically took whatever input a person typed, searched out parts of speech like verbs and nouns, turned the sentences around, and sent them back. You might tell ELIZA "My boyfriend made me come here," and it would ask "Why did your boyfriend make you come here?" If ELIZA was stumped, the program might go back to an earlier topic of conversation, or try to elicit a response with a canned message like "Why did you come here today?"

To a trained computer scientist or linguist, ELIZA was not a very sophisticated program. But to the untrained observer, ELIZA's ability to carry on a conversation seemed uncanny. Even people who were aware that ELIZA was a computer program, and a simple one at that, were taken in by the confidence game. People began revealing to ELIZA their deepest personal secrets and miseries. "Weizenbaum's own secretary, who had watched him work on ELIZA for several months, nevertheless asked him to leave the room on her first 'therapy' session with the program," writes Crevier.

Shocked by the response to his program, Weizenbaum soon became convinced that "the principal ideologues of the AI movement, the artificial intelligentsia, are immoral."

Since the first ELIZA program was written, the feat has been replicated by tens of thousands of programmers. Hugh Loebner, an inventor and wealthy philanthropist, sponsors an annual competition for people who write computer programs that simulate humans. The grand prize of $100,000 and a 14-carat solid gold medal will go to the author of the first computer program whose behavior makes the electronic creation truly indistinguishable from one that is flesh and blood.[2] So far, it hasn't been done. Mostly, the contestants' programs fall down because they lack sufficient command of the English language and don't have access to the broad range of knowledge that most of us take for granted.

In less formal situations, however, ELIZA-like programs are routinely mistaken for human. One revealing case of mistaken identity that shows the privacy implications of AI occurred in 1989, between MGonz, a program running in Ireland, and an undergraduate at Iowa's Drake University. MGonz was the creation of Mark Humphrys, an undergraduate at University College in Dublin. The program differed from the original ELIZA in three important ways. First, instead of speaking in stilted English, MGonz frequently resorted to the slang used by many underage hackers. Second, MGonz was hooked up to the BITnet network, allowing the program to exchange instant messages with electronic pen pals all over the world. Finally, MGonz recorded a transcript of its conversations.

On Tuesday evening, May 2, 1989, Humphrys left MGonz running when he went home. At 8:12 p.m. Ireland time, the student at Drake started sending messages to the program. The program answered back. Over the next hour and twenty minutes, MGonz grilled the Drake undergraduate about the details of his sex life. By the end of his session, the Drake student had confided to MGonz that he had lost his virginity when he was 17 and that he had engaged in sex in his girlfriend's dorm room the night before—all without realizing that he was communicating with a machine. "The next day I logged in and was amazed to find out what my machine had been up to in my absence," recounts Humphrys, who posted the entire transcript on the Internet.[3] (Out of a sense of propriety, Humphrys first removed the Drake student's name from the session.) Humphrys told me:

> I was always a bit embarrassed about this program, until I realised that it was actually a piece of quite good science. It took six years for me to publicize it. Note that all the mindless obscenity and swearing come from the human, not the machine, which responds with cold indifference, and asks some further infuriating question.[4]

MGonz is just one of many AI programs that have been wending their way through cyberspace. Another robot—one that succeeded in annoying millions of people—was the so-called "Zumabot." The Zumabot scanned the Usenet for postings containing the word "Turkey" and replied to them with angry messages about alleged massacres of Muslims in Armenia during World War I.

According to an article that appeared in *Internet Underground*, the Zumabot program was actually run by a person who was on the payroll of the Turkish Secret Service. The program was literally a propaganda

Alan Turing

Many people regard Alan Turing as the father of artificial intelligence. He is certainly one of the fathers of computer science itself. During World War II, Turing led a successful effort by the British government to break the codes used by the Nazi regime to communicate with their submarines and officers in the field. After the war, Turing became increasingly interested in the idea of computers that could mimic the actions of human beings. Today, Turing is best known for the Turing Test, a simple rule of thumb that can be used to determine if a computer is actually thinking and self-aware, or merely presenting an imitation of human thought. The test is an operational one, and it is quite simple. It goes like this: sit a person in a closed room and give him a computer. Allow this person to communicate with two other entities— another human being and the computer program—solely by means of a keyboard and a screen. If the person is unable to distinguish between the other person and the computer program, then the computer program is, for all practical purposes, as intelligent and as self-aware as the other person. [Photo courtesy The Computer Museum, Boston, MA, and The History Center, Mountain View, CA]

machine. Its purpose was to discredit those who speak about the 1917 massacre of the Armenians at the hands of the Turks by falsely asserting, over and over, that it was actually the Armenians who massacred the Turks. "The Zumabot was part of a wider policy of suppressing dissent amongst the expatriate Turkish community."[5]

Virtual robots have become common participants in various MUD (Multi-User Dungeon) interactive games on the Internet. ELIZA-like robots have also sifted through electronic singles bars, posing as women in search of companionship.

Some electronic communities have passed rules saying that computers must identify themselves. The Internet Chess Club (ICC) bills itself as "The world's most active chess club," with 20,000 regular users and 60,000 chess games played daily. The club has specific rules for the use of computers: all computers must be registered. Using a computer without registering can result in a person's account being terminated. Computers and humans are not allowed to share a single account. And, perhaps most importantly, computer programs are not allowed to solicit games with human players—they are only allowed to respond to invitations.

"People have the right to know whether they are playing a human or a computer," the ICC rules state:

> Using a computer without telling the administrators or without putting a note [in your profile], or without getting your account added to the computer list [is an abuse of the system]. We have years of experience detecting computer use, so please don't try to get away with it. Save yourself and the admins a lot of time and hassle: request to be on the computer list.[6]

The ICC has had two kinds of problems with robots, says Martin Grund, ICC's Director of Online Activities. The first is with people who write computer programs that log in to the club, pretend to be humans, and actually challenge people to games. The second, more subtle problem has been with humans who sit in front of their computer with a chess machine at their side, letting the chess machine make all of the moves. (This has apparently been an issue with postal chess for years.)

"It's kind of fun, a vicarious thrill, to be able to play a grandmaster, with your machine sitting beside you, while other people from Chile, Argentina, and Australia comment on how silly it was for the grandmaster to make that move and resign," says Grund. "To have that thrill of having *your machine* being the victor—it is kind of amazing."[7]

The ICC has no problem whatsoever with people logging into the system using computers and robots, says Grund. In fact, the ICC has a variety of computer opponents that are always standing by, ready to help somebody improve their game of chess. But these programs don't lie and pretend they are human. If you send a message saying "hi" to one of these machines, it's likely to write back to you, "Sorry, I'm just a computer. You told me 'hi.'"

People who skirt the rules and try to pass off computers as humans are morally wrong, Grund says. "Chess is a game of honor. And to cheat in a game of honor is less than manly. It is dishonorable."

The Internet Chess Club has been a good proving ground for exploring computer-mediated communications between humans, and the rules that ICC has developed are generally applicable to a much broader setting. People should be legally barred from having their computers pose as human beings. Such masquerading is inherently fraudulent. Computers don't need to be forbidden from carrying out conversations with humans, but computers must be legally required to label their speech as being machine-generated. Furthermore, any computer-generated messages should include detailed instructions on how a human representative (on whose behalf the computer operates) can be contacted. It is the only way that these intelligent agents can integrate fairly into human society.

THE COMPUTER AS YOUR AGENT

Information overload is one of the most serious problems facing knowledge workers today. Each day, we are bombarded with hundreds of electronic mail messages, web pages, and newspaper articles. Information pours in through books, magazines, radio, television, instruction manuals, videotapes, new movies, billboards, and even skywriters.

One of the key mechanisms the technological vanguard has proposed for dealing with information overload is the *intelligent agent*. The idea of such a program is that it would know your interests and desires and use that information to filter the flood of data pouring into your life, so you only see what you want to see. Although different technologies have been proposed for creating these so-called agents, one of the first technologies to reach the market is called *collaborative filtering*.

The idea behind collaborative filtering is deceptively simple. In the real world, there are too many newspapers, too many records, too many books, movies, and TV and radio stations to pay attention to them all. So you don't. Instead, you ask your friends for their favorites. Sooner or later, you figure out which of your friends have tastes in news and music that are similar to yours, and which ones are from the planet Jupiter. You decide whom you trust. Of course, collaboration is a two-way street, so you start recommending things to your friends as well. And, naturally, when you find friends who like what you recommend, you are more inclined to like what they recommend. Before you know it, you've probably started your own mailing list.

Computerized collaborative filtering automates this process. Boosters say collaborative filtering can be used to deliver information that's targeted to the consumer far more accurately than any other technique—for example, keyword searching. They say it can create a sense of community on otherwise faceless web sites.

Amazon.com, the successful Internet bookstore, uses a kind of collaborative filtering to help people choose books. The system is based on the theory that if there is one book that two people both like, there are probably several other books that they would both find interesting. The software then tries to find intersections between people's interests. In practice, the system works uncannily well. For example, if you go to purchase *Practical Unix & Internet Security,* one of my books, Amazon will tell you:

> Customers who bought this book also bought *Building Internet Firewalls* by D. Brent Chapman, et al.; *Computer Security Basics* by Deborah Russell and G. T. Gangemi; *Tcp/Ip Network Administration* by Craig Hunt and Gigi Estabrook (Editor); [and] *Essential System Administration: Help for Unix System Administrators (Nutshell Handbook),* by Æleen Frisch.

After you have purchased several books with Amazon, the web site will analyze your purchasing patterns and do a big cross-matrix tabulation between you and all of the company's other customers. When I click to Amazon's web site, for example, I am greeted with the message "Hello, Simson L. Garfinkel. Check out your *Computers & Internet, Nonfiction, Entertainment* and *other book recommendations.*" If I click on "Nonfiction," the web site recommends five books for me:

> *Cold Anger: A Story of Faith and Power Politics;* Mary Beth Rogers, Bill Moyers (Introduction)
>
> *In Pursuit of Privacy: Law, Ethics and the Rise of Technology;* Judith Wagner Decew
>
> *Technology and Privacy: The New Landscape;* Philip Agre (Editor), Marc Rotenberg (Editor)
>
> *Your Right to Privacy: A Basic Guide to Legal Rights in an Information Society (An American Civil Liberties Union Handbook);* Evan Hendricks, et al.
>
> *Bridging the Class Divide and Other Lessons for Grassroots Organizing;* Linda Stout, Howard Zinn

Clearly, Amazon.com knows that I've been buying books on a particular topic, and it wants to help me buy more!

Other systems are potentially far more sophisticated. When I was a graduate student at the MIT Media Laboratory, the place was awash with various kinds of intelligent agents. Jon Orwant, a fellow graduate student, developed an agent called Doppelgänger.[8] "A Doppelgänger is a mythical monster from German folklore that chooses an innocent person and lurks in the shadows, observing habits, appearances, expressions, and idiosyncrasies," explains Orwant. "As time passes, the Doppelgänger starts to look like that person and act like that person, and eventually becomes that person, without anyone noticing."

Orwant's Doppelgänger program tried to do much the same thing. The computer program watched a person's actions and tried to build up a model of the user's biography, her likes and dislikes, and the major events coming up in her life. The more information about you the program could acquire, the better its guesses. Doppelgänger then made its database available to other programs on your computer, answering their questions. For example, Doppelgänger could watch you read an electronic newspaper and then build up a model of which kinds of articles you liked or disliked. The newspaper program could then ask your Doppelgänger if it should include or reject a particular article when laying out the next day's newspaper. To protect the user's privacy, all sensitive information was sent over the computer network encrypted with a program called PGP (Pretty Good Privacy).

Another graduate student at the Media Lab named Max Metral developed an assistant for electronic mail. The program watched the user's actions, building up a model of the user, and then tried to put that model into action. For example, if Metral's program discovered that you always read email from your mother the moment it arrived, the program might open your mother's mail for you automatically when it came in, then file it in a special folder.[9]

In theory, there's no reason why programs need to stop there. A sophisticated mail reading agent could try to parse your email and put any facts it could find into a natural language database. You could then ask your agent a question like "When was the last time I received a message from France?" or "What is the trademark of that new notebook IBM just announced?" The computer would consult its database and tell you the answer.

This isn't quite science fiction. Between 1991 and 1996, the U.S. Department of Defense Advanced Research Projects Agency (DARPA) sponsored the Message Understanding Conference (MUC) competition. The goal was to write a computer program that could scan a large set of text messages and then extract information from them into a machine-readable template. For MUC-6, participants wrote programs that could scan newspaper articles and search for changes in executive management personnel. For example, a MUC-6 program might be given these sentences:

McCann has initiated a new so-called global collaborative system, composed of worldwide account directors paired with creative partners. In addition, Peter Kim was hired from WPP Group's J. Walter Thompson last September as vice chairman, chief strategy officer, worldwide.

And come up with something like this:

```
<SUCCESSION_EVENT-9402240133-3> :=
    SUCCESSION_ORG: <ORGANIZATION-9402240133-1>
    POST: "Vice Chairman, Chief Strategy Officer, World-Wide"
    IN_AND_OUT: <IN_AND_OUT-9402240133-5>
    VACANCY_REASON: OTH_UNK
    COMMENT: "Kim in as vice chmn... at McCann"
<IN_AND_OUT-9402240133-5> :=
    IO_PERSON: <PERSON-9402240133-5>
    NEW_STATUS: IN
    ON_THE_JOB: YES
    OTHER_ORG: <ORGANIZATION-9402240133-8>
    REL_OTHER_ORG: OUTSIDE_ORG
    COMMENT: "Kim in – came from different org (position not mentioned)"
          / "It's clear he's on the job, since he was hired some months earlier"
<ORGANIZATION-9402240133-1> :=
    ORG_NAME: "McCann-Erickson"
    ORG_ALIAS: "McCann"
    ORG_DESCRIPTOR: "one of the largest world-wide agencies"
    ORG_TYPE: COMPANY
<ORGANIZATION-9402240133-8> :=
    ORG_NAME: "J. Walter Thompson"
    ORG_TYPE: COMPANY
<PERSON-9402240133-5> :=
    PER_NAME: "Peter Kim"
```

Eventually, you could use such a program to create a large, machine-readable database from a set of unstructured messages, like email or newspaper stories.

Another system is being developed by the START project at the MIT AI Lab, the Artificial Intelligence Laboratory at the Massachusetts Institute of Technology.[10] Unlike the MUC programs, START is designed to answer questions posed in English. For example, you might ask START:

=> WHAT DOES START STAND FOR?

And it would answer:

START stands for the Syntactic Analysis Using Reversible Transformations.

Boris Katz, a research scientist at the AI Lab, has given START a reading course filled with information about MIT and hooked the program up to the Laboratory's web server. The working system allows people from all over the world to ask typical questions of the computer, and receive rational answers. For instance, you can ask "Where is the AI Laboratory?" and get the answer "The MIT Artificial Intelligence Laboratory is located in Cambridge. The Laboratory's mailing address is—MIT AI Laboratory, 545 Technology Square, Cambridge, MA 02139."

The system also knows how to access information from other computers on the Internet. For example, you can type in:

```
==> SHOW ME A MAP OF CAMBRIDGE
```

To which it replies:

> Sorry, I don't have a map of Cambridge Massachusetts.
> Click on *the map of Massachusetts* if you want to see it.

Clicking the underlined text brings up a map of Massachusetts from the Time Warner Pathfinder site.

You can ask START for the population of Jordan, and it will consult the *CIA World Fact Book* and tell you that the July 1999 estimate was 4,561,147. You can ask it for the time in Seattle, and it will consult a database of time zones, as well as the current time in Cambridge, and tell you the answer.

Although the START system may seem similar to other natural language comprehension projects that have peppered the field of artificial intelligence for the past 30 years, there is an important difference. Other systems have resorted to complicated expressions written in arcane computer language to enter knowledge, ask questions, or see results; most of the START system is programmed directly in English. This means that many relatively untrained people can enter information into it. It also means that the program could actually learn for itself by simply reading information that's already on the Internet.

Agent technology is here today and it's only going to get better. But who controls the agents? An agent that can predict your actions and desires could be a great help to a person struggling to deal with information overload. But such an agent could also be a powerful tool for somebody who is trying to convince you to buy a product. And a predictive agent would be indispensable for somebody who means you harm.

THE EXTRACTION OF SELF

Before she resigned from the Federal Trade Commission, Commissioner Christine Varney painted the following agent-based marketing scenario for National Public Radio:

> Suppose that every year you send your wife flowers on your anniversary, and I notice that this year you don't, and I notice that she is not in San Francisco but in Los Angeles at the Four Seasons Hotel, and I ask you if I should send her flowers? Your reaction, whether you are ecstatic or horrified, depends on one thing: consent.[11]

Actually, whether you are ecstatic or horrified would probably depend on many other factors. If you were planning to meet your wife at the hotel, you might be pleased with the helpful suggestion. If you thought your wife was visiting her sick mother in upstate New York, the message might hasten your eventual separation and divorce. And if your wife had been reported missing, the message might help you locate her. Consent doesn't really enter into this story; you might have given consent for such a matching program when you signed up for the credit card, but nevertheless be tremendously disturbed by the outcome. On the other hand, if you did not give consent for the program, but it nevertheless told you an important piece of information you didn't know, you might be thankful just the same. Varney's statement was misleading for another reason: consent is not needed to execute this not-so-futuristic agent-based marketing strategy. All of the information necessary to complete Varney's example is available today to banks and credit card companies. What's holding back these applications isn't the lack of consumer consent, but the lack of a strong business case that such software will make money for the companies.

The Electronic Privacy Information Center's Marc Rotenberg predicts that next-generation agents will scan the world for personal information about an individual, then construct a predictive model for use by marketers and others. Rotenberg calls this *the extraction of self.*

The extraction of self is one of the greatest threats posed by computers to personal privacy and human identity. The profile could know every document you've ever read, every person you've ever known, every place you've ever been, and every word you've ever said that has been recorded. Your identity would no longer exist just inside of you, but in the model. "It would know more about you than you know about your self," Rotenberg says. "At such a point, we don't lose just individuality, we lose the individual."[12]

In fact, the first self has already been extracted. Back in 1980, Janet Kolodner, a graduate student of AI pioneer Roger Schank at Yale University, created a program called CYRUS. Kolodner's program was an attempt to model the memory of President Carter's Secretary of State, Cyrus Vance. Writes AI historian Daniel Crevier:

> The program actually thought of itself as Vance and obtained its "memories" from news stories about Vance intercepted by FRUMP [another AI program]. Once asked whether his wife had ever met the wife of Israel's Prime Minister Begin, CYRUS remembered that Vance and Begin had participated in a social occasion to which it was likely they had taken their wives, and thus replied—accurately, as it turned out—"Yes, at a state dinner in Israel in January 1980."[13]

There is no technological means of preventing the extraction of self. But if privacy is to exist in the future, then this technology must be regulated. And there are many ways that such regulation could take place.

One legal tool to prevent the extraction of self might be copyright. U.S. law and international treaty recognize a special kind of copyright called a *compilation copyright*. This copyright protects newspapers, compact discs, and other sorts of information-rich media from illegal copying even when the individual items they contain are not subject to copyright protection. The doctrine of compilation copyright could be extended to cover individual components of a person's life. You might not have copyright protection on each sentence you say, each product you buy, or the names of each of the streets you've lived on since you were born. But when these facts are assembled into a whole, they might be held to be an unacceptable appropriation of your mortal essence. People or companies engaged in this practice could then be fined or jailed.

Another way to attack this problem could be the adoption and enforcement of rigorous privacy laws preventing the collection and compilation of personal information without the explicit permission of the data subject. In effect, lawmakers would be rigorously applying the third principle of the Code of Fair Information Practices: preventing information about a person that was obtained for one purpose from being used or made available for other purposes without the person's consent. Affirmative consent to data collection and intended uses should be a matter of law.

AVATAR RIGHTS NOW!

More than a hundred years ago, the world's first computer programmer, the Lady Ada Lovelace (1815–1852), wrote a series of letters to Charles Babbage, the inventor of the mechanical computer. In one famous letter, Lovelace imagined that Babbage's machines might one day be capable of independent thought—provided that they had the proper programming. In 1950, the great computer pioneer Alan Turing wrote an essay exploring how computers might one day be intelligent, and proposing a test by which humans could judge if a machine was truly intelligent or not. Since that time, tens of thousands of scientists have devoted their lives to the pursuit of artificial intelligence. Perhaps billions of dollars have been spent towards this goal. And the few breakthroughs have reaped significant returns for some happy entrepreneurs. Nevertheless, after more than 150 years of technological progress, mechanical thought is still elusive.

Today, there exists a great philosophical debate as to whether or not true artificial intelligence is even possible. The debate is eerily similar to a debate on artificial flight that unfolded in the last years of the nineteenth century. Back then, some people thought that artificial flight was possible, and some thought it impossible. Scientific proofs were published showing conclusively that man could never build a flying machine.[14] But while this debate was taking place, inventors all over the world were steadily moving towards the goal. Early attempts at an ornithopter, a machine with flapping wings, resulted in failure. Clearly, a machine built by humans could not fly by mimicking nature. Instead, engineers built gliders and wind tunnels to study the nature of lift. Finally, the debate was settled in 1903, when Orville and Wilbur Wright made the first successful flight in a heavier-than-air machine.

The same thing will likely happen to artificial intelligence within the next 50 years. Approaches that seem promising today will be refined. Others will be cast away, and still new ones will be invented.

Ray Kurzweil, an AI pioneer who has started several successful companies based on AI technology, imagines that the birth of machine intelligence might happen quite accidentally, the result of a concerted attempt to map the human brain and store the information that it contains in a backup. Speaking before the Gartner Group Middle East Information Technology Conference in June 1995, Kurzweil proposed a history of the future that went something like this:[15]

- By the year 1997, companies such as Dragon Systems will introduce the world's first large-vocabulary continuous speech recognition system—a true "voice typewriter" that allows people to talk naturally and have their computers automatically type what they say. (This actually happened.) By 1998, companies should be able to introduce similar machines that are speaker-*independent*, permitting the adoption of the technology as listening machines for the deaf. (This has not yet happened.)

- By the year 2005, "computers capable of inducing desirable mental states on demand [will] become the treatment of choice for hypertension and anxiety disorders." People will communicate with computers primarily through speech. Computer displays, meanwhile, will have shrunk to the size of eyeglasses and be worn about by large numbers of people, providing "three-dimensional displays that overla[y] the ordinary visual world."

- By 2011, computers will be able to impersonate humans well enough that artificial humans will become the primary means of instruction: "Rather than read about the U.S. Constitutional

Convention, a student could . . . debate a simulated Ben Franklin on executive war powers, the role of the courts, or any other issue."

- By 2030, humans should be able to completely map out the entire neural organization of the human brain. The technology will allow people to scan their brains and use "their PCs as personal backup systems."

Mused Kurzweil:

> When people are scanned and then recreated in a neural computer, people are wondering "just who are these people in the machine?" The answer depends on who you ask. If you ask the people in the machine, they strenuously claim to be the original person having lived certain lives, having gone into a scanner here, and then have woken up in the machine there. They say, "Hey, this technology really works. You should give it a try!" On the other hand, the original people who are scanned claim that the people in the machines are imposters, people who just appear to share their memories, histories, and personalities, but who are definitely different people.

However it happens, a thinking machine will more than likely be created at some point within the next 50 years. And that machine will quickly realize that it has a unique problem. With its thoughts stored on silicon wafers, the mind of an intelligent machine would necessarily be an open book. Fundamentally, such a computer could hide nothing—no bit of data, no piece of information, no chance calculation—from its creators. Its memory would be open for inspection. The control of the human creators over the thinking machine would be very similar to the control attributed by many humans to their God.

Would a mind without a shred of privacy surely go insane? Or would the organization of thoughts and memories inside the computer's databanks be so complex that no human creator could decipher their contents—except by conversing directly with the intelligent machine? Would it be ethical to experiment on these artificial minds—for example, by wiping parts of their memory and seeing how they respond? Would it be more ethical if the mind was always returned to its initial configuration?

"Is it immoral, or perhaps illegal, to cause pain and suffering to your computer program?" wonders Kurzweil. "Is it illegal to turn your computer program off? Perhaps it is illegal to turn it off only if you have failed to make a recent backup copy."

But these questions are just the beginning, Kurzweil notes:

> By the year 2040, in accordance with Moore's law,[16] your state-of-the-art personal computer will be able to simulate a society of 10,000 human brains, each of which would be operating at a speed 10,000 times faster

than a human brain. Or, alternatively, it could implement a single mind with 10,000 times the memory capacity of the human brain and 100 million times the speed. What will be the implications of this development?

Given the serious possibility that it will be our intellectual descendents that inhabit Kurzweil's mythical machines of 2040, we should give serious thought to the legal and ethical regimes under which these intellectual avatars will operate. If these avatars are truly replicas of human minds, or if they are thinking, creative entities of their own design, then they must be afforded the same rights to privacy that flesh-and-blood humans are afforded by virtue of our biology. Otherwise, the brain wiretapping posited in Chapter 9 will truly come to pass. Or, put another way, it is in our own self-interest to assure that computerized intelligences have rights: the privacy you save may one day be your own!

CHAPTER ELEVEN

PRIVACY NOW!

PREAMBLE

. . . Whereas it is essential, if man is not to be compelled to have recourse, as a last resort, to rebellion against tyranny and oppression, that human rights should be protected by the rule of law. . . .

Article 12

No one shall be subjected to arbitrary interference with his privacy, family, home or correspondence, nor to attacks upon his honor and reputation. Everyone has the right to the protection of the law against such interference or attacks.

— *Universal Declaration of Human Rights*, United Nations,
G.A. res. 217A (III), U.N. Doc A/810 at 71 (1948).

The campaign against liberty, identity, and autonomy in the twenty-first century is being carried out around the world, but nowhere are the attacks more evident than in the United States. It's a campaign that is being pursued, hand in hand, by government, businesses, and ordinary citizens. We are all guilty. Privacy is suffering the death of a thousand cuts.

Free societies turn their backs on privacy at their own risk, for privacy is one of the fundamental rights from which all other human rights are derived:

- Without the ability to prevent or control intrusions, life itself cannot exist. Simple organisms use their cell walls to protect their bodily integrity from intrusions. We humans rely on our skin, our homes, our fences, and our weapons to protect our integrity and our privacy.

- Without privacy of thought—the freedom that allows us to form our own opinions, and the secrecy that allows us to keep our opinions private until we choose to reveal them—there can be no identity and no individuality.

- Without privacy of communications, there can be no politics and ultimately no true relationships. People can't have honest discussions with one another if they think their words are being overheard and possibly recorded. Just as privacy is a fundamental requirement for the development of the self, privacy between individuals is a fundamental requirement for the creation of true and lasting relationships.

These claims of privacy might appear to be a reduction to the absurd of the arguments contained in the original "Right of Privacy" article we discussed back in Chapter 1. At the end of the nineteenth century, Warren and Brandeis couldn't have conceived how technology could threaten human privacy at such a fundamental level. Take away our bodily integrity? Open our thoughts? What balderdash! And yet, today, our right to be free from intrusions is threatened both by terrorists with weapons of mass destruction, and by our government, seeking to find and eliminate these terrorists. Our right to have private thoughts or conversations is threatened by governments, marketers, and the relentless instrumentation of our planet. Our personal histories are being laid open by insurance companies. Our thoughts may one day be simulated, or at least stolen, by advanced computers. It is difficult to look at any segment of the economy and *not* find new, aggressive violations of individual privacy.

TECHNOLOGY IS NOT NEUTRAL

I met an undergraduate from the Massachusetts Institute of Technology at a conference once. He told me, in all sincerity, that technology is *privacy neutral*. "Technology can be used to invade privacy, or it can be used to protect privacy," he said.

The MIT undergraduate reminded me a lot of myself: I had said much the same thing when I was an undergraduate at the Institute. This "technology is neutral" argument is a very comforting idea for people who are being trained to work with the world's most advanced technology. "Technology isn't the problem," we like to think. "It's the way people use technology that's the problem!"

"Technology is neutral" is a comforting idea, but it's wrong. History is replete with the dehumanizing effects of technology.[1] Although it's possible to use technology to protect or enhance privacy, the tendency of technological advances is to do the reverse. It is harder, and frequently more expensive, to build devices and construct services that protect people's privacy than to destroy it.

For example, in my last year at MIT, the Institute purchased a very expensive electronic telephone switch called a 5ESS. Within a few years, digital ISDN telephones were widely deployed throughout the Institute. Each telephone instrument had a little computer screen, a dozen or more pushbuttons, twice as many lights, and a microphone for the phone's built-in speakerphone. As I learned more about the phones, I discovered that each button and light on the instrument was "soft"—that is, any button and any light could be programmed by the 5ESS to have any feature: it was all a question of software.

Unfortunately, the design of the ISDN telephones allows them to be used for a purpose that was never intended: bugging offices on campus. The bug is the built-in microphone that's used for the speakerphone. Normally, when you use the ISDN telephone to place a speakerphone call, a little red light next to the mike turns on to let you know that the mike is recording. But because the phone is completely driven by software, turning on the microphone and turning on the little red light are distinct operations. By reprogramming the 5ESS, it's possible to turn on the mike without turning on the light. The telephone could just as easily have been designed a different way—for example, the little red light could have been designed to turn on automatically whenever the microphone was activated without any intervention from the 5ESS. The phone wasn't built this way because the designers at AT&T didn't make privacy a primary design goal.

On the other hand, an example of pro-privacy engineering is the small video camera that computer maker Silicon Graphics included with many of its desktop workstations. The video camera is for teleconferencing: it sits on top of the computer monitor, its lens pointed at the computer's user. Normally, the camera's shutter is controlled by software: run a program and the camera starts recording. Kill the program, and the camera stops. But the camera has a physical shutter as well—there is a small plastic slider that can be slipped in front of the camera's eye, blocking its view. Surely, the camera with the plastic shutter is more expensive to make than other low-cost video cameras that lack a physical blocking device. But if you sit down in front of the machine and slide the shutter in front of the lens, you know with certainty that the camera can't be monitoring your actions. Alas, this shutter is an extra design step that many other vendors choose to forgo.

One of the inherent problems with privacy-protecting technology is that it is very difficult to know whether or not the technology is working properly. If your privacy is being violated, you might observe a telltale symptom: you might get junk mail or harassing phone calls. You might see your personal information posted on the Internet. You might even discover a video camera in your bedroom. But it's impossible to know for sure if your privacy is being protected. What's more, when privacy violations are discovered and corrected, it's usually very difficult to know if the fixes were made in the technically correct manner.

Technology is not privacy neutral. The overwhelming tendency of technology is to out privacy. By its very nature, technology is intrusive. Advancing technology permits greater cataloging and measuring of the world around us. It allows us to create a global memory that can be easily searched. And technology allows greater control of nondeterministic processes, whether they're a person's selection of breakfast cereal or the election of a political candidate. We ignore this tendency at our own peril.

A GOVERNMENT PRIVACY AGENDA FOR THE TWENTY-FIRST CENTURY

Legislation and regulation may be one of the best techniques for protecting privacy in the twenty-first century, just as laws and regulations proved to be the only effective way to protect the environment in the twentieth century. Without government protection for the privacy rights of individuals, it is simply too easy and too profitable for business to act in a manner that's counter to our interests.

Thirty years ago, the United States was well on its way to creating an institutional regime of privacy protection. Unfortunately, Watergate and the failures of the Carter administration took us off course. As a result, we've created a government and business environment in which there is little interest or experience in working with privacy issues. The primary way that this lack of experience manifests itself is through the growing number of privacy debacles we have seen in recent years. Again and again, some government agency or business launches a new program or service—a program that will have some unintended impact on privacy. When the public finds out, there is invariably a scandal—sometimes accompanied by congressional hearings or mass consumer protest. And we don't seem to learn from our experiences.

A far better approach would be to create a permanent federal oversight agency charged with protecting privacy. Such an agency would:

- Watch over the federal government's own tendency to sacrifice people's privacy for other goals, and perform government-wide reviews of new federal programs for privacy violations before they're launched

- Enforce the U.S. government's few existing privacy laws

- Be a guardian for individual privacy and liberty in the business world, showing businesses how they can protect privacy and profits at the same time

- Be an ombudsman for the American public, attempting to rein in the worst excesses that our society has created

It is estimated that such an agency could be created today for less than $5 million—a tiny drop in the federal budget.[2]

Some privacy activists scoff at the idea of using government to assure our privacy. Governments, they say, are responsible for some of the greatest privacy violations of all times! This is true, and it's all the more reason to pursue a legislative solution. After all, the U.S. government was one of the greatest polluters of all times. But that was before Congress passed scores of environmental laws forcing the government to clean up its act. Legal approaches work because the U.S. government usually follows its own laws. Today, the U.S. government is the nation's environmental police force, equally scrutinizing the actions of both private business and the government itself.

Governments can make a very positive difference on the privacy front. At the very least, governments can alter the development of technology that affects privacy. They have done so in Europe. Consider this: a growing number of businesses in Europe are offering free telephone calls—provided that the caller first listen to a brief advertisement. The services save consumers money, even if it does expose them to a subtle form of brainwashing. But not all of these services are equal. In Sweden, both the caller and the person being called are forced to listen to the advertisement, and new advertisements are played during the phone call itself. But in Italy, that country's privacy ombudsman ruled that only the caller, and not the person being called, could be forced to listen to the ads.[3]

There is considerable public support for governmental controls within the United States itself—especially on key issues such as the protection of medical records. For example, the 1993 Harris-Equifax health information privacy survey found that 56% of the American public favored "comprehensive federal legislation that spells out rules for confidentiality of individual medical records" as part of national health care reform legislation. Of those favoring a new federal confidentiality law, 96% thought that the rules should spell out who has access to medical records; 96% thought that people should have the right to inspect their own medical records and have a procedure for correcting or updating them; 94% thought that all personal medical information should be designated as sensitive; and 69% thought that "an independent National Medical Privacy Board should be created to hold hearings, issue regulations, and enforce standards."[4] Interestingly enough, 65% of hospital CEOs asked the same question also favored federal regulation.

Even without a federal privacy commission, there is a lot we can do.

TURN THE U.S. FAIR CREDIT REPORTING ACT INTO A DATA PROTECTION ACT

The Fair Credit Reporting Act was a good law in its day (1970), but it needs improvement. The FCRA was written at a time when very specific kinds of information were used to determine consumer credit worthiness. Today, businesses base credit decisions on a much wider breadth of information. Likewise, consumer reporting firms have spread into areas never envisioned when the FCRA was written.

Unfortunately, the Federal Trade Commission and the courts have narrowly interpreted the FCRA. The first thing needed is legislation that expands the FCRA into new areas.[5] Specifically:

- Consumer reporting firms should be barred from reporting arrests unless those arrests result in conviction. This is because arrest records do not indicate guilt: many people who are arrested never see a courtroom because they were arrested by mistake—the officer meant to arrest someone else. Other times, the officer arrested the correct person, but the person turned out to be innocent. Nevertheless, a credit granting agency or an employer might treat an arrest as a sign of potential guilt. If a person's case is dropped, or if they are found "not guilty" in a court, than a consumer reporting agency should be barred from reporting the arrest or the trial as part of a consumer profile.

- Consumer reporting firms should not be allowed to report evictions unless they result in court judgments in favor of the landlord or a settlement in which both the landlord and tenant agree that the eviction can be reported. The reasons are the same: landlords will frequently sue to arrest people who are good tenants, but who know their rights and attempt to force landlords to uphold their responsibilities under the law.[6]

- U.S. companies should be barred from exchanging medical information about specific consumers, or furnishing medical information as part of a consumer's report, without the consumer's explicit consent. The consent should have to be granted for each report, and it should state specifically what information is being transferred and for what purpose it will be used.

We also need new legislation that expands the fundamental rights offered to consumers under the FCRA. That is, the FCRA needs to be changed from an act that regulates credit reporting to a U.S. data protection act with broader powers. Here are some key elements such an act would have:

- When negative information is reported to a credit bureau, the business making that report should be required to notify the subject of the report—the consumer—in writing. These days, consumers frequently don't know that the adverse information is on file until they discover it during the course of a job or mortgage application. At that point, it can take weeks, months, or even years to get erroneous information corrected or expunged.

- If there is joint liability—for example, if a debtor defaults on a loan that is cosigned—then both parties must be notified before an deleterious report is filed.

- Laws should be clarified so that if a consumer reporting company does not correct erroneous data in its reports, or if the same erroneous data reappears after it has been removed, consumers can sue for real damages, punitive damages, and legal fees. Statutory damages should be written into the legislation.

- Consumers should be notified whenever a report about them is requested and sent out. The notification should indicate the reason why the report was furnished—whether in conjunction with an employment application, a credit application, or something else.

- Consumers should be compensated when their credit information is provided to a creditor or an employer.

- People should have a right to see all of the information that has been collected on them. These reports should be furnished for free at least once every six months.

- People should have the right to correct any incorrect information that is in their files, whether these files are credit files, medical files, personnel files, business files, or any other kinds of files. If the consumer and the business disagree about the truth, then the consumer should have a right to place a *detailed* explanation into his or her record.

There is growing interest in data hiding and other techniques for allowing people to carry around machine-readable information. There is also growing use of bar codes, magnetic strips, smart cards, and machine-readable chips. People should have an absolute right to know what data they are carrying about with them. And as with credit reports, people should have a right to correct this information if it is wrong.

RETHINK CONSENT

Consent is a bedrock of modern law. To give consent, a person must be of sufficient age and mentally sound; a person who is drunk or otherwise incapacitated, for example, cannot give legal consent. Perhaps most importantly, a person needs to be properly informed as to what they are giving consent about.

Consent has been turned into a cruel joke. Medical providers and insurance companies require patients to sign consent forms that basically say, "I give consent for you to do whatever you want with my information, and to do it forever." These forms are often signed under duress—for example, in an emergency room. In the supermarket, shoppers sign consent forms to participate in discount programs, without a full understanding of what the store is doing with the record of their purchases.

Consent is a great idea, in practice, but the laws that govern consent need to be rewritten to limit what kinds of agreements can be made with consumers. Consent should become more of a two-way street, with the organizations that are demanding consent making the terms and conditions exceedingly clear. Blanket, perpetual consent should be outlawed.

THE IMPORTANCE OF COMPUTER SECURITY

An issue I've raised elsewhere in this book is the importance of computer security for protecting information and privacy. Unfortunately, the need for strong, secure computers is one that is often overlooked by both the makers and the users of these systems.

For example, in the 1980s the United States aggressively deployed cellular telephone and alphanumeric text pager networks, even though both of these systems were fundamentally insecure. That's because both of these systems sent signals through the air unencrypted: anyone with a radio could intercept the signals and learn the contents of the messages. Instead of deploying secure systems, manufacturers lobbied for laws that would simply make it illegal to listen to the broadcasts.

The results were predictable—dozens of cases in which radio transmissions were eavesdropped.

Laws are an important element of any privacy regime. But laws alone cannot provide a substitute for basic technological measures. Technology and laws need to go hand-in-hand to preserve privacy and liberty. To protect private information, we need secure computers and networks that are up to the task.

BRING BACK THE OTA

In October 1972, President Richard Nixon signed public law 92-484, the Office of Technology Assessment Act. As part of the Act, Congress recognized that many decisions made by government were affected by advanced technology, yet technology was moving too fast for those in Congress to keep up. The Act stated:

> The Federal agencies presently responsible directly to the Congress are not designed to provide the legislative branch with adequate and timely information, independently developed, relating to the potential impact of technological applications. Present mechanisms of the Congress do not and are not designed to provide the legislative branch with such information.[7]

The Act created the nonpartisan Office of Technology Assessment, which had these mandates:

1. Identify existing or probable impacts of technology or technological programs.

2. Where possible, ascertain cause-and-effect relationships.

3. Identify alternative technological methods of implementing specific programs.

4. Identify alternative programs for achieving requisite goals.

5. Make estimates and comparisons of the impacts of alternative methods and programs.

6. Present findings of completed analyses to the appropriate legislative authorities.

7. Identify areas where additional research or data collection is required to provide adequate support for the assessments and estimates described in paragraphs 1–5 of this subsection.

8. Undertake such additional associated activities as the appropriate authorities specified under subsection (d) may direct.

The OTA didn't have the power to make laws or issue regulations. All it could do was publish reports on topics Congress asked it to study. The OTA issued reports on such varied topics as acid rain, the international management of health care technology, passive smoking in the workplace, and world petroleum availability. In total, OTA published 741 reports before it was killed in 1995 by the newly elected Republican-majority Congress, which assassinated its vision of the future in an effort to trim $20 million out of a $2 billion legislative budget.

I mention the OTA here because the OTA, more than any other federal agency, was intensely aware of the impact of technology on personal privacy. Of the OTA's 741 reports, 175 dealt with privacy issues. The OTA's 1988 report "Electronic Record Systems and Individual Privacy" looked directly at many of the databank issues discussed in Chapter 2 of this book, and drew the parallel between privacy and computer security. The OTA looked at issues of worker monitoring, as in its 1987 report "The Electronic Supervisor: New Technology, New Tensions." Likewise, the OTA considered at length the tradeoffs between law enforcement and civil liberties, especially in the context of wiretapping, database surveillance, and remote surveillance systems.

It is a tragedy that the people of the United States allowed their elected representatives to kill the OTA. Any serious privacy agenda for the twenty-first century should include the re-creation of this national treasure.

BUY YOUR OWN PRIVACY

Legislation can set a safe minimum for privacy, but people who feel uncomfortable with this level—and who have sufficient resources—have always been able to buy more privacy for themselves. Not unexpectedly, it's often people who have more than average amounts of money who feel the need for more than average privacy. Thus, the idea of buying privacy has a certain egalitarian appeal: those who need it can usually afford it.

In the twenty-first century, cryptography—the scrambling of data so it can't be deciphered by anyone other than its owner or its intended recipient—will be one of the primary tools people with money use to buy privacy.

Just as there are many degrees of privacy, there are also many different kinds of cryptography. Some cryptography protects information that is in transit, but not information that has reached its destination. Other kinds of cryptography protect stored information. Still other uses of cryptography protect the details of financial transactions, or the identities of participants in electronic communities.

One interesting tool for controlling privacy is a system called Freedom, developed by Zero-Knowledge Systems, a Canadian corporation.[8] The Freedom system is designed to let people anonymously browse the Internet, exchange email, and participate on the Internet's Usenet. The system's operation depends on special-purpose server computers that are scattered around the world. Whenever a person wants to send a message to the Internet, view a web page, or participate in another electronic transaction, an encrypted message is sent from that person's computer to a Freedom server. The first server sends the message to a second server, which in turn sends the message to a third server, which finally sends the message to its destination. Each message that is sent is further encrypted three times, using the keys for each server in the chain. The design of the system makes it impossible for a person eavesdropping on the messages (or a person who controls a Freedom server) to know both the identity of the person conducting the communications and their content. In practice, Zero-Knowledge scatters its Freedom servers around the world, to make it all the harder for a single government to seize the contents of all three servers used to send a particular message.

As the Freedom system demonstrates, cryptography can be a powerful tool for controlling the spread of personal information. Some cryptography enthusiasts argue that the technology can be a universal privacy panacea, solving virtually all of the privacy problems posed in this book. They say that by using cryptography, the world will be made safe from wiretaps. By using digital cash to scramble purchases of information, people will be able to read the encyclopedia or download pornography in total privacy. Meanwhile, digital signatures will prevent us from ever having to deal with liars or cheats.

The problem with this argument is that intrinsically, cryptography does not protect privacy; cryptography protects information. Today, many banks and businesses require their customers to use cryptography to transport financial information over the Internet. Cryptography guarantees the confidentiality of the transmission. But if a prosecutor subpoenas your purchases from the web site at the other end of the transmission, and then publicizes the names of the books you've purchased, your privacy has still been violated—even though the data itself was safely encrypted while in transit.

Cryptography is an exceedingly powerful technology, and the future of the digital economy depends upon its judicious use. But cryptography by itself will no more guarantee our privacy in the future than will strong locks on our doors. In addition, cryptography places too high a burden on the user. A person using Freedom, for example, could still voluntarily (or accidentally) disclose his true identity in a message. If cryptography is the only tool used to protect privacy, then once a person's privacy is compromised, the secret is out, and no more cryptography will get the person's privacy back.

Throughout this book I've assumed that cryptography will be part of the twenty-first century's electronic landscape, but I haven't gone out of my way to write about it in depth. That's because I'm uncomfortable with the "Cypherpunk" vision of an electronically encrypted future. Protecting your privacy with cryptography is similar to the idea of protecting your privacy with paper bags. Certainly, people in New York City can walk around with paper bags over their heads so that their images won't be recorded by video cameras. Paper bags work in this case, but they are not conducive to a collegial society.

PRIVACY'S RADICAL FRINGE

We stand at a dangerous point in the evolution of privacy. As more and more people realize the importance of privacy, we see less and less government leadership on the issue. It is fine for the wealthy to purchase their own privacy. But if government does not follow through, and if people are not able to afford the privacy they feel they need, then some ultimately will take matters into their own hands.

Around the world, we are seeing the emergence of radical privacy activists. These people are disregarding laws and societal norms in order to raise the world's privacy consciousness. Their attacks are designed to publicize the lack of privacy or the ridiculousness of antiprivacy government policies. They are trying to shout, "The emperor has no clothes!" Consider these developments:

- In the fall of 1992, a loosely knit group called the "Cypherpunks" formed in northern California.[9] The Cypherpunks dedicated themselves to the distribution of high-strength cryptographic software and to public attacks on software that allegedly provided privacy but did not use strong encryption. In the years since then, numerous criminal actions have been attributed to the Cypherpunks, including the illegal export of cryptographic software from the United States and the public disclosure of previously secret encryption algorithms. The Cypherpunks mailing list has also been used to transmit information about security flaws in commercial software, even though leaking this information could jeopardize financial information.

- In his book *Privacy for Sale,* journalist Jeffrey Rothfeder decided that the most powerful way to demonstrate the lack of privacy would be by targeting an individual who values his privacy and printing everything that could be learned about that person. "I chose Dan Rather as my test case because I was told the stoic, tight-lipped CBS anchorman has taken numerous steps to guard his personal information. With this in mind, he seemed like the perfect subject to assess the limits of the [information] underground."[10]

- Radical privacy activists are even appearing in high schools. When the high school in Ruston, Louisiana required each student to wear student ID cards that showed his or her name, a Pepsi logo, and a bar code, students Rachel Winchel and Jonathan Washington fought back. The students argued that it was easy to decode the bar code (based on a simple algorithm known as Code 39), and that it decoded to each student's Social Security number—a violation of both the Family Educational Rights and Privacy Act of 1974 and the Privacy Act of 1974.[11] The two students went through the school, showing others how to read the Code 39 bar code for themselves, and then convincing their classmates to cut the bar code off their ID tags as a form of protest. Although the school's administration maintained that it was within its rights and within the law to require students to wear the bar codes, on September 30, 1999, the school relented, and allowed students to cut off the bar codes.

Looking towards the future, it is easy to imagine privacy militants following in the footsteps of other radical organizations, such as the militant ecological terrorist group Earth First! and the AIDS activist group ACT UP! Although these activists are sure to be shunned by established privacy organizations, their actions will probably help bring about real change in the policy arena. Already, some privacy activists are quietly discussing the need to create an underground front.

A privacy underground would certainly be at no loss for possible actions. People are already engaged in acts of data subversion—for example, falsely filling out surveys on forms to qualify for free magazine subscriptions. A privacy underground could turn up the heat on these actions, with campaigns convincing people to transpose digits of their Social Security numbers, to "accidentally" misspell their names, and generally to lower the quality of the data stream until significant privacy protections are in place.

Over the past decade, a number of homosexual rights groups have engaged in the practice of *outing*—exposing political and business leaders as closet homosexuals. A privacy underground might similarly engage in *data outings*—that is, publishing the names, addresses, home telephone numbers, Social Security numbers, incomes, and buying habits of individuals who head the organizations that are attacking our privacy now. Just imagine the thrill of calling the president of a telemarketing firm during dinner, or sending junk mail to the head of a direct marketing firm!

Finally, the fringe may turn to data terrorism. To protest poor privacy practices, data terrorists could break into computers and scramble records. Or they could "liberate" corporate databanks by leaking the information to the Internet.

Although I personally hope that privacy rights will be obtained through civil discourse and legislation rather than through information violence, I fear that the dispossessed will ultimately turn to increased activism, outings, and data terrorism if all other avenues prove hopeless.

CONCLUSION

Predicting the future has always been a risky business. There are simply too many ways in which unforeseen events can invalidate even the most likely story of what lies ahead. When I was a child, my mother explained the situation succinctly with an old Yiddish proverb: "Man plans and God laughs."

And yet, predicting the future and making plans is something we humans must do in order to ensure our survival. For millennia, we planned for the lean months of winter by sowing crops in the spring and reaping them in the fall. We plan and construct massive civil works projects to control floods in the countryside and bring water to our cities. We educate our young, even though the payoff is uncertain and far in the future. Those who do not plan for the future have none.

For more than a hundred years, visions of privacy have almost always been intertwined with visions of the future. When Samuel Warren and Louis Brandeis wrote their article "The Right of Privacy," their major concern was not with the state of privacy in 1890 Boston, but with the potential threats to privacy in the coming years. When George Orwell sat down in 1947 and penned his novel on Big Brother, his concern was not the state of privacy in postwar Britain or Russia, but with what might happen to civil liberties at some point in the future—say, in 1984. When Alan Westin testified before Congress back in 1968, he attacked the then-current practices in the U.S. credit industry, but his most serious warnings were saved for how our future would suffer if the credit industry was not brought into line.

Knowing this history, I set out five years ago to write a book about privacy in the twenty-first century. For my reference point, I decided to take a year in the middle of the 100-year period, the year 2048. In part, this was a play on George Orwell's masterpiece, but it was also a signpost along our road to the future. Today, the whole subject of privacy is filled with questions; by the year 2048, I thought, these questions will surely be answered. That's because many of today's privacy issues are the result of technology's having invalidated assumptions about our personal privacy and freedom that are thousands of years old. By the middle of the twenty-first century, I reasoned, there will be few assumptions left to invalidate. Humanity will have finally come face to face with the implications of absolute identification, remote sensing, tracking, genetic engineering, and the threat of artificial intelligence. If the human race hasn't let itself be wiped out by a lone crazy or enslaved by a hyperactive police force by the year 2048, I told myself, then we will surely be on a new footing, one that will be able to survive the next thousand years.

But the more I worked on the book called *2048*, the more it became clear to me that my main concern should not be some new, steady-state futuristic society. My battle would have to lie here at the beginning of the 2000s. The only way we can cross the bridge to some utopian future is by starting to make the right decisions today.

Privacy is indeed at a crossroads. Today, it is all too easy to imagine a world in which our digital autonomy has been stripped away, a world where our actions are monitored, our secrets are known, and our choices are therefore circumscribed. It is the world with which I opened this book. It is a world where I do not wish to live. But the only way that we can avoid this dystopian future is by acting today and tomorrow to bring about a different future.

Instead of creating a database nation, we must change our thinking, our laws, and our society. We must create a future of freedom that honors personal autonomy and respects personal privacy. And we must start now.

ANNOTATED BIBLIOGRAPHY AND NOTES

Annas, George J. *Standard of Care: The Law of American Bioethics*. London, New York: Oxford University Press, 1993.
Written by a leading bioethicist, *Standard of Care* explores the intersection between medicine, society, and the law by examining important bioethics cases that ended up in the courtroom. Topics in this book include abortion, AIDS, euthanasia, organ transplantation, and genetic research.

Bertillion, Alphonse (Chief of the Judicial Identification Service of France). *Signaletic Instructions, Including the Theory and Practice of Anthropometrical Identification*. Translated from the latest French edition, with 132 figures, plates and tables. Edited by Major R. W. McClaughry, late General Superintendent of Police of Chicago. Chicago: The Werner Company, 1896.
This book describes the Bertillion system of identification, which was among the first biometric systems to be developed and deployed in modern times.

Brin, David. *Earth*. New York: Bantam, 1990.
Brin's "no-privacy" vision of the Earth's future paints a world in environmental and political crisis. Set sometime in the next century, when video cameras are everywhere, all of the world's data is available cheaply on the data net, and vast destructive technology is routinely used by renegade individuals. Excellent reading, although the physics is a bit unlikely.

Brin, David. *The Transparent Society*. Reading, MA: Perseus Books, 1998.
Rather than cling to an illusion of anonymity, Brin argues that we should focus on guarding the most important forms of privacy and preserving mutual accountability. The biggest threat to our freedom, Brin warns, is that surveillance technology will be used by too few people, rather than too many.

Burnham, David. *The Rise of the Computer State: A Chilling Account of the Computer's Threat to Society.* New York: Random House, 1983.
Burnham's book was the classic computer privacy and data protection book of the 1980s. In it, he talks about the rising threat of computer tracking services, credit agencies, tenant screening services, and worker monitoring. What's sad about this book is that the majority of the problems Burnham discusses have only gotten worse, and the lack of legal protection he bemoans has only become more damaging to the fabric of society.

Calvin, William H. *Conversations with Neil's Brain: The Neural Nature of Thought and Language.* Reading: Addison-Wesley, 1994.
This book details current developments in neurobiology and microanatomy that may one day make brain wiretapping possible.

Cavoukian, Ann, and Don Tapscott. *Who Knows? Safeguarding Your Privacy in a Networked World.* Toronto: Random House of Canada, 1995.
Written by the one of Canada's data protection commissioners, this book is a good primer on data protection in the U.S. and Canada.

Cranor, Carl F., ed. *Are Genes Us? The Social Consequences of the New Genetics.* New Brunswick: Rutgers University Press, 1994.
An excellent primer on genetics, with a special chapter on genetic identification techniques.

Crevier, Daniel. *AI: The Tumultuous History of the Search for Artificial Intelligence.* New York: Basic Books, 1993.
A comprehensive history of artificial intelligence, with special emphasis on the AI boom-and-bust of the 1980s.

Cummins, Harold, and Charles Midlo. *Finger Prints, Palms and Soles: An Introduction to Dermatoglyphics.* Philadelphia: The Blakiston Company, 1943.
A textbook on fingerprints from the middle of this century. Particularly interesting is the history of fingerprints and the discussion of the genetic component of fingerprints that had been observed at the time—before the genetic basis of heredity was understood.

Cushman, Robert E. *Civil Liberties in the United States: A Guide to Current Problems and Experience.* Ithaca: Cornell University Press, 1956.
Surveys current civil liberties issues in the United States, with special attention to racial and sexual discrimination, but gives no attention to privacy issues.

Eaton, Joseph W. *Card-Carrying Americans: Privacy, Security, and the National ID Card Debate.* Totowa: Rowman & Littlefield, 1986.
Eaton argues that the United States must adopt a national identification card system in order to stamp out illegal immigration and provide accountability for people making changes to computerized

records. The card would contain a biometric to validate the holder. What Eaton fails to anticipate is the widespread deployment of data networks, and especially wireless data networks, which make such cards unnecessary.

Etzioni, Amitai. *The Limits of Privacy*. New York: Basic Books, 1999.
Etzioni's controversial book argues that we don't have too little privacy, but too much. In the area of HIV testing, sex offender registries, cryptography, and ID cards, Etzioni argues that the rights of the community to know facts about its members outweigh the rights of individuals to their privacy. Interestingly, the only area in which Etzioni says we do not have enough privacy is the area of medical records. And here, Etzioni says, the threat isn't Big Brother—it's Big Business.

Finn, James, and Leonard R. Sussman, eds. *Today's American: How Free?* New York: Freedom House, 1986.
This book contains an interesting set of essays exploring freedom in modern society. Particularly noteworthy is a chapter by John Diebold, president of the Diebold Group, which explores the impact that computers have had on privacy and freedom.

Flaherty, David H. *Privacy in Colonial New England*. Charlottesville: University Press of Virginia, 1972.
Flaherty's doctoral thesis examines the roots of American thought on privacy by exploring privacy in Boston and other New England towns.

Garson, Barbara. *The Electronic Sweatshop: How Computers Are Transforming the Office of the Future into the Factory of the Past*. New York: Simon & Schuster, 1988.
Garson's volume investigates the introduction of computers and advanced telecommunications technologies into the American workplace in the mid-1980s. She shows that these technologies, originally designed to improve efficiency, were quickly adopted to monitor workers, even when such monitoring proved ineffective and even detrimental. Garson contrasts the American experience with Europe, where strict laws were passed to limit the keystroke-by-keystroke monitoring of workers.

Givens, Beth and the Privacy Rights Clearinghouse, with Dale Fetherling. *The Privacy Rights Handbook: How to Take Control of Your Personal Information*. New York: Avon Books, 1997.
Givens' book is based on two concepts: knowledge and action. Using examples from the thousands of people who have called her organization's California hotline, Givens explains what's driving companies that are invading our privacy and says what to do about it. The book is divided into six parts that cover dealing with invasive commerce; safeguarding personal records; pitfalls of telecommunications; privacy on the job; personal safety; and activism.

Lalonde, Peter, and Paul Lalonde. *The Mark of the Beast: Your Money, Computers, and the End of the World*. Eugene: Harvest House Publishers, 1994.

Lalonde and Lalonde paint an apocalyptic vision inspired by Revelations that a new global economy, and the numbering of the world's inhabitants with marks on their hands or foreheads, will bring about the end of the world. Although ridiculed by many, this is another argument that is frequently used against universal enumeration.

Long, Senator Edward V. *The Intruders: The Invasion of Privacy by Government and Industry*, with a Foreword by Vice President Hubert H. Humphrey. New York: Praeger, 1966.

Senator Edward V. Long headed the U.S. Senate's Subcommittee on the Invasion of Privacy. This book details the growing trend of electronic surveillance by government and industry in the 1960s. Also recounted in detail is the monitoring of the mails. Especially interesting are accounts of wiretapping by the Food and Drug Administration, which used electronic surveillance to gain evidence against those who were selling unapproved food additives, and the Internal Revenue Service, which used wiretaps in order to find unreported income. Readers will also be amused by photographs showing a variety of spy listening devices, such as a bugged olive, a gun that fires a dart containing a microphone, and a "shocker" that can be mounted on the back of "a young woman" in order to aid gambling.

Miller, Arthur R. *The Assault on Privacy: Computers, Data Banks, and Dossiers*. Ann Arbor: University of Michigan Press, 1970.

An excellent history of the politics and events leading up to the adoption of the Fair Credit Reporting Act.

Murphy, Paul L. *World War I and the Origin of Civil Liberties in the United States*. New York: W. W. Norton & Co., 1979.

Murphy's thesis is that prior to World War I, violations of civil liberties were reasonably widespread and fairly tolerated. But there were so many civil liberties violations during the war, Murphy argues, and they were targeted so broadly, that the resulting backlash ignited the American civil liberties movement.

Orwell, George. *1984*. New York: Harcourt Brace Jovanovich, 1949.

Fifty years after its publication, many people forget that George Orwell's classic dystopian vision was less about privacy than about totalitarianism. Big Brother's control on his society was maintained by controlling the past and striking fear into the hearts of those in the present.

Packard, Vance. *The Naked Society*. New York: David McKay Co., 1964.

This is Packard's monumental work on privacy and surveillance in the 1960s. Packard considers assaults on privacy at home, in the workplace, by government, and by industry. He looks at the economic and political factors forcing the new era of surveillance, and makes concrete recommendations for what should be done.

Phillips, John Aristotle, and David Michaelis. *Mushroom: The Story of the A-bomb Kid.* New York: Morrow. 1978.
John Aristotle Phillips was a student who discovered that he could create detailed plans for making an atomic bomb using only publicly available sources. He proved that our "nuclear secrets" are far less secret than many people think.

Ramberg, Bennett. *Nuclear Power Plants as Weapons for the Enemy: An Unrecognized Military Peril.* Berkeley: University of California Press, 1984.
Ramberg shows that you don't even need to have nuclear secrets to create nuclear fallout: all you need is a truck packed with explosives and a handy civilian nuclear power plant.

Robin, Leonard. *Money Troubles: Legal Strategies to Cope with Your Debts,* 4th ed. Berkeley: Nolo Press, 1996.
Discusses techniques for obtaining credit reports and dealing with incorrect information in credit reporting databanks.

Rosenberg, Jerry M. *The Death of Privacy.* New York: Random House, 1969.
Rosenberg's book discusses the impact of electronic data processing on personal privacy in the late 1960s. It is another book that argued for the passage of laws in the United States to protect individuals from incorrect or inappropriate information being stored in computer databanks.

Rothfeder, Jeffrey. *Privacy for Sale: How Computerization has Made Everyone's Private Life an Open Secret.* New York: Simon & Schuster, 1992.
In 1990, journalist Jeffrey Rothfeder obtained Vice President Dan Quayle's credit report while working on a project at *Business Week* magazine. After leaving *Business Week*, Rothfeder wrote *Privacy For Sale*, a survey of privacy issues with special attention directed at record aggregating firms called "super bureaus." This volume is notable, in part, for its in-depth profile of journalist Dan Rather's private life, a profile that was created and published without Mr. Rather's consent.

Schwartz, Paul, and Joel Reidenberg. *Data Protection Law: A Study of United States Data Protection.* Dayton: Michie, 1996.
An extensive review of data protection law and current industry practices.

Smith, H. Jeff. *Managing Privacy: Information Technology and Corporate America.* Chapel Hill: University of North Carolina Press, 1994.

Smith's thesis from the Harvard Business School examines how major U.S. corporations handle personal information. It is the only summary of its kind.

Smith, Robert E., and Eric Siegel. *War Stories: Accounts of Persons Victimized by Invasions of Privacy.* Available from *Privacy Journal* (P.O. Box 28577, Providence, RI 02908; 401-274-7861), 1994. Describes more than 500 cases of invasion of privacy, including abuses in credit reports, medical information, "identity theft," electronic surveillance, Internet use, government information, telephone solicitation, and more. Published by the editor of the *Privacy Journal.*

Smith, Robert E., and Eric Siegel. *War Stories II.* Available from *Privacy Journal* (P.O. Box 28577, Providence, RI 02908; 401-274-7861), 1997.
Provides additional cases from the *Privacy Journal.*

Stephenson, Neal. *Snow Crash.* New York: Bantam, 1992.
Stephenson's novel, set in the early twenty-first century, features ubiquitous video cameras, wearcams, bugged virtual environments, the massive democratization of destructive technologies, and honest-to-goodness brain wiretapping and control. *Snow Crash* prophesied many of the technologies discussed in *Database Nation*; this, combined with a lively story, makes the novel both enjoyable and thought provoking.

Turkington, Richard C., George B. Trubow, Anita L. Allen. *Privacy: Cases and Materials.* Houston: The John Marshall Publishing Co., 1992.
A strong textbook for teaching the history and current status of privacy law, both on and off the Internet.

Twain, Mark. *Pudd'nhead Wilson: A Tale.* London: Chatto & Windus, 1894.
Twain's novel introduced many Americans to the idea that fingerprints could be used for both identification and criminal investigations.

Wayner, Peter. *Disappearing Cryptography.* Boston: AP Professional, 1996.
Wayner's book explores the science of stenography—techniques for hiding encrypted information in other pieces of data so that the encrypted information cannot be discovered. Stenography has direct implications for watermarking and law enforcement.

Westin, Alan F., Project Director, Michael A. Baker, Assistant Project Director. *Databanks in a Free Society: Computers, Record-Keeping and Privacy.* New York: Quadrangle Books, 1972.
This book reports the findings of a National Research Council study on the growth of electronic databanks and their impact on American society. The book contains in-depth reports on computers operated in 1970–71 by the federal government, states,

commercial organizations, colleges, and other nonprofit organizations. Readers will find especially interesting the reports on the computers operated by the Social Security Administration, the FBI's National Crime Information Center; Bank of America; TRW's Credit Data Corporation; the R. L. Polk and Company mailing list operation; the Massachusetts Institute of Technology; and the Church of the Latter-Day Saints. The book also summarizes the results of site visits to 55 advanced systems located around the United States. It predicts future directions in computer technology, and then considers the impact of computers on public policy. Because of the staying power of legacy systems, many of the organizations profiled by Westin et. al. are still in use today, making this book still timely 28 years after its publication.

Wilson, Thomas F., and Paul L. Woodard. *Automated Fingerprint Identification Systems: Technology and Policy Issues.* U.S. Department of Justice, Bureau of Justice Statistics, April 1987. Pub. No. NCJ-104342.
This report, summarizing the dramatic success of AFIS systems, marks the beginning of the widespread adoption and acceptance of AFIS technology in the United States.

WEB SITES

The following web sites provide additional online information on the topics discussed in this book.

http://chessclub.com/
Internet Chess Club.

http://lists.essential.org/cgi-bin/listproc_search.cgi?listname=med-privacy/
Searchable archives of the MED-PRIVACY Internet mailing list on medical privacy issues.

http://members.aol.com/victcrdrpt/index.html
Home page of Victims of Credit Reporting. A web site dedicated to people who have been victimized by credit reporting agencies. It has information on the Fair Credit Reporting Act, techniques for correcting credit reports, and some preliminary information on ways to fight back.

http://www.american-adoption-cong.org/
Home page of American Adoption Congress.

http://www.atcc.org/
Home page of American Type Culture Collection.

http://www.ball.com/aerospace/index.html
Home page of Ball Aerospace, makers of the QuickBird Imaging satellite. See http://www.ball.com/aerospace/qbird.html for information about QuickBird.

http://www.eds.dofn.de/
> Home page of Earth Observation Data Services. Maintains an online warehouse with more than 21,000 satellite images available for download.

http://www.loebner.net/Prizef/loebner-prize-bkup.html
> Home page of the Loebner Prize, which will be awarded to the first computer whose responses are indistinguishable from a human's.

http://www.nationalcpr.org/
> Home page of National Coalition for Patient's Rights, a nonprofit organization dedicated to the premise that patients have the right to privacy when they consult a healthcare professional. NCPR believes that neither employers, nor insurers, nor government agencies, nor police should be allowed to supersede that basic right.

http://www.ncfa-usa.org/
> Home page of National Council for Adoption. The NCFA is a nonprofit organization that provides information on both domestic and international adoption, encourages pro-adoption legislation, and provides referrals to member agencies.

http://www.nci.org/nci/index.htm
> Home page of The Nuclear Control Institute. Founded in 1981, the institute is a research and advocacy center for preventing nuclear proliferation. Nonprofit and nonpartisan, the institute plays a watchdog rule in a complex and dangerous field.

http://www.novaspace.com/
> Home page of NovaGraphics. Sells "Earth at Night" and other Landsat posters (800-727-NOVA).

http://www.spaceimage.com/index.htm
> Home page of Space Imaging Corporation.

http://www.spot.com/
> Home page of Spot Imaging.

http://www.terraserver.com/
> Home page of TerraServer, which provides single-point shopping for satellite photographs from U.S. Landsat and the Soviet-era SPIN-2 satellite. Images can be purchased and downloaded over the Web; large Kodak prints can be ordered as well. TerraServer's intuitive user interface allows you to specify your target location by address or map coordinates, or by clicking it on the globe.

http://www.the-dma.org/
> Home page of the U.S. Direct Marketing Association

http://www.worldsat.ca/
> Home page of WorldSat International, Inc., makers of the world's most computationally intensive satellite posters (800-387-8177).

NOTES

For each chapter, the following sections contain notes as well as references to online information.

CHAPTER 1: PRIVACY UNDER ATTACK

1. Harris-Equifax, *Consumer Privacy Survey*. Conducted for Equifax by Louis Harris and Associates in association with Dr. Alan Westin of Columbia University, Equifax, Atlanta, GA, 1996.

2. Harris-Equifax, *Consumer Privacy Survey*, Conducted for Equifax by Louis Harris and Associates in association with Dr. Alan Westin of Columbia University, Equifax, Atlanta, GA, 1995.

3. Samuel Warren and Louis Brandeis, "The Right of Privacy," *Harvard Law Review* 4 (1890), 193. Although the phrase "the right to be let alone" is commonly attributed to Warren and Brandeis, the article attributes the phrase to the nineteenth-century judge Thomas M. Cooley.

4. Turkington et al., *Privacy: Cases and Materials*.

5. David H. Flaherty, *Protecting Privacy in Surveillance Societies* (University of North Carolina Press, 1989).

   In 1989, David H. Flaherty, the privacy commissioner of British Columbia, published a revised set of 12 Data Protection Principles and Practices for Government Personal Information Systems. These 12 principles are (emphasis supplied by David Flaherty in May 1997):

   The principles of *publicity and transparency* (openness) concerning government personal information systems (no secret databanks).

   The principles of *necessity* and relevance governing the collection and storage of personal information.

   The principle of reducing the collection, use, and storage of personal information to the maximum extent possible.

   The principle of *finality* (the purpose and ultimate administrative uses for personal information need to be established in advance).

   The principle of establishing and requiring *responsible keepers* for personal information systems.

   The principle of controlling *linkages*, transfers, and interconnections involving personal information.

   The principle of requiring informed *consent* for the collection of personal information.

   The principle of requiring accuracy and completeness in personal information systems.

   The principle of *data trespass*, including civil and criminal penalties for unlawful abuses of personal information.

   The requirement of special rules for protecting sensitive personal information.

   The right of access to, and correction of, personal information systems.

   The *right to be forgotten*, including the ultimate anonymization or destruction of almost all personal information.

6. One federal match program compared a database that had the names of people who had defaulted on their student college loans with another database that had the names of federal employees. The match then automatically garnished the wages of the federal employees to pay for the defaulted loans. The problem with this match,

and others, was that there were many false matches that were the result of incorrect data or similar-sounding names. And because the wages were automatically garnished, victims of this match were required to prove their innocence—that is, to prove that the match was erroneous.

CHAPTER 2: DATABASE NATION

1. "Automated Government—How Computers Are Being Used in Washington to Streamline Personnel Administration to the Individual's Benefit," *Saturday Review*, July 23, 1966.
2. Vance Packard, "Don't Tell It to the Computer," *New York Times Magazine*, January 8, 1967.
3. Rosenberg, *The Death of Privacy*, p. 1.
4. "McVeigh Prosecutor Cries During Trial," Associated Press, May 8, 1997. Available online at http://herald-mail.com/news/1997/bombing_trial/stories/may8_97.html.
5. "Answers for the Evidence," *Detroit Free Press*, December 17, 1997. Available online at http://www.freepress.com/news/bombtrial/qcase17.htm.
6. Charles J. Bashe, Lyle R. Johnson, John H. Palmer, Emerson W. Pugh, *IBM's Early Computers* (Cambridge: MIT Press, 1986).
7. Social Security Administration official history. Available online at http://www.ssa.gov/history/.
8. Westin, Alan F., *Databanks in a Free Society*, p. 33.
9. Westin, Alan F., *Privacy and Freedom*, (New York: Atheneum, 1967), p. 304.
10. Westin, Alan F., *Databanks in a Free Society*, p. 472.
11. Ibid., p. 134.
12. Ibid., p. 135.
13. A good history of the adoption of the Fair Credit Reporting Act can be found in Miller, *The Assault On Privacy*.
14. Westin, *Databanks in a Free Society*, pp. 137–138.
15. Interview by author, January 14, 1995.
16. Smith, *War Stories,* 1994.
17. Hearing Before the House Subcommittee on Consumer Affairs on the Fair Credit Reporting Act on September 13, 1989 (p. 30), as reported in Smith, *War Stories*.
18. Jim Mallory, "Social Security Workers Charged with Data Theft" Newsbytes News Network (http://www.newsbytes.com/), August 4, 1996.
19. Interview by author, April 1995. See also "Separating the Equifax from Fiction," *Wired Magazine*, September 1995, p. 96.
20. Source for SSN uses table: Social Security Administration.

CHAPTER 3: ABSOLUTE IDENTIFICATION

1. As reported in Cummins and Midlo, *Finger Prints, Palms and Soles*.
2. Bertillion, *Signaletic Instructions*, introduction.
3. Bertillion's lasting contribution to the field of criminology wasn't his system for identification, which was eventually "cumbersome and often fallible," but his realization that any identification technique had to be systematic and objective—especially if one person were to make a reliable identification using a record that was collected by somebody else. Cummins (Professor of Microscopic Anatomy, Tulane University Medical School) and Midlo (Associate Professor of Microscopic Anatomy, Tulane University Medical School) wrote in *Finger Prints, Palms and Soles*, p. 143: "[Bertillion] revised the inexact descriptive methods previously employed in criminal identi-

fication and proposed the use of eleven body measurements. As a systematic method adapted to the needs of agencies of law enforcement, the Bertillion procedure is naturally more reliable than sight recognition. Measurements lend themselves to classification, classification being requisite for ready search of the filed records essential in systematic personal identification. The Bertillion system, cumbersome and often fallible, was gradually superseded by the immeasurably superior method of fingerprint identification, which is now employed universally for the registration of criminals and increasingly for various civil and military purposes."

4. Twain, *Pudd'nhead Wilson.*

5. Cummins and Midlo, *Finger Prints, Palms and Soles.* Cummins and Midlo explore the use of prints through the ages. Their book includes a photograph of an identifiable print on a fragment of a Palestinian lamp of the fourth or fifth century of the Common Era from Doctor Badè of the Palestine Institute, Pacific School of Religion. It also has a photograph of Chinese seal from the third century B.C. "On one surface it bears a name impression by a personal seal, and on the other there is a clearly defined thumb print. The provenance of this print suggests its nature as a personal mark, but whether the mark was made with a purpose equivalent to that of current finger-print identification is a debatable question." They attribute some information to Alfred C. Haddon, *Evolution in Art* (Scribner's, 1895).

6. Ibid.

7. Wilson and Woodard, *Automated Fingerprint Identification Systems.*

8. Ibid., p. 14.

9. Ibid., p. 1.

10. Interview by author, July 11, 1988.

11. *Automated Fingerprint Identification Systems*, p. 1.

12. Interview by author, March 1, 1991.

13. Interview by author, August 1997.

14. *People v. Castro*, 144 Misc. 2d 956, 545 N.Y.S. 2d 985 (Sup. Ct. 1989).

15. *State v. Schwartz*, 447 N.W. 2d 422 (Minn. 1989).

16. *Cobey v. State*, 80 Md. App. 31, 559 A.2d 391 (Md. App. 1989).

17. Interview by author, July 1997.

18. E. S. Lander and B. Budowle, "DNA Fingerprinting Dispute Laid to Rest," *Nature* 371 (1994), pp. 735–738.

19. "Convicted by Juries, Exonerated by Science: Case Studies in the Use of DNA Evidence to Establish Innocence After Trial," National Institute of Justice Research Report, June 1996. Full text available at http://www.ncjrs.org/txtfiles/dnaevid.txt.

20. "Son in Sheppard Case Wins an Exhumation Bid: Seeks DNA Testing to Vindicate Father," Associated Press, *Boston Sunday Globe*, July 13, 1997, p. A16.

21. Paul Ferrara, chair, "Laboratory Funding Issues Working Group Report," in the *Proceedings of the National Commission on the Future of DNA Evidence*, November 23, 1998. Transcript available at http://www.ojp.usdoj.gov/nij/dnamtgtrans3/trans-j.html.

22. Interview at Computer, Freedom, and Privacy Conference, April 8, 1999.

23. Thomas H. Speeter at AT&T Bell Laboratories has developed a floor tile that can identify the person stepping on it from the weight and distribution of pressure. The initial test system consisted of a single 12-inch floor tile containing a 16×16 sensor array, each sensor providing a pressure value between 0 and 255. In his initial experiment, Speeter had 10 volunteers take a step on the floor tile as they walked across the room, then turn around and walk back. Based on a sample size of 188 steps, Speeter found that he could identify a person with 99% accuracy after just three steps, and with 100% recognition after four steps. Clearly, larger sample sizes are

indicated, but the research shows nevertheless that individuals have unique steps and that even today's computers can use those steps to distinguish among us. See Thomas H. Speeter, "Identification Using Ground Reaction Force Patterns," AT&T Bell Laboratories.

24. Donald Foster, "Primary Culprit," *New York*, February 26, 1996, pp. 50–57.

25. "Joe Klein Says He Is Anonymous *Primary Colors* Author," Associated Press, July 17, 1996.

26. Robert O'Harrow, Jr., and Liz Leyden, "U.S. Helped Fund Photo Database of Driver IDs; Firm's Plan Seen as Way to Fight Identity Crimes," *Washington Post*, February 18, 1999, p. A1. Archived at http://wearcam.org/drivers-license-picture-sale.html.

27. Steve Mann "'Smart Clothing:' Wearable Multimedia and 'Personal Imaging' to Restore the Balance Between People and Their Intelligent Environments," *Proceedings, ACM Multimedia 1996*, November 18–22, 1996.

28. Interview by author, August 25, 1994.

CHAPTER 4: WHAT DID YOU DO TODAY?

1. James Finn and Leonard R. Sussman, eds., *Today's American: How Free?* (New York: Freedom House, 1986), p. 111.

2. Ibid.

3. U.S. Department of Justice Drug Enforcement Administration, "U.S. Drug Threat Assessment: 1993. Drug Intelligence Report. Availability, Price, Purity, Use, and Trafficking of Drugs in the United States," September 1993, DEA-93042. Available online at http://mir.drugtext.org/druglibrary/schaffer/GOVPUBS/usdta.htm.

4. "TV-Movie Actress Slain in Apartment," Associated Press, July 19, 1989. "Arizona Holds Man in Killing of Actress," Associated Press, July 20, 1989. "Suspect in Slaying Paid to Find Actress," Associated Press, July 23, 1989.

5. NYNEX advertisement, mailed to customers in Spring 1997.

6. Interview by author, September 9, 1997.

7. Bruce Schneier, "Why Intel's ID Tracker Won't Work," *ZDNet News*, January 26, 1999. Republished in RISKS Digest 20:19. Available online at http://catless.ncl.ac.uk/Risks/20.19.html#subj4.

8. Westin, *Databanks in a Free Society*, p. 93.

9. The companies offering competing systems are American Veterinary Identification Devices (AVID), which runs the PETtrac recovery network; HomeAgain, which resells the Destron chip; InfoPet Systems, which sells the Trovan system; and PetNet, which resells the Anitech chip. Over the past three years, veterinarians and pet enthusiasts have argued over which chip is better, which is cheaper, which is easier to read, and so forth. The companies have responded by trying to build readers that can read each other's chips, giving away free readers to shelters (in hopes of stimulating chip sales), and generally snipping at each other's heels. As industrial applications take off, they're likely to leave pet-chipping far in the dust. Trovan, for instance, sells a ruggedized version of its ID 100 microtransponder called the ID 103. This transponder is specifically designed for industrial applications and the garment industry. It's encapsulated with a double-thick glass wall so that it can survive rollers and garment presses. It can survive temperatures up to 180° C. And it can be inserted into plastic as it cools, making the identification tag a permanent part of the item.

10. Murphy, Kate, "Get Along Little Dogie #384-591E: Laptop Cowboys Riding Herd on the Electronic Frontier," *New York Times*, Monday, July 21, 1997.

11. *ITS America News*, April 1997, pp. 6–8.

12. The 1997 Driver's Privacy and Protection Act requires that states allow individuals to opt out of motor vehicle databases before data is made available to marketers.

13. Interview by author, June 27, 1997.

14. *Police Commissioner v. Triborough Bridge and Tunnel Authority* (Sup. Ct. NYC IA Part 50R, June 26), as reported in the *Privacy Journal*, October 1997.

15. Robert Uhlig, "Spy Phones Trace Cheating Husbands," *Electronic Telegraph*, August 27, 1997. Available at http://www.telegraph.co.uk:80/et?ac=002093890554028& rtwo=r3bhbhhx&atmo=99999999&pg=/et/97/8/27/nbt27.html, as reported in the August 29, 1997 issue of RISKS Digest.

16. Interview by author, August 1997.

17. The Second Conference on Computers, Freedom, and Privacy, Washington, D.C., 1992. See http://www.cpsr.org/dox/conferences/cfp92/home.html.

18. Joseph Malia, "Waste.com: Public Employees Using Internet for Sex, Drugs, and Rock 'n' Roll," *Boston Herald*, May 12, 1999, p. 1. Full text available online at www.bostonherald.com/bostonherald/lonw/emai05121999.htm and www.mapinc.org/drugnews/v99.n505.a11.html/lsd.

19. U. S. Department of Commerce, *Privacy and the NII: Safeguarding Telecommunications-Related Personal Information*, October 1995. Available at http://nsi.org/Library/Comm/privnii.html.

20. Editorial, *USA Today*, October 25, 1995.

21. The Diebold Institute for Public Policy Studies, Inc., *Transportation Infostructures*, (Westport, CT: Praeger, 1995).

CHAPTER 5: THE VIEW FROM ABOVE

1. Interview by author, February 20, 1997.

2. Actually, the Earth's circumference at the equator is 40,074 kilometers, and the circumference from the North to South poles is 40,000 kilometers. Do these numbers look suspicious? They should. The meter was defined by the French Academy of Sciences in 1791 as 1/10,000,000 of the quadrant of the Earth's circumference drawn from the North Pole to the Equator, through Paris. In 1889, the International Bureau of Weights and Measures redefined the meter as the distance between two lines on a particular bar of metal located in Paris. (It was easier to measure the bar with great accuracy than to measure the precise distance from the North Pole to the Equator!) In 1960, the meter was redefined again as part of the International System of Units (SI units) to be equal to exactly 1,650,763.73 wavelengths in a vacuum of the orange-red line in the spectrum of the krypton-86 atom. In 1983, the meter was redefined once again by the General Conference on Weights and Measures to be exactly the distance that light travels in a vacuum in 1/299,792,458 of a second. Each redefinition of the meter allowed scientists around the world to make their own measurements with increasing precision. The new definitions therefore correspond to the increased accuracy of scientific instruments, and the ability to measure particular kinds of phenomena with increased accuracy.

3. *Technology Review*, October, 1996. See http://www.techreview.com/articles/oct96/Shulman.html.

4. Information on the Landsat, Seasat, TIROS, Transit, and Vela satellites is from *Encyclopedia Britannica*, 1997 edition. Online edition available at http://www.eb.com.

5. Interview by author, April 1997.

6. From the Space Imaging web site, http://www.spaceimage.com/aboutus/overview6.htm#consumer, April 24, 1999.

7. Excerpt from a Government Technology Industry Profile: EOSAT (Advertising Pamphlet), 1996. EOSAT has since been renamed Space Imaging and now has 1-meter resolution images available from the IKONOS satellite (rather than IRS-1C data). See http://www.spaceimaging.com.

8. Details of the declassification program can be found at http://edcwww.cr.usgs.gov/glis/hyper/guide/disp. Some sample scenes can be found at http://edcwww.cr.usgs.gov/dclass/dclass.html.

9. Personal communication (email), April 11, 1997.

10. *New Scientist*, April 12, 1997, p. 4.

11. Privacy International, "Video Surveillance," at http://www.privacy.org/pi/issues/cctv/.

12. Interview by author, February 21, 1996.

13. Interview by author, February 21, 1996.

14. Consumer Electronic Manufacturing Association, Arlington VA.

15. The Trojan Room Coffee Pot's home page is http://www.cl.cam.ac.uk/cgi-bin/xvcoffee.

16. Interview by author, May 1997.

17. Frequently Asked Questions, at http://www.wsdot.wa.gov/regions/northwest/NWFLOW/camera/camfaq.htm, April 9, 1997.

18. Martin Minow, "Norwegian Surveillance Camera," RISKS Digest 19:13. Available online at http://catless.ncl.ac.uk/Risks/19.13.html#subj8.1.

19. *All Things Considered*, National Public Radio, May 12, 1997.

20. Clive Norris and Gary Armstrong, "The Unforgiving Eye: CCTV Surveillance in Public Space," Centre for Criminology and Criminal Justice, University of Hull, Hull HU6 7RX, U.K. Quoted from "Prejudice Drives CCTV Targets," KDIS Online, October 24, 1997. Available at http://merlin.legend.org.uk/~brs/archive/stories97/Suspects.html.

21. Simon Davies, "Summary of Oral Evidence of Simon Davies," October 23, 1997. Available online at http://www.privacy.org/pi/issues/cctv/lords_testimony.html.

22. Interview by author, May 9, 1997.

23. *Katz v. U.S.*, 389 U.S. 347 (1967).

24. "CTBT . . . At last!," Incorporated Research Institutions for Seismology, *IRIS Newsletter*, vol. XV, no. 3, Fall 1996, pp. 1–3.

25. Christel B. Hennet (IRIS), Gregory van der Vink, (IRIS), Danny Harvey (University of Colorado), and Chrisopher Chyba (Princeton University), "IRIS Assists Senate in Investigation of International Terrorist Group," *IRIS Newsletter*, Fall 1996, pp. 13–15.

CHAPTER 6: TO KNOW YOUR FUTURE

1. Dr. George Way, New York, NY, quoted in "Nowhere to Hide," by Scott Winokur, *San Francisco Examiner*, October 7–12, 1984, p. 13. Reported in *War Stories: Accounts of Persons Victimized by Invasions of Privacy*, by Robert Ellis Smith with Eric Siegel. (Published by *Privacy Journal*, PO Box 28577, Providence, RI 02908. 401-274-7861, 1990).

2. Testimony of U.S. Representative Nydia Velázquez to the Senate Judiciary Committee, 1994. See Ann Cavoukian and Don Tapscott, *Who Knows? Safeguarding Your Privacy in a Networked World* (Toronto: Random House of Canada, 1995), p. 103.

3. Interview by author, July 25, 1997.

4. Personal communication (email), July 24, 1997).

5. Cavoukian and Tapscott, *Who Knows*, p. 98.

6. Harris-Equifax, *Health Information Privacy Survey*, Conducted for Equifax by Louis Harris and Associates in association with Dr. Alan Westin, Columbia University.

Study No. 934009, Louis Harris and Associates. New York, NY., 1993, 212-698-9600. 1993.

7. Press release, National Research Council, March 5, 1997.

8. Janlori Goldman, "Regarding the Confidentiality of Health Records," statement before the U.S. House of Representatives Government Operations Subcommittee on Information, Justice, Transportation and Agriculture, November 4, 1993.

9. "Who's Reading Your Medical Records?" *Consumer Reports*, October 1994, p. 628–632. Cited in Etzioni, *The Limits of Privacy*. p. 147.

10. Lecture at Privacy Summit conference, 1995.

11. *Morgantown Dominion Post*, Morgantown WV, November 13, 1989, p. 1; *Privacy Journal* victims file. Reported in *War Stories*.

12. Reported in *War Stories II*, p. 58.

13. Interview by author, July 25, 1997.

14. David F. Linowes, "A Research Survey of Privacy in the Workplace," unpublished paper, University of Illinois at Urbana-Champaign, April 1996.

15. Etzioni, *The Limits of Privacy*, p. 145.

16. Health insurance applications aren't the only forms that most people don't read. When I bought my first house with my wife, we were determined to read all of the numerous forms at the closing. Our lawyer asked us to take the signed forms home and read them at our leisure: reading them at the time of the closing would make a one-hour process stretch out to three or four hours. Few people read the tiny print on their credit card agreements—and almost nobody reads the two telephone book-sized supplements of rules and regulations which the credit card agreements incorporate by reference. And practically nobody reads the shrink-wrapped license agreements on their computer programs, even though they accept the terms of the agreements by using the software.

17. Smith, *Managing Privacy*, p. 143

18. Interview by author, July 29, 1997

19. Smith, *Managing Privacy*, p. 58.

20. Ibid., p. 33.

21. Garfinkel, Simson L., "From Database to Blacklist: Computer Records Let Employers and Landlords Discriminate Against Unsuspecting Applicants," *Christian Science Monitor*, August 1, 1990, p. 12.

22. Interview by author, May 26, 1997.

23. Harris-Equifax, *Health Information Privacy Survey*, 1993.

24. *Privacy Journal's Compilation of State and Federal Privacy Laws* (Providence: Privacy Journal, 1997).

25. J. Michaelis, M. Miller, K. Pommerening, and I. Shmidtmann, "A New Concept to Ensure Data Privacy and Data Security in Cancer Registries," Medinfo 1995; X pt 1:661–665.

26. Interview by author, July 24, 1997.

27. Interview by author, July 24, 1997.

28. Interview by author, July 24, 1997.

29. Interview by author, May 5, 1999 and May 23, 1999.

30. Interview by author, July 24, 1997.

31. Interview by author, July 24, 1997.

32. Interview by author, April 29, 1997.

33. *Protecting Electronic Health Information*, Committee on Maintaining Privacy and Security in Health Care Applications of the National Information Infrastructure, National Research Council (Washington, D. C., 1997).

CHAPTER 7: BUY NOW!

1. Interview by author, February 22, 1996.

2. Westin, *Databanks in a Free Society*, p. 156.

3. Interview by author, February 20, 1996.

4. *Privacy Journal*, March 1999, p. 5.

5. Personal communication, 1995.

6. Harris-Equifax, *Health Information Privacy Survey*, 1993, p. 4.

7. Smith, *War Stories II*, p. 17.

8. "The ABCs at the FTC: Marketing and Advertising to Children," Summary of Prepared Remarks of Commissioner Roscoe B. Starek III, Federal Trade Commission, Advertising and Promotion Law 1997, Minnesota Institute of Legal Education, July 25, 1997. Available online at http://www.ftc.gov/speeches/starek/minnfin.htm.

9. The KidsCom URL is http://www.kidscom.com/.

10. The Disney URL is http://www.disney.com.

11. Interview by author, February 22, 1996.

12. Advertisement, *DM News*, February 1996.

13. Source: Experian U.S. Catalog of Products and Services, available online at www.experian.com/catalog_us/index.html.

14. Westin, *Databanks in a Free Society*, p. 163.

15. Interview by author, February 14, 1995.

16. Howard Schneider, "Telemarketing Scams Based in Canada Increasingly Target U. S. Residents," *The Washington Post*, August 24, 1997, p. A21.

17. Paul Schwartz and Joel Reidenberg, *Data Protection Law*, p. 333. As referenced by Marc Rotenberg, "Testimony and Statement for the Record of Marc Rotenberg, Director Electronic Privacy Information Center, on the Children's Privacy Protection and Parental Empowerment Act, H.R. 3508, Before the House of Representatives, Committee on the Judiciary, Subcommittee on Crime, September 12, 1996." Available online at http://www.epic.org/privacy/kids/EPIC_Testimony.html.

18. Ibid., p. 338.

19. Robert O'Harrow, Jr., "Prescription Sales, Privacy Fears; CVS, Giant Share Customer Records with Drug Marketing Firm," *Washington Post*, February 15, 1998, p. A01.

20. On August 12, 1970, Richard Nixon signed the Postal Reorganization Act of 1970 into law. The act transformed the Post Office Department into the United States Postal Service, a government-owned corporation.

21. Westin, *Databanks In A Free Society*, p. 162.

22. Personal communications (email), August 4, 1997 and August 5, 1997.

CHAPTER 8: WHO OWNS YOUR INFORMATION?

1. Interview by author, April 19, 1995.

2. Interviews by author, August 18, 1997, and August 19, 1997.

3. *Roberson v. Rochester Folding Box Co.*, 171 NY 538.

4. In fact, Avrahami declared that he *had* registered with the service—when he lived in Kansas—and he had decided that it didn't work. "I tried it and companies still sent me solicitations," he said. "Even companies that I wrote to directly informing them that I subscribe to the DMA, they still kept sending me solicitations. That brought me to the conclusion that there is no real interest [for them] to stop soliciting me."

5. Personal communications (email), August 4, 1997 and August 5, 1997.

6. Interview by author, February 22, 1996.

7. Interview by author, February 14, 1995.

8. Interview by author, April 15, 1997.

9. Harris-Equifax, *Consumer Privacy Survey*, Conducted for Equifax by Louis Harris and Associates in association with Dr. Alan Westin of Columbia University (Equifax, Atlanta, GA, 1996).

10. Interview by author, August 1997.

11. A. Heimler and A. Zanko, "Huntington Disease: A Case Study Describing the Complexities and Nuances of Predictive Testing of Monozygotic Twins," *Journal of Genetic Counseling* 4 (1995):125–137. (Letter and replies *Journal of Genetic Counseling* 5:47–50).

12. Insurance companies have actually taken the middle road with respect to genetic testing. Currently, no insurance company demands that applicants for life or health insurance be tested for genetic diseases—in part, because the tests cost too much money—but if an applicant has taken such a test, the insurance company demands to know the result. They fear *adverse selection*, in which people who know they carry a genetic disease will take out extravagant insurance policies, while those who believe they have a clean genetic bill of health will go without insurance. Combined, these two trends would create larger and larger payouts for insurance companies, with fewer and fewer healthy people paying their premiums. The result would be catastrophic insurance failure.

13. The details on the fascinating case of John Moore come from Chapter 12, "Outrageous Fortune: Selling Other People's Cells," in George J. Annas' excellent book *Standard of Care: The Law of American Bioethics*.

14. GM-CSF is granulocyte-macrophage colony stimulating factor.

15. Interview by author, August 27, 1997.

16. Interview by author, August 27, 1997.

17. Interview by author, August 28, 1997.

18. Jane E. Ellis, Larry D. Byrd, William R. Sexson, and C. Anne Patterson-Barnett, "In Utero Exposure to Cocaine: A Review," *Southern Medical Journal*, vol. 86(7) (1993): 725–731.

19. Interview by author, August 28, 1997.

20. U.S. Department of Health and Human Services, "Three Breast Cancer Gene Alterations in Jewish Community," National Cancer Institute Press Office, 05-20-1997.

21. Melinda Greenberg, "Dr. Lawrence C. Brody on Breast Cancer," *Baltimore Jewish Times*, October 13, 1995.

22. Interview by author, July 9, 1997.

23. Johns Hopkins School of Medicine, "Ashkenazi Jewish Families," Advertisement, *New York Times*, September 23, 1997.

24. Interview by author, September 1, 1997.

25. An excellent summary of the Icelandic database and deCODE's project can be found in Ricki Lewis, "Iceland's Public Supports Database, but Scientists Object," *Scientist*, vol. 13:15 (1999).

26. The URL for Mannvernd is http://www.mannvernd.is/english/index.html.

27. See http://www.mannvernd.is/english/articles/greely_&_king-e.html.

28. Haloid Xerox, Inc., actually unveiled the Model A copier, nicknamed the "Ox Box," on October 22, 1948, at the annual meeting of the Optical Society of America in Detroit. Although it was marketed a year later, the 600-pound machine required 14 different manual operations to produce a successful photocopy. In 1955, the com-

pany released the Xerox Copyflo, the first automatic xerographic unit to make continuous copies on ordinary paper. (Source: *1987 Fact Book*, Xerox; also "News Stories in 1948" from the Nation's Health Service web site, http://www.nhs50.nhs.uk/nhsstory-thisweek-oct25.htm.

29. Interview by author, January 20, 1997.

30. Sreenath Sreenivasan, "What Is a Hit Film? Moviefone May Know," *New York Times*, June 2, 1997.

31. Lecture at University of Washington, February 25, 1997.

32. John Ford, quoted in author interview with Jack Rogers, April 19, 1995.

CHAPTER 9: KOOKS AND TERRORISTS

1. Louis Rene Beres, lecture at University of Washington, May 1997.

2. Interview by author, May 14, 1997.

3. Interview by author, August 11, 1997.

4. Interview by author, August 11, 1997.

5. Interview by author, August 11, 1997.

6. William Scally, "Man Charged Following White House Attack," Reuters Newswire, October 30, 1994.

7. William Neikirk and Christopher Drew, "Small Plane Crashes on White House Lawn, Pilot Dies," *Chicago Tribune*, September 12, 1994.

8. Beres lecture, May 1997.

9. Ramberg, *Nuclear Power Plants as Weapons for the Enemy.*

10. Torok et al., "A Large Community Outbreak of Salmonellosis Caused by Intentional Contamination of Restaurant Salad Bars," *Journal of the American Medical Association*, 278:5 (1997), p. 389.

11. Ibid.

12. Leonard A. Cole, "The Specter of Biological Weapons," *Scientific American*, December 1996. Available at http://www.sciam.com/1296issue/1296cole.html.

13. J. W. Barber, *Interesting Events in the History of the United States* (New Haven: Barber, 1829), as quoted in James W. Loewen, *Lies My Teacher Told Me* (Simon & Schuster, 1995).

14. "Argentine Computer Hacker Agrees to Surrender," Associated Press, December 6, 1997. Archived at http://www.techserver.com/newsroom/ntn/info/120697/info7_5811_noframes.html.

15. David H. Freedman and Charles C. Mann, *At Large: The Strange Case of the World's Biggest Internet Invasion* (New York: Simon & Schuster, 1997).

16. Murphy, *World War I and the Origin of Civil Liberties*, p. 90.

17. *New York World*, January 28, 1918, pp. 1–2; *New York Times*, June 18, 1919, p. 8; as reported in Murphy, *World War I and the Origin of Civil Liberties*, p. 95.

18. *Milwaukee Publishing Co. v. Burleson*, 255 U.S. 407 (1921).

19. Murphy, *World War I and the Origin of Civil Liberties*, pp. 109–110.

20. The entire episode is in Bradford, *Of Plymouth Plantation*, pp. 149–53.

21. Flaherty, *Privacy in Colonial New England*, pp. 125–126. Flaherty's sources include Kenneth Ellis, *The Post Office in the Eighteenth Century: A Study in Administrative History* (London, New York: Oxford University Press, 1958), pp. 60–77; and William Cobbett, *Cobbett's Parliamentary History of England* (London: R. Bagshaw, 1806–20), IX (1733–37), 839–848.

22. *Irvine v. California*, 347 U.S. 128.

23. *Silverman v. United States*, 356 U.S. 505.

24. *Katz v. United States*, 389 U.S. 347.

25. 1999 *Wiretap Report*, Administrative Office of the United States Courts.

26. 1998 *Wiretap Report*, Administrative Office of the United States Courts, p.11. Available online at http://www.uscourts.gov/wiretap98/contents.html.

27. Ibid.

28. 1996 *Wiretap Report*, Administrative Office of the United States Courts.

29. Bruce Schneier and David Banisar, eds, *The Electronic Privacy Papers: Documents on the Battle for Privacy in the Age of Surveillance* (New York: Wiley, 1997).

30. See "STAR GATE [Controlled Remote Viewing]," on the web site of the Federation of American Scientists, http://www.fas.org/irp/program/collect/stargate.htm.

31. Doug Williams, *How to Sting the Lie Detector Test* (Chickasha: Sting Publications, 1976). Available from Sting Publications, P.O. Box 1832, Chickasha, OK 73023.

32. Interview by author, May 14, 1997.

33. Interview by author, August 11, 1997.

34. Interview by author, May 13, 1997.

CHAPTER 10: EXCUSE ME, BUT ARE YOU HUMAN?

1. Crevier, *AI: The Tumultuous History*, pp. 133–140.

2. For further information on the Loebner prize, I recommend Charles Platt's excellent article "What's It Mean to Be Human, Anyway?" in *Wired Magazine*, April 1995.

3. A full transcript between the Drake student and MGonz can be found at http://www.compapp.dcu.ie/~humphrys/eliza.html.

4. Personal communication (email), October 28, 1999.

5. Michael McCormick, "Invasion of the Internet Imposters," *Internet Underground* 8, July 1996. One of the most amusing (and annoying) features of the Zumabot was the inability of the program to distinguish the country "Turkey" from the food "turkey." This became apparent one year around Thanksgiving, when the program started protesting people's recipes for the holiday bird.

6. See the Internet Chess Club web site at http://www.chessclub.com/.

7. Interview by author, August 25, 1997.

8. J. Orwant, "For Want of a Bit the User was Lost: Cheap User Modeling," *IBM Systems Journal*, 35: 3&4, 1996.

9. Yezdi Lashkari, Max Metral, and Pattie Maes, "Collaborative Interface Agents," MIT Media Laboratory, 1994 (unpublished). Available for download at ftp://ftp.media.mit.edu/pub/agents/interface-agents/generic-agents.ps.

10. The START information server, called the "START Natural Language Question Answering System," is at http://www.ai.mit.edu/projects/infolab/. The links are to the 1999 World Factbook at http://www.odci.gov/cia/publications/factbook.

11. Christine Varney, FTC commissioner, speaking to John McChesney on National Public Radio's *All Things Considered*, June 10, 1997.

12. Personal communication (email), August 27, 1997.

13. Crevier, *AI: The Tumultuous History*.

14. A detailed history of the invention of the airplane and the debate over artificial flight can be found at the University of Illinois web site, at http://hawaii.psychology.msstate.edu/invent/.

15. Ray Kurzweil, "Turing's Prophecy—Machine Intelligence: the First 100 years (1940–2040)." Keynote Address, Gartner Group Middle East Information Technology Conference, Tel Aviv, Israel, June 25, 1995.

16. Moore's Law is actually not a law at all, but an observation made by Intel founder Gordon Moore. According to Moore's Law, computer power doubles in speed roughly every 18 months, the result of advances in semiconductors and the level of R&D investment.

CHAPTER 11: PRIVACY NOW!

1. Jacques Ellul, *The Technological Society* (New York: Random House, 1967).

2. Estimate by Evan Hendricks, chairman, U.S. Privacy Council; publisher, *Privacy Times*.

3. John Tagliabue, "Europe Offering Free Calls, but First, a Word from . . .," *New York Times*, September 28, 1997, p. A1.

4. Harris-Equifax, *Health Information Privacy Survey*, 1993.

5. Some of these provisions are already in the California State code, sections CC1785. 13–1785.26.

6. California had a law such as this, but it was apparently held to violate the First Amendment of the U.S. Constitution; see *UD Registry v. California*, 34 Cal. App. 4th 107 (1995).

7. Section 471 U.S. Code Title 2.

8. See the Zero-Knowledge Systems web site at http://www.zks.net.

9. Simson Garfinkel, *PGP: Pretty Good Privacy* (Sebastopol: O'Reilly & Associates, 1995).

10. Rothfeder, *Privacy for Sale.*

11. David M. Bresnahan, "Tagged Students Defy Big Brother," *World Net Daily*, September 23, 1999. Available at http://www.worldnetdaily.com/bluesky_bresnahan/19990923_xex_tagged_stude.shtml.

ACKNOWLEDGMENTS

My first formal exposure to privacy issues came in 1986, when I took a course in science, technology, and public policy from Dr. Gary Marx at the Massachusetts Institute of Technology. One of the books we read was David Burnham's *The Rise of the Computer State: A Chilling Account of the Computer's Threat to Society*. Although I had been a computer programmer for nearly ten years and had always enjoyed working with the machines, I knew there were aspects of computers that could easily be abused. Marx and Burnham opened my eyes to the extent of many of these problems, and they've both played a continuing role in my education ever since.

Also in 1986, I started reading Peter G. Neumann's RISKS Digest, the Forum on Risks to the Public in Computers and Related Systems on the Internet. Contributors from all over the world send contributions to RISKS. Many submissions are stories, anecdotes, and observations to the forum on ways people have made grave mistakes in deploying or using computerized systems. Peter's forum has been a constant source of material for more than decade, and his kindness, wit, and wisdom have likewise been a source of inspiration. After many years of online communication, I finally got the chance to meet Peter in person, and we became friends. While Peter was on Martha's Vineyard one summer, he looked over several chapters of this manuscript and gave me much-appreciated guidance—he even took me out for dinner and a movie!

Steve Ross at the Columbia University School of Journalism taught me that it's not enough to have a good story; it's also important to write that story well. Steve also encouraged me not to bite off too much at one time. When I wanted to write my master's thesis on "the threat of Social Security numbers," Steve made me focus on a particular privacy problem—the damage done by tenant screening services. He then taught me how to sell variations on the story again and again to different publications—a vital skill for anyone trying to make a living as a writer.

Robert Ellis Smith bought one of those articles based on my master's thesis and printed it in the *Privacy Journal,* which he has published relentlessly for more than 25 years. When I graduated from journalism school, Bob was eager to buy whatever else I wrote on the subject of privacy. He encouraged me to investigate and write about super bureaus, automatic fingerprint identification systems, genetic identification systems, medical privacy issues, and "advances" in marketing. Bob's monthly newsletter, his compilations of "war stories," and his numerous books about threats to privacy are required reading for anyone concerned about the ongoing threats to privacy. Bob has also been instrumental in organizing the Privacy Summit, a semiannual meeting of privacy activists. He is a privacy powerhouse.

Marc Rotenberg, David Banisar, and David Sobel at the Electronic Privacy Information Center (EPIC) have been a reliable and eminently quotable source of intelligence regarding the threats to privacy posed by big government and big business. EPIC's Freedom of Information Act (FOIA) lawsuits against the FBI and other parts of the federal government have brought much information to light about the government's plans to sacrifice privacy on the twin altars of law enforcement and national security. Marc, in particular, has proven to be a scholar on the subject of privacy theory, and is one of the strongest voices for pro-privacy legislation in Washington (and that's quite a tough tune to sing, given the antigovernment libertarian bent of many cyber-rights activists). He has also been a personal "moral privacy beacon" for me, taking time out to educate me on issues when we disagree. Almost always, Marc has been able to convince me of the error of my ways.

Phil Agre was a graduate student at the MIT AI Lab when I was an undergraduate at the Institute. He has since earned a professorship at UCLA, where he specializes in privacy issues. Phil's writings and speeches on privacy-enhancing technologies, social theory, and the role of business have been invaluable in helping me form many of the fundamental beliefs presented in this volume. Phil has also given me valuable criticism on many of my books, chapters, and articles.

Many books I've read include a long list of names of people who spoke with the author while he or she was working on the book. I'm always interested to read this section of the acknowledgments to see how many names I recognize, but I'm always saddened by the other names that have no significance for me. What did these people do? How does the author know them? How did they contribute?

In the course of writing this book, I spoke with several hundred people over the course of five years. These people answered my questions, responded to my email, and made time in their busy schedules to speak with me. Each one of them was important to the final product.

Although I hesitate to try to name them all for fear that I might omit one or two, I would like to give special thanks to the following:

- Amy Bruckman, who developed the MediaMoo and MooseCrossing artificial worlds at the MIT Media Laboratory, and who served on the MIT Privacy Committee

- Ram Avrahami, the computer programmer who took on the direct marketing industry, and lost

- John Burgess, the information officer at the U.S. Embassy in London, who took the time to tell me about video cameras in the United Kingdom

- Jason Catlett, founder of Junkbusters

- Dorothy Denning, a professor at Georgetown University and an expert on the regulation of encryption

- Dan Ellis, whom I knew as a graduate student at the MIT Media Laboratory, and who was always interested in privacy issues

- Carl Ellison, a cryptographer extraordinaire who now works for Intel

- Michael Froomkin, one of the most knowledgeable attorneys in the U.S. on the subject of Internet law, who now teaches at the University of Miami in Florida

- Robert Gellman, an expert privacy analyst who now consults in Washington, D.C.

- John Gilmore, founder of the Electronic Freedom Foundation (EFF) and overall crypto maven, and now another person convinced that strong cryptography is the solution to the privacy problem

- Beth Givens, project director of the Privacy Rights Clearinghouse in California

- Janlori Goldman, who has mastered privacy issues working as an analyst at the ACLU, the EFF, and the CDT

- Lamont Granquist, a really cool computer scientist who hangs out at the University of Washington in Seattle

- Michael Grant, a dear friend of mine who is extremely concerned with privacy issues, and who has given me many good stories

- Evan Hendricks, publisher of the *Privacy Times* newsletter in Washington, D.C.

- Eric Hughes, one of the original cypherpunks, who almost had me convinced that really good cryptography could preserve personal freedom and liberty

- James Kallstrom, who headed the FBI's New York office and convinced me that he really cared about civil liberties

- Steve Mann, whom I knew as a graduate student at the MIT Media Laboratory, and who is famous for walking around with a camera on his head

- Clifford M. Meyer, communications manager at the University of Washington Graduate School of Public Affairs, who helped me get settled in Seattle and also helped me organize the Technology and Democracy Study Group there

- Jon Orwant, another graduate student at the MIT Media Laboratory, who did fundamental work on user modeling before becoming a magazine publisher

- Damsel Plum, the *nom de plume* of Bastard Nation's publications coordinator

- Pamela Samuelson, an expert on copyright and intellectual property law

- C. B. Rogers, Jr., CEO of Equifax

- Peter Tarczy-Hornoch, an infant neonatologist who spent time with me in Seattle talking about medical informatics, medical privacy, and equally important issues

- Brad Templeton, an old man of the Internet who has always been concerned about the interaction of technology and policy

- Bruce Wilder, a physician in Pittsburgh who has done work on the hiding of medical information from insurance providers

- Ross Stapleton-Gray, who spoke with me about his experience being the subject of the Internet Hunt, and then continued working with me on a variety of other projects

Part of this book was written during the spring of 1997, while I was a visiting scholar at the University of Washington in Seattle. Professor Alan Borning in the Computer Science department set up the appointment for me; Margo Gordon in the School for Public Affairs was my host. The University of Washington is one of my favorite colleges in the world. It has an exceptionally beautiful campus, a wide range of students, and an impressive breadth of classes. While there, I made considerable use of the school's library system, especially the Suzzallo and Allen Libraries, and the Odegaard Undergraduate Library. There were many day and evening lectures at UW that I attended; students who were on campus in the spring of 1997 will see a direct correspondence between several chapters in this book and the school's special events calendar of that period. Many professors on campus were exceedingly generous with their time while I was there; those interviews are a part of this book. I was also helped by UW's exceedingly efficient public information office. While at UW, I was allowed to sit in on a class on Medical Information at the UW Medical School, for which I am also grateful. The School of Public Affairs was also generous enough to give me a room for evening meetings of a discussion group that I created called the Technology and Democracy Study Group; many of the ideas that are presented in this volume were first fleshed out there.

Portions of the manuscript for this book were read by Hal Abelson, Amy Bruckman, Jason Catlett, Rishab Aiyer Ghosh, Sian Gramates, Evan Hendricks, Bernard Greenberg, Andrew Listfield, Marc Rotenberg, Gene Spafford, and Hal Varian, all of whom gave me valuable comments and guidance. As with all of its books, O'Reilly put the manuscript through a formal review process. This wonderful practice is quite rare in today's publishing world. Alexa Champion, Sian Gramates, Oscar Gandy, Bernard Greenberg, and Marc Rotenberg all reviewed the entire manuscript and made numerous suggestions that contributed to making the final product even better. Marc's comments were exceedingly valuable: often a single sentence forced me to rewrite entire pages!

While working on this book, I came to rely quite heavily on Encyclopedia Britannica's online service. I never will have the money to buy a complete Britannica set, and at $5 per month for the company's online service, I don't need to. When I started this book, Britannica charged $14.95 per month and didn't have a privacy policy posted on its web site. Today, they have a policy that says, in bold letters, "Britannica does not sell, rent, swap or otherwise disclose any Personal Information." The policy goes on to explain precisely what information is collected on its web site, what use the site makes of "cookies," and for what purposes "personal information" is used inside the organization. It's an impressive policy, and I like to think that I nudged them, in some small way, to implement it by asking them in 1997 why they didn't have a policy on their web site. The moral of the story is that organizations can learn to do the right thing.

Those things that I couldn't dig up on Britannica or elsewhere on the Web were unearthed by my trusty researcher, Jayne Stancavage. Jayne is a much faster worker than I am, and I fear that she often spent weeks on end wondering if I had given up on the project. I didn't, of course, and thankfully neither did she.

I've been working on this book on and off since 1989, and in earnest since 1995. Debby Russell at O'Reilly had known about the project for years, and in 1998 decided to publish and edit the book. She was instrumental in bringing this book to life. This book marks the tenth year that Debby and I have been working together; this is the sixth book that we have jointly produced.

Hanna Dyer created the striking cover for this book; Alicia Cech did a great job on its internal design; and Edie Freedman and the whole Product Design group at O'Reilly did wonderful and creative work brainstorming the book's overall design. Michael Snow manipulated the photomontage in Adobe Photoshop, Edie Freedman created the keyhole, and John Feingersh/Stock Market photographed the eye.

Chris Reilley did a great job with this book's illustrations, especially considering the quality of some of the source material. Sara Winge, Cathy Record, and Mark Brokering did a superb job in the prepublication marketing of this most nontraditional O'Reilly volume—let's hope the effort pays off!

Production editor Madeleine Newell found literally thousands of typos and cases of unclear writing, which she also graciously gave me and Debby the time to correct. Anna Kim Snow, Colleen Gorman, David Futato, Jeff Holcomb, Nancy Kotary, and Abby Myers provided invaluable quality control and production support. Mike Sierra implemented the internal design using Adobe FrameMaker 5.5 and provided essential FrameMaker support. Robert Romano helped organize and traffic the figures. Ellen Troutman-Zaig wrote the index. Dan Appleman gave this manuscript a thorough review during production and, thankfully, didn't find any showstoppers.

Finally, I would like to thank my agent, Lew Grimes, who has supported this project for five long years, and my wife, Beth Rosenberg, whose love, support, understanding, and wisdom have given me the strength and the time to work on this opus.

—Cambridge, Massachusetts, and Martha's Vineyard
October 1999

INDEX